CASE STUDIES
IN SEXUAL DEVIANCE

The assessment and treatment of sexual deviance can be very difficult tasks, and it can be hard to find mentors to provide initial skills training and help in navigating the many complexities of a particular case. This book presents a series of case studies from international experts in the field that depict the evidence-based assessment and treatment of a variety of paraphilias. Intended as learning tools that readers can use as models and from which they can gain insight, these case studies are offered as exemplars of clinical problem solving. The authors of each chapter provide research evidence that justifies treatment decisions, explain their assessment strategies and case formulations, and provide information about how to navigate common problems a clinician will encounter, such as denial, poor motivation, and co-morbid problems. A variety of assessment instruments and treatment strategies are also illustrated. Both new and experienced clinicians will find this book to be an invaluable resource in their own work.

William T. O'Donohue, PhD, is a professor of psychology at the University of Nevada, Reno, and the director of the Victims of Crime Treatment Center, which provides free assessment and treatment for children who have been sexually abused and women who have been sexually assaulted. He has published over 70 books and 200 journal articles and book chapters, and has served on the American Psychiatric Association's Advisory Group for revising the *DSM* diagnosis of pedophilia.

D1519733

Humber College Library
3199 Lakeshore Blvd. West
Toronto, ON   M8V 1K8

INTERNATIONAL PERSPECTIVES ON
FORENSIC MENTAL HEALTH
A Routledge Book Series
Edited by Ronald Roesch and Stephen Hart
Simon Fraser University

The goal of this series is to improve the quality of health care services in forensic settings by providing a forum for discussing issues related to policy, administration, clinical practice, and research. The series will cover topics such as mental health law; the organization and administration of forensic services for people with mental disorder; the development, implementation and evaluation of treatment programs for mental disorder in civil and criminal justice settings; the assessment and management of violence risk, including risk for sexual violence and family violence; and staff selection, training, and development in forensic systems. The book series will consider proposals for both monographs and edited works on these and similar topics, with special consideration given to proposals that promote best practice and are relevant to international audiences.

Published Titles

Learning Forensic Assessment
Rebecca Jackson

Handbook of Violence Risk Assessment
Randy K. Otto & Kevin S. Douglas

Dangerous People: Policy, Prediction, and Practice
Bernadette McSherry & Patrick Keyzer

Risk Markers for Sexual Victimization and Predation in Prison
Janet I. Warren & Shelly L. Jackson

How to Work With Sex Offenders: A Handbook for Criminal Justice, Human Service, and Mental Health Professionals, Second Edition
Rudy Flora & Michael L. Keohane

Managing Fear: The Law and Ethics of Preventive Detention and Risk Assessment
Bernadette McSherry

Case Studies in Sexual Deviance: Toward Evidence Based Practice
William T. O'Donohue

Forthcoming Titles

Forensic Psychological Assessment in Practice
Corine De Ruiter & Nancy Kaser-Boyd

Handbook of Forensic Social Work with Children
Viola Vaughan-Eden

Sex Offender Risk: An Indeterminate Preoccupation
Robert Prentky & Howard Barbaree

CASE STUDIES IN SEXUAL DEVIANCE

Toward Evidence Based Practice

Edited by
William T. O'Donohue

Routledge
Taylor & Francis Group

NEW YORK AND LONDON

First published 2014
by Routledge
711 Third Avenue, New York, NY 10017

Simultaneously published in the UK
by Routledge
27 Church Road, Hove, East Sussex BN3 2FA

Routledge is an imprint of the Taylor & Francis Group, an informa business

© 2014 Taylor & Francis

The right of the editor to be identified as the author of the editorial material, and of the authors for their individual chapters, has been asserted in accordance with sections 77 and 78 of the Copyright, Designs and Patents Act 1988.

All rights reserved. No part of this book may be reprinted or reproduced or utilised in any form or by any electronic, mechanical, or other means, now known or hereafter invented, including photocopying and recording, or in any information storage or retrieval system, without permission in writing from the publishers.

Trademark notice: Product or corporate names may be trademarks or registered trademarks, and are used only for identification and explanation without intent to infringe.

Library of Congress Cataloging in Publication Data
O'Donohue, William T.
    Case studies in sexual deviance : toward evidence based practice / William T.
    O'Donohue.
    pages cm
    Includes bibliographical references and index.
    1. Paraphilias—Case studies. I. Title.
    HQ71.O396 2013
    616.85'83—dc23
    2013011701

ISBN: 978-0-415-88048-0 (hbk)
ISBN: 978-0-415-88049-7 (pbk)
ISBN: 978-1-315-89013-5 (ebk)

Typeset in Garamond
by EvS Communication Networx, Inc.

Printed and bound in the United States of America by
Edwards Brothers Malloy

CONTENTS

CONTENTS

ABOUT THE CONTRIBUTORS

Chi Meng Chu, PhD, is currently the Assistant Director of Forensic Health Services at the Clinical and Forensic Psychology Branch, Ministry of Social and Family Development, Singapore. He also heads the Centre for Research on Rehabilitation and Protection at the Ministry of Social and Family Development, and is a Research Affiliate with the Centre for Forensic Behavioural Science, Monash University. In addition, he is an Adjunct Assistant Professor with the Department of Psychology, National University of Singapore.

David L. Delmonico, PhD, is a Professor at Duquesne University in Pittsburgh, Pennsylvania. Dr. Delmonico, a graduate of Kent State University's Counseling and Human Development Services Program, conducts research, consultation, and training on topics such as cybersex, cyberoffense, and cybersafety. Dr. Delmonico is co-author of *In the Shadows of the Net, Cybersex Unhooked,* and *Cybersex Unplugged.* He has published numerous scholarly articles on a variety of technology and sexuality topics. Dr. Delmonico is Director of the Online Behavior Research and Education Center (OBREC) at Duquesne University and Associate Editor of the Sexual Addiction & Compulsivity journal.

Lawrence Ellerby, PhD, CPsych, is a Forensic Psychologist in private practice with Forensic Psychological Services, Ellerby, Kolton, Rothman & Associates in Winnipeg, Manitoba, Canada. He has been involved in the development and delivery of assessment and treatment services for violent and sexual offenders since 1987 and has published articles and book chapters related to these issues. In addition to his clinical practice he is Lecturer for the Department of Psychiatry at the University of Manitoba, a consultant to the Canadian Center for Child Protection, a trainer for the Canadian Police College, a member of Interpol's Specialist Group on Crimes against Children, and past President of the Association for the

Treatment of Sexual Abusers. His practice was also the recipient of the Canadian Criminal Justice Associations Crime Prevention Award.

Elizabeth J. Griffin, MA, is a licensed Marriage and Family Therapist with over 27 years of experience treating individuals with sexually problematic behaviors, especially those that involve the Internet. She has worked in outpatient, inpatient, military, and prison settings. Ms. Griffin lectures nationally on the assessment and treatment of sexual offenders and those with sexually compulsive behavior, as well as issues related to cybersex. She is co-author of *In the Shadows of the Net, Cybersex Unhooked,* and *Cybersex Unplugged.* Ms. Griffin is the founder of Internet Behavior Consulting, a company focused on issues related to problematic online behavior.

Ashley Haidle is a Marriage and Family Therapist Intern who graduated with her MA from the University of Nevada, Reno, in 2011. She has worked in a residential program for juveniles who offend sexually, assisting with program development, case consultation, and treatment planning while providing direct clinical services to program residents.

Stephen J. Hucker, MD, is Professor of Psychiatry in the Forensic Psychiatry Division at the University of Toronto and associated with the Centre for Addiction & Mental Health. He works in the areas of general forensic and correctional psychiatry but has had a longstanding interest in sexual disorders. He has made a particular study of sexual masochism and asphyxiophilia.

Elizabeth J. Letourneau, PhD, is Associate Professor, Department of Mental Health, and Director, Moore Center for the Prevention of Child Sexual Abuse, Johns Hopkins Bloomberg School of Public Health. Dr. Letourneau has studied sexual offending and sexual victimization for more than 20 years and is focused on primary prevention of child sexual abuse. She has completed several investigations on the effects of sex offender registration and community notification policies and was an investigator on the largest randomized controlled trial of treatment effectiveness for juvenile sex offending. Currently, Dr. Letourneau is involved in projects ranging from development of family-focused primary prevention strategies through identification of high risk Internet Crimes Against Children offenders. Dr. Letourneau has presented her research nationally and internationally, recently at the invitation of Interpol.

Jill S. Levenson, PhD, is currently an Associate Professor of Psychology and Human Services at Lynn University in Boca Raton, FL. She is also a licensed clinical social worker with over 20 years of experience treating sexual offenders. Dr. Levenson's area of research involves studying the impact and effectiveness of social policies and therapeutic interventions designed to reduce sexual violence. She has been a co-investigator or consultant on four grants funded by the U.S. Department of Justice investigating the effectiveness of sex offender registration and notification in preventing recidivism. She has published over 80 peer-reviewed articles and book chapters and has co-authored three books on the treatment of sex offenders and their families.

Amy Lykins, PhD, is currently Senior Lecturer in the School of Behavioural, Cognitive, and Social Sciences at the University of New England, Armidale, New South Wales, Australia. She is also a registered Clinical Psychologist in both Canada and Australia. Her primary research interests are in the areas of human sexuality and sexual health, particularly the role of cognitive processes in the evaluation of sexual information related to sexual attraction and orientation.

Diane G. Mercier, PhD, is a licensed Psychologist with a private practice in Reno, Nevada. She has specialized in the field of sexual abuse for over 30 years, providing assessments and treatment for sexual offenders, as well as treatment for child and adult victims of sexual abuse. Diane assisted in the development of a statewide network to address the problem of juvenile sexual offending aimed at promoting training and interagency networking.

Kirk A. B. Newring earned his PhD from the University of Nevada, Reno, and has worked in total confinement facilities with adolescents and adults with sexual offense behaviors. For the past few years, Dr. Newring has led Forensic Behavioral Health, a private practice group near Omaha, Nebraska, whose emphasis is working with court-involved youth and adults. Dr. Newring is an adjunct faculty member at Nebraska Wesleyan University, teaching several courses in the Master's of Forensic Science program.

William T. O'Donohue, PhD, is a Professor of Psychology at the University of Nevada, Reno. He has published over 70 books and 200 journal articles and book chapters. He is the Director of the Victims of Crime Treatment Center, which provides free assessment and treatment for children who have been sexually abused and women who have been sexually assaulted. He has served on the American Psychiatric Association's Advisory Group for revising the *DSM* diagnosis of pedophilia.

Cindy M. Schaeffer, PhD, is a Child-Clinical Psychologist and Associate Professor of Psychiatry in the Family Services Research Center at the Medical University of South Carolina. Her areas of expertise include youth antisocial behavior, adult and adolescent substance abuse, child maltreatment, youth peer relationships, Multisystemic Therapy (MST), and longitudinal data analysis. Dr. Schaeffer is involved in numerous research projects developing, evaluating, and disseminating ecologically based interventions for youth and families involved in the juvenile justice and child welfare systems.

Robert P. Stuyvesant, LCSW, ACSW, is a Clinical Social Worker in private practice. Since 1981 he has worked extensively in the evaluation and treatment of adults and juveniles who have sexually offended. He has provided an outpatient treatment program for adults and adolescents over the past 30-plus years in Reno, Nevada, while providing consultation and training to various programs and agencies responding to the problem of sexual abuse. He has been a clinical member of the Association for the Treatment of Sexual Abusers for 23 years.

Jo Thakker, PhD, is a Senior Lecturer in Psychology at the University of Waikato in Hamilton, New Zealand. She received her PhD in psychology from Canterbury University in New Zealand in 1997 and has since worked in both clinical and university settings. Most of her clinical work has been with offenders in Australia and New Zealand. Her key research areas include sexual and violent offenders, substance use and abuse, and cultural psychology. Dr. Thakker also has a background in theoretical research.

Tony Ward, PhD, DipClinPsyc, is a Clinical Psychologist by training and has been working in the clinical and forensic field since 1987. He is currently Professor of Clinical Psychology at Victoria University of Wellington, New Zealand. Dr. Ward was formerly Director of the Kia Marama Sexual Offenders' Unit at Rolleston Prison in New Zealand, and has taught both clinical and forensic psychology at Victoria, Deakin, Canterbury, and Melbourne Universities. He is currently the Director of Clinical Training at Victoria University, Wellington. Dr. Ward's research interests fall into four main areas: correctional and clinical rehabilitation models and issues; cognition and sex offenders; ethical issues in clinical and forensic psychology; and evolutionary explanations of crime and mental disorders. He has over 330 academic publications and his most recent book is *Foundations of Offender Rehabilitation* (Routledge, 2012; coauthored with Sharon Casey, Andy Day, and Jim Vess).

1

INTRODUCTION TO CASE STUDIES IN SEXUAL DEVIANCE
Improving the Quality of Services

William T. O'Donohue

The Value of the Case Study Approach

This book presents a series of case studies that depict the evidence based assessment and treatment of a variety of paraphilias. It is not intended to present these case studies as additional evidence for the effectiveness of these treatments. Unfortunately, this has been an all too common mistake in the history of mental health treatment—case studies have been over-valued as evidence for conclusions about treatment efficacy. The reader is cautioned not to make this mistake with the case studies presented in this book. All of the authors of these chapters acknowledge that their case studies ought not to have this function.

However, case studies are valuable—and perhaps even invaluable—for other reasons. First and foremost, they illustrate the concrete application of abstract information usually derived from research studies to a particular clinical situation. One can read the assessment or treatment outcome literature and come to general conclusions that a therapist ought to use, for example, Relapse Prevention in the treatment of some paraphilias, but this still leaves many open questions regarding how exactly to accomplish this. What assessment ought to be conducted first? What intervention steps ought to be conducted and in what sequence; for example, are offense claims targeted before problems of immediate gratification? What ought a therapist to do with common problems that occur in therapy such as problematic client motivation? Case studies can illustrate possible solutions to these sorts of practical and important questions.

Thus, the case studies in this book are presented as exemplars of clinical problem solving in assessing and treating paraphilias. They are presented as learning tools that give readers the opportunity to model their behavior after that of experienced experts. It is important to note that these cases have been disguised to protect client confidentiality—many authors achieved this by blending two cases. However, the chapter authors tried to provide practical and concrete cases that are realistic depictions of how an actual case would unfold.

Another important reason why case studies can be useful is that there is simply much missing information in the field of sexual deviancy. Some key paraphilias have few or no randomly controlled outcome studies (Laws & O'Donohue, 2012). These problems are to some extent "orphaned" and if the clinician decides to treat he or she usually extrapolates what has worked for other similar problems. However, this extrapolation requires some clinical ingenuity and the ability to adapt and translate these principles to a new therapy target. Thus, at times the case studies in this book review this kind of extrapolation.

In addition, case studies can be helpful because the treatment of the paraphilias is very difficult. This will be discussed more fully below but suffice it to say at this juncture that clinicians in this field are often working over a quite prolonged treatment period (treatment can last for several years), with complicated clients (legally and clinically). Clinicians will be using assessment devices with unknown or problematic error terms, with clients who display various levels of treatment motivation and various and often unknown levels of accurate disclosure. Clinicians will be battling powerful motivating forces (deviant sexual urges), with treatment targets such as sexual self-control and sexual orientations that are, at best, highly resistant to change, with a host of comorbid problems (e.g., alcohol abuse, misogyny, or even Anti-Social Personality Disorder). In addition, clinicians will be dealing with problems that have a high relapse rate, in domains that have a number of legal consequences and that are some of the most socially stigmatized problems, and with treatments that are not all that powerful (Marques, Wideranders, Day, Nelson, & Ommeren, 2005).

Finally, case studies can assist in the problem of training—they can be a part of how students can learn to skillfully and faithfully implement evidence based techniques. It appears that we have a bit of a workforce problem in this area—there are too few therapists trained to provide high quality treatment given the unfortunate need revealed by the epidemiology of sexual victimization. Reading case studies is a method that can partially help with this problem because it provides a concrete illustration by these experts of the methods that have been shown to work. Clinicians seem to like to read case studies: perhaps because it so clearly mirrors their day-to-day experience and perhaps because if a case study is well written it unfolds as an interesting and even compelling narrative.

The chapter authors were asked to write their chapters to have some sort of similar structure. They were asked to include these elements in their chapters:

1. Provide a brief background/description of the case.
2. Present a clinical assessment (include a rationale for the psychometrics of measurement strategies used).
3. Case formulation (demonstrate how they came to conceptualize the case); arrive at conclusions (however preliminary); any diagnoses; rule in or rule out any comorbid issues and how they plan to deal with these.
4. Treatment plan and implementation (again, with a rationale that this is reasonably evidence based).
5. Deal with complications in treatment (denial, nonattendance, lapses, etc.).
6. Terminating treatment and developing a relapse plan or any other issues for post-treatment.
7. Conclusions and any general advice or perspectives.
8. How nonspecifics were dealt with in this case (e.g., the therapeutic relationship)?
9. What would the clinician have done if therapy wasn't working as it should?
10. What ethical or legal considerations came into play?
11. What common "mistakes" were avoided in treatment?
12. What is the "art" of this case, and how was it (if at all) informed by scientific evidence?
13. What cultural factors did the clinician consider and what difference did these make (if relevant in this case)?

General Problems in the Assessment and Treatment of Sexual Deviance

There are a variety of factors that contribute to this difficulty. Below is a partial list:

1. Clients can be in (full or partial) denial.
2. Clients can lie (paraphilias are stigmatized and are difficult to admit to).
3. Clients often are not highly motivated to be in treatment or do not stay motivated (perhaps treatment is legally mandated).
4. Clients are often highly heterogeneous—from juveniles to the elderly, with a wide range of status on variables such as SES, intelligence, and general social skills. Kiesler (1966) years ago astutely warned about client uniformity myths.
5. Clients can be entwined in complicated family systems that impact treatment progress.

6. Much rides on the success of treatment because treatment failures can mean that another child is molested or another woman is raped. It can also mean that the client must go back to prison perhaps for decades.

7. Treatment often occurs in a variety of settings and must be adapted for these settings (e.g., prisons, outpatient therapist offices, or special inpatient settings).

8. Assessment often involves domains that force us to rely on problematic self-report such as sexual fantasy. Assessment is often multifaceted and requires the measurement of many domains, and these results must be synthesized. These measurements often have to occur many times if treatment progress is to be measured.

9. The psychometric instruments that we use often have important missing psychometric information or problematic psychometric information—we know too little about the error terms of these instruments. There is often reason to believe that the error terms are large or unacceptable. Some of this is often due to the complex and difficult objective of assessment: it is simply very complex to accurately measure risk of reoffending over a 5-year period.

10. Some psychometric instruments are controversial because of what is involved in their procedures (e.g., the penile plethsymograph requires the presentation of deviant stimuli and requires a strain gauge to be placed on the client's penis; O'Donohue & Letourneau, 1992). This is quite different from usual assessment procedures carried out by mental health professionals.

11. Treatments are provided by a wide variety of professionals from psychiatrists to psychologists to social workers, who have a wide variety of general clinical experience, and a wide variety of personal characteristics. Kiesler (1966) also warned against therapist uniformity myths.

12. Treatment is often very long term, with Relapse Prevention modules it can even been construed as lasting an entire lifetime.

13. Treatments are complicated to implement. They often do not rely on single components such as contingency management or exposure therapy for anxiety but rather are multifaceted. Thus, the therapist must have a wide range of skills.

14. Some treatment targets are just very difficult to change (e.g., sexual orientation). It may be said that it is even unclear what all the practical goals of therapy ought to be. For example, is the goal to change a deviant orientation, or because of practical limitations allow the deviant sexual interest to remain, but work to have the client not act on the deviant orientation?

15. Important controversies exist regarding these treatment goals. Is it permissible, for example, in a Harm Reduction Model, to allow the client to masturbate to deviant fantasies (in the hopes that this will

decrease further acting out on these), or is this unacceptable deviance in and of itself?

16. Treatment often takes place in a legal context and these vary across states and nations. Thus, the clinician often has to attend to unique forensic parameters or requirements.

17. Treatment effects are weak (Marques et al., 2005). Some have even claimed that they are so weak that it is wrong to claim that a treatment is evidence based (Laws & O'Donohue, 2012).

18. Relapse is very common. It is possible to think that the only reasonable goal is zero future occurrences (as opposed to say a Harm Reduction Model) and this can be a very hard goal to achieve. If it is not achieved, many would then regard treatment as a failure.

19. There are multiple models of treatment and controversies exist regarding which ought to be implemented (e.g., Relapse Prevention Therapy vs. Good Lives Model of therapy).

20. Clients often present with serious comorbid problems. They may have a long standing substance abuse problem or a personality disorder such as Anti-Social Personality Disorder. They may have other problems such as anger control, problematic attitudes toward women, or poor social skills. These problems complicate treatment and sometimes even obviate it. However, questions remain regarding case formulation: when should comorbid problems be treated: one at a time at the outset of treatment, simultaneously, or should they be ignored for the time being? Should the therapist coordinate treatment with another therapist or try to treat these problems him- or herself?

21. Quality treatment is expensive partly due to its length and partly due to the rarity of high quality therapists given the demand; in these economic times there can be insufficient funds to properly treat individuals. Often taxpayers are involved in this because treatment may be provided in a correctional institute or under the conditions for probation and parole. Taxpayers can ask legitimate questions about the value they are receiving for their money.

22. Diagnostic criteria are changing in the fifth edition of *The Diagnostic and Statistical Manual of Mental Disorders* (*DSM-V*; American Psychiatric Association, 2013) and some have argued not for the better. It seems that the diagnosis of the paraphilias in the *DSM-V* will require at least two actual victims. Thus, the old distinction between a pedophile (one who has a deviant sexual orientation toward children) and a child molester (one who has actually abused a child) will be lost. In general it seems, without sound argument, that the *DSM-V* has moved from pathologizing say a sexual orientation toward children as deviant to only pathologizing the actual victimization of a child. This has a serious negative consequence in that it normalizes a sexual attraction to children.

23. There is a wide variety of quality among evaluators and therapists. There are few barriers to claiming expertise, and like other areas of specialty practice, there can be a disturbingly large amount of variance in practice patterns.

24. There are few experts in academia who can provide this training, which makes it difficult to obtain quality training in this field. It is also a legitimate question about what specialized skill sets are needed in this field (say, being able to implement the Good Lives Model) and what more general skills sets are needed (e.g., being able to make judgments about the accuracy of self-report; being able to synthesize a wide variety of assessment material; being able to come up with a sound case formulation and treatment plan with a complex presentation; being able to help with problematic motivation; being able to interface with legal professionals; being able to strike a balance between support and confrontation; being able to handle stress and burnout).

25. There can be burnout and a need that is not fully recognized for therapist and staff support. This is a difficult problem to treat and other treatment modalities such as dialectical behavior therapy (Linehan, 2006) have mechanisms to support clinicians. More research is needed in this area.

26. There is little known about culturally sensitive assessment and treatment approaches—although this is ethically required by organizations such as the American Psychological Association.

27. There are some strange and potentially dangerous ideas in the field such as the permissibility and even the optimality of adult–child sexual contacts (Sanfort, 1987). Values and norms are involved in our field and these are beyond the ability of science to adjudicate (O'Donohue, in press).

28. There is a need for quality improvement (QI) philosophy and technology to be applied to this domain. We need to increase stakeholder literacy on what constitutes evidence based assessments and treatments. We need to increase transparency on key measures such as success and failure rates of individual therapists and programs. We need to look at stakeholder satisfaction and the value proposition that we are offering. We need to conduct research that gives much more practical information, such as the probability of relapse, so key decision makers have clear data upon which to make their decisions.

The Quality Improvement Agenda in the Assessment and Treatment of the Paraphilias

To argue for a QI commitment in the assessment and treatment of the paraphilias is not to say that it currently has an exceptional quality problem.

Unfortunately, because so little data have been collected regarding quality in this area we are not actually in a position to say much about its quality, and this itself is a problem. As a profession we cannot simply assume sufficient general quality, especially given both the importance of the issue as well as some inkling (e.g., discouraging outcome data; Marques et al., 2005) that suggests that quality might need to be improved.

Also, a QI commitment will bring a number of distinct advantages, and there is a trend to commit to QI in healthcare (Berwick & Nolan, 1998) and it would be disadvantageous for those assessing and treating paraphilias to miss this important movement. If it does, funding and acceptance will grow to be even greater problems.

The basic idea in QI is to detect problems in a product or service and to try to continuously improve these. Berwick and Nolan (1998) have astutely argued that in general the healthcare professions rely on the "bad apples" approach to quality. That is, the healthcare professions develop ethical codes and then seek, with various levels of stringency, to identify those that are violating these, and then attempt to punish these bad apples. There are a number of problems with relying on this approach to quality. First, it tends to surveill only fairly egregious violations of quality (e.g., sex with clients or intermingling funds). Second, it promotes fear and escape in healthcare professionals—they seek to hide their errors instead of exposing these and trying to learn from them so that they can be avoided in the future. Moreover, this is a fairly qualitative and static approach. If one is not violating an ethical standard, then there is no additional improvement beyond this categorical classification. Finally, questions can be raised about the sensitivity and specificity of the system—how accurately is this system detecting quality violations? Certainly there are no data on this and much of the evidence based practice movement is based on the premise that there are a fair number of services that are not evidence based.

On the other hand a QI perspective seeks to expose errors so that processes can be studied to eliminate these. It does not blame individuals but rather fallible production processes that result in errors. In embracing this orientation, clinicians are encouraged to expose problems so that they can be studied in QI evaluation cycles.

What Is Quality Improvement? A Primer

First we will review some of the classic theorists in QI:

Shewhart

Shewhart proposed that a high quality product need not be "perfect" (the standard expectation of the factory's engineers) but "in control." He proposed that the finished product or service ought to meet specifications that would vary to a certain small but irreducible extent. He called this normal difference "common cause" variation. Common cause variation can be reduced by understanding the variables in the processes that produce it (e.g., in healthcare it may be implementing treatments for which there is no evidence of their efficacy). On the other hand, he also described "special cause" variation, which is a difference in an outcome of a process that is due to causes that are intermittent (e.g., a stressed clinician due to suffering from the flu). Unfortunately, when most individuals think of quality problems they mistakenly think about special cause variation. According to Shewhart attempts to eliminate special cause variation are time consuming, costly, wasteful, and make things worse rather than better. In order to differentiate common cause variation from special cause variation, Shewhart uses a "control chart"; a statistical process control chart depicts variation as a function of common and special causes, which also includes statistically generated upper and lower limits.

Malcolm Baldrige

The Baldrige program identifies seven key action areas or categories regarding quality:

Leadership.   Leadership involves efforts by senior leadership and management to lead by example to integrate quality improvement into the strategic planning process, hiring, training, and processes throughout the entire organization to promote a commitment to quality and QI techniques.

Information and Analysis.   Information and analysis concerns managing and using the data needed for effective QI. Because quality improvement is based on management by fact, sound information and analyses are critical to QI success.

Strategic Quality Planning.   Strategic quality planning involves three major components: (1) developing long- and short-term organizational objectives for structural, performance, and outcome quality standards; (2) identifying ways to achieve those objectives; and (3) measuring the effectiveness of the system in actually achieving quality standards.

Human Resource Development and Management.   Human resource development and management involves working to develop the full potential of the workforce. This effort is guided by the principle that the entire workforce is motivated to achieve new levels of service and value.

Process Management. Process management concerns the scrutiny and continual improvement of the processes related to the creation and maintenance of high quality services. Within the context of quality improvement, process management refers to the improvement of work activities and workflow across functional or department boundaries.

System Results. System results entails assessing the quality results achieved and examining the organization's success at achieving quality improvement.

Satisfaction of Patients and Other Stakeholders. Satisfaction of patients and other stakeholders involves ensuring the gathering of data that measure ongoing satisfaction by those internal and external to the behavioral healthcare system with the services provided.

W. Edwards Deming

Deming made an important contribution to the philosophy and technology of quality improvement by recognizing that there is certain key knowledge that underpins all improvements. He called these elements the "System of Profound Knowledge." According to Deming, in order to comprehend the workings of a system and thus be able to improve it, one has to have an appreciation of the system as an entity unto itself, have an understanding of its sources of variation, a theory of knowledge of how to bring about change, and an understanding of the psychology of the personnel involved in the functioning of the system. We are helped to understand why all processes in a healthcare delivery system constantly exhibit variation if we comprehend the nature of variation.

The pursuit of improvement relies on cycles of learning. But it is not sufficient to show in a QI trial that a change is an improvement. The change must be fully and faithfully integrated into the system of production. This takes some careful planning, including some additional learning in regard to dealing with those who will be affected by the change and those who will implement the change and make these changes sustainable. Deming (Walton, 1996) developed his famous "14 points" to transform management practices:

1. *Create constancy of purpose.* A healthcare delivery organization's highest priority is to provide the best quality care at the lowest cost possible. A healthcare organization must strive to maximize efficiency and effectiveness through constant improvement.
2. *Adopt the new philosophy.* Everyone working in the organization can find ways to promote quality and efficiency, to improve all aspects

of the system, and to promote excellence and personal accountability. Pride of workmanship must be emphasized from recruitment to retirement.

3. *Cease dependence on inspection to achieve quality.* Reliance on routine inspection to improve quality assumes that error is highly likely (i.e., a search for errors, problems, or deficiencies; the "bad apples" approach). Instead, there should be a continuous effort to minimize error. As Deming points out, "Inspection (as the sole means) to improve quality is too late!" Lasting quality comes not from inspection, but from substantive improvements in the system.

4. *Do not purchase on the basis of price tag alone.* Purchasers must account for the quality of the item being purchased, as well as the cost. High quality organizations tend to think of their suppliers as "partners" in their operation. Successful partnerships require clear and specific performance standards and feedback on whether those standards are being met. Supplier performance can also be improved through an understanding of the supplier's QI efforts; longer-term contracts that include explicit milestones for improvement in key features; joint planning for improvement; and joint improvement activities. Of course, in service delivery regarding the paraphilias a key resource purchased is labor. There is a saying in law that there is nothing so expensive as a cheap lawyer. There might be an equivalent adage in this area: "There is nothing so expensive as a cheap paraphilia assessor or treatment provider."

5. *Constantly improve the system of production and service.* Quality can be built into all health delivery activities and services and can be maximized by continuous examination to identify potential improvements. This requires close cooperation between those who provide and those who consume services. Improved efficiency and service can result from focusing not only on achieving present performance targets, but more importantly, by breaking through existing performance levels to new, higher levels.

6. *Institute QI training on the job.* On-the-job QI training ensures that every worker has a thorough understanding of: (a) the needs of those who use or pay for our services; (b) how to meet those needs; and (c) how to improve the system's ability to meet those needs. Incorporating QI into the fabric of each job can speed learning.

7. *Institute effective leadership.* The job of management is leadership. Effective leaders are thoroughly knowledgeable about the work being done and understand the environment and complexities with which their workers must contend. Leaders create the opportunity for workers to suggest improvements and act quickly to make needed changes in production process. Leaders are concerned with success as much as with failure and focus not only on understanding "substandard,"

but also "superstandard" performance. The effective leader also creates opportunities for below- and above-average performers to interact and identify opportunities for improvement.

8. *Drive out fear.* The Japanese have a saying: "Every defect is a treasure," meaning that errors and failures are seen as opportunities for improvement. Errors or problems can help identify more fundamental or systemic root (common) causes and ways to improve the system. Yet, fear of identifying problems or needed change can kill QI programs. Also, some may feel that the idea of making improvements is an admission that the current way of doing things is flawed or that those responsible are poor performers. Improved performance cannot occur unless workers feel comfortable that they can speak truthfully and are confident that their suggestions will be taken seriously.

9. *Break down barriers between departments.* Barriers between organizations or between departments within one organization are obstacles to effective QI. Interdepartmental or intraorganizational friction or lack of cooperation result in waste, errors, delay, and unnecessary duplication of effort. QI requires that all workforce members, departments, and units share a unified purpose, direction, and commitment to improve the organization. Intraorganizational pathways are developed and cultivated as mechanisms by which to improve performance.

10. *Eliminate slogans, exhortations, and targets for the workforce for zero defects and new levels of productivity.* The problem with such exhortations is that they place the burden for quality on worker performance instead of poor system design. QI requires that the organization focus on improving its work processes. In so doing, service quality will increase, productivity and efficiency will rise, and waste will diminish.

11. *Eliminate management by numbers and objective—Substitute leadership.* Work production standards and rates, tied to incentive pay, are inappropriate because they burn out the workforce in the long run. Alternatively, according to Deming, a team effort should be marshaled to consistently increase quality, which will lead to increased profits/savings that can then be translated to, for example, higher salaries or better benefits. Improvement efforts should emphasize improving processes; the outcome numbers will change as a consequence.

12. *Remove barriers to pride of workmanship.* The workforce is the most important component of a healthcare delivery system because it cannot function properly without workers who are proud of their work and who feel respected as individuals and professionals. Managers can help workers be successful by making sure that job responsibilities and performance standards are clearly understood; building strong relationships between management and the workforce; and providing

11

workers with the best tools, instruments, supplies, and information possible.

13. *Institute a vigorous program of continuous education and self-improvement.* Healthcare workers can improve their lives through education and ever-broadening career and life opportunities. The field needs not just good people; it needs people who are growing through education and life experiences.

14. *Put everybody to work to accomplish this transformation.* The essence of QI is an organization-wide focus on meeting the needs of those who use or pay for healthcare services. Effective quality management programs go beyond emphasizing one or two efforts or areas to improve performance. Every activity, every process, and every job in behavioral healthcare can be improved. Everyone within the organization can be given an opportunity to understand the QI program and their individual role within that effort. Improvement teams that include broad representation throughout the organization can help ensure success of initial efforts and create opportunities for cross-disciplinary dialogue and information exchange.

Quality Objectives

The Institute of Medicine examined the U.S. healthcare system over the last few decades and published a series of reports that were a strong indictment of the safety and quality of the system. In December 1999 for example, the IOM released a report estimating that 98,000 people die each year in the United States from medical errors made by healthcare professionals. The IOM argued for the adoption of systematic QI techniques to make the system safer but also to institute the following objectives.

(1) access, (2) timeliness, (3) equitableness, (4) safety, (5) efficiency, (6) consumer centricity (7) good value, (8) effectiveness, (9) transparency, (10) evidence based.

What Do We Know about Quality in the Assessment and Treatment of the Paraphilias? An Important but Unmet Agenda

These quality objectives as a whole indicate the multiple dimensions and scope of the quality agenda and they are listed below in no particular order. What is most urgently needed in our field is a broad, comprehensive strategic plan to enable us to begin work on these quality objectives. We need baselines, profound knowledge about the processes that affect these; leadership in instituting a QI process related to this; and then training in QI tools and methods to begin the actual work on these.

Access

We need to know barriers to access and attempt to minimize these. In healthcare in general geography is seen as presenting access problems— practitioners are generally congregated in cities rather than rurally. In addition, for obvious reasons, the poor have more access problems as do non-English speakers. As a field we need to measure these barriers and to devise innovations to reduce their impact; teletherapy is one such innovation (O'Donohue & Draper, 2010).

Timeliness

We need to assess how quickly assessment and treatment takes place when someone requests this. Are there long waits? What can be done to decrease this waiting time?

Equitableness

Are there differences in quality of services to the poor vs. those in higher SES strata? Are there differences in quality of services to those from historically disadvantaged groups vs. those from the majority culture? What is to be done internationally, particularly with second and third world countries? Again, we need to develop benchmarks and start to reduce these differences in quality.

Safety

We need to develop measures of the safety of our assessments and treatments. What are the kinds of things that cause harm and what kinds of harm are there? Certainly, either the client or others (e.g., victims) can be harmed when assessments are incorrect (both in sensitivity and specificity errors). Treatment failures can involve further victims, which also is an obvious class of harm. We need to make a list of the kinds of harm that can be associated with our professional activities so that we can begin to understand the problematic processes that produce these and innovate to reduce their frequency.

Efficiency

How efficient are our services? Often our interventions can take years and maybe even decades with Relapse Prevention. How can we make these interventions more efficient? Do some treatment models have equivalent success rates but achieve these more efficiently (e.g., which is more efficient, the Good Lives Model or Relapse Prevention)?

Consumer Centricity

We need to understand who are our consumers and look at our services from their perspectives. Certainly, the client is one of our consumers—how do we provide information to him that allows him to act as an intelligent and empowered consumer? Therapist ratings, clear informed consent that accurately depicts risk and success rates, are steps in the right direction. Payers are also our consumers and we need to provide important information to third party payers: how we arrive at our diagnoses; how do we provide a good rationale for a treatment plan; what is the probability of success they are paying for; why they ought to believe that they are paying for the more efficient and effective therapy or assessment? And finally, society is also one of our consumers and as a whole society wants to be safe from further victimization. How do we properly take into account the legitimate interests of our society and provide services and information to address this?

Good Value

How do we drive down the cost of our services while driving up effectiveness? How do we give payers good value for their dollar? How do we demonstrate this in a fair and complete way? We need to start addressing these questions and providing information to stakeholders.

Effectiveness

We need to provide clear information on the effectiveness of our services, even when this is problematic (Marques et al., 2005). There are concerns about the general effectiveness of treatment and these must be honestly addressed. What is the evidence for effectiveness? What are the limitations? What are our failure rates? What are our success rates? How do these vary given type of client, problem, and therapist? What can be done to benchmark these and improve them?

Transparency

We need to provide this information in easily accessible ways. Therapist ratings and effectiveness results can be displayed on websites. The Association for the Treatment of Sexual Abusers (ATSA) can do a lot by providing consumer centric information about these issues (e.g., safety and cost). We need to empower all stakeholders with this information so they can make decisions. It is my hypothesis that it will be very good for our field when this information is displayed in a QI system and over the years when trends show that these quality indicators are showing continuous improvement.

Evidence Based

What are evidence based treatments and assessments in our field? The American Psychological Association (APA) convened an important committee and came up with a list of evidence based treatments, often known as the Chambless list. Should we do something similar? What criteria should be used? Once such a list is established, then as a field we can start to measure to what extent services are evidence based in the field.

Summary and Conclusions

Clearly there are many important and unanswered questions in the field of the assessment and treatment of sexual deviance. It would behoove us to understand important trends in healthcare and begin to consider the implications of these to our field. We need to frankly address quality dimensions and problems in our field and to embrace technologies and philosophies that will allow us to constantly improve our services. Our services need to be undertaken at the highest levels of quality possible because so much rides on these.

References

American Psychiatric Association. (2013). *Diagnostic and statistical manual of mental disorders* (*DSM-V*; 5th ed.). Washington, DC: Author.

Berwick, D., & Nolan, T. (1998). Physicians as leaders in improving health care. *Annals of Internal Medicine, 128*(4), 289–292.

Kiesler, D. A. (1966). Some myths of psychotherapy research and the search for a paradigm. *Psychological Bulletin, 65*(2), 110–136.

Laws, D. R., & O'Donohue, W. T. (2012). *Sexual deviance* (2nd ed.). New York, NY: Guilford.

Linehan, M. (2006). Two year randomized control trial and followup of dialectical behavior therapy. *Archives of General Psychiatry, 64,* 202–224.

Marques, J. K., Wideranders, M., Day, D. M., Nelson, C., & Ommeren, A. (2005). Effects of a relapse prevention program on sexual recidivism: Final results from California's sex offender treatment and evaluation project (SOTEP). *Sexual Abuse: A Journal of Research and Treatment, 17,* 79–107.

O'Donohue, W. T. (2010). A critique of the proposed *DSM-V* diagnosis of pedophilia. *Archives of Sexual Behavior, 39*(3), 587–590.

O'Donohue, W. T. (in press). *Clinical psychology and the philosophy of science*. New York, NY: Springer.

O'Donohue, W. T., & Draper, C. (2010). *Stepped care and ehealth*. New York, NY: Springer.

O'Donohue, W. T., & Letourneau, E. (1992). The psychometric properties of the penile tumescence assessment of child molesters. *Journal of Psychopathology and Behavioral Assessment, 14,* 123–174.

Sandfort, T. (1987). The argument for adult child sexual contact. In J. H. Geer & W. O'Donohue (Eds.), *The sexual abuse of children* (pp. 38–48). Hillsdale, NJ: Erlbaum.

Walton, M. (1986). *The Deming management method.* New York, NY: Perigee.

2

MULTISYSTEMIC THERAPY FOR YOUTH PROBLEM SEXUAL BEHAVIOR
A Case Example

Elizabeth J. Letourneau and Cindy M. Schaeffer

In this chapter, we describe an empirically supported intervention for youth with criminal and noncriminal sexual behavior problems; that is, multisystemic therapy for problem sexual behavior (MST-PSB). We also present a case example of the approach. MST-PSB is the only treatment for youth problem sexual behavior to have its effectiveness evaluated through randomized clinical trials (RCT), the gold standard for treatment outcome research (Reitzel & Carbonell, 2006). Indeed, three randomized clinical trials support the efficacy of MST-PSB. In the first of these (Borduin, Henggeler, Blaske, & Stein, 1990), 16 youth with sexual offenses were randomly assigned to MST-PSB or usual services, typically individual treatment. Across a 3-year follow-up, relative to youth in the usual services condition, youth in the MST-PSB condition had significantly lower sexual recidivism rates (12% vs. 75%) and lower, though not statistically significant lower general recidivism rates (25% vs. 50%). In the second RCT (Borduin, Schaeffer, & Heiblum, 2009), 48 youth with sexual offense adjudications were randomized to MST-PSB or usual services, typically group cognitive-behavioral therapy or individual therapy. Across an 8.9-year follow-up, relative to youth in the usual services condition, youth in the MST-PSB condition had significant lower rates of sexual recidivism (8% vs. 46%), general recidivism (29% vs. 58%), and spent 80% fewer days in detention facilities. In the most recent RCT, 127 youth were randomized to MST-PSB or usual services, typically specialized sex offender cognitive-behavior therapy that could be augmented with individual or family therapy (Letourneau et al., 2009). Across a 12-month follow-up, relative to youth in the usual services condition, youth in the MST-PSB condition had significantly greater improvement on measures of deviant sexual interest/risk, general delinquency, and substance use, and also were significantly less likely to spend time in costly out-of-home placements. We contend that the effectiveness of MST-PSB demonstrated by these three randomized controlled trials is due to its focus on ameliorating the broad range of known (i.e., established through research) correlates of sexual misbehavior.

The term *problem sexual behavior* (PSB) describes non-normative sexual behaviors by youth under the age of 18, whether formally adjudicated or not, which either victimize others or place others at risk of victimization. The range of deviant sexual behavior encompassed by this term includes nonaggressive sexual acts against others such as the fondling of a younger child in the context of an ongoing relationship, and aggressive sexual acts against others such as the violent rape of a peer. Under this definition, other non-normative sexual behaviors, such as excessive or public masturbation, would not be considered a PSB unless it did or had the potential to victimize others, or was part of a larger pattern of behaviors involving sexual victimization of others. We feel that use of the term *problem sexual behavior* is less stigmatizing and pejorative than the term *sexual offender*. However, in light of the fact that the term *juvenile sexual offender* abounds in the empirical literature, we will use this term when citing specific studies that defined their samples in this way (as do most of the studies on correlates of sexual offending).

Empirical and Theoretical Foundations of MST-PSB

MST-PSB is an adaptation of standard MST for youth who have engaged in nonsexual delinquent behavior (Henggeler, Schoenwald, Borduin, Rowland, & Cunningham, 1998, 2009). The treatment involves all components of the standard MST model (i.e., clinical interventions, staffing, quality assurance mechanisms), plus several additional clinical procedures to address the unique needs of youth with problem sexual behaviors and their families. Throughout the sections that follow, we use the term *standard MST* when referring to issues related uniquely to MST for nonsexual offenders; the term *MST-PSB* when referring uniquely to MST for problem sexual behaviors; and the term *MST* when speaking generally about both versions.

The effectiveness of standard MST has been established with chronic and violent juvenile delinquents and substance abusing youth (for reviews, see, e.g., Eyberg, Nelson, & Boggs, 2008; Henggeler, 2011; National Institute on Drug Abuse, 1999; U.S. Public Health Service, 2001; Waldron & Turner, 2008). Standard MST is designed to address the array of risk factors commonly associated with conduct problems among youth. Decades of cross-sectional and longitudinal research have shown that risk factors for conduct problems involve influences at multiple individual and environmental levels (Deater-Deckard, Dodge, Bates, & Pettit, 1998; Elliott 1994; Loeber, Farrington, Stouthamer-Loeber, & Van Kammen, 1998; Thornberry & Krohn, 2003).

Schoenwald and Rowland (2002) summarized the evidence for risk and protective factors associated with serious adolescent antisocial behavior. As indicated in their review, conduct problems are associated with low IQ, cognitive biases about the advantages of aggression, and social skill deficits (individual level risk factors), parental substance abuse, low parental supervision, and inconsistent family discipline (family level), association with deviant peers (peer level), low academic achievement and low commitment to education (school level), and neighborhoods characterized by high levels of poverty, residential mobility, and drug availability (community level).

Although the empirical literature regarding risk factors for youth problem sexual behavior is much less extensive, a consensus is emerging among reviewers that like other youth conduct problems, juvenile sexual offending is multidetermined and results from risk factors similar to those related to juvenile nonsexual offending (Borduin & Schaeffer, 2001; Seto & Lalumière, 2010; van Wijk, Vermeiren et al., 2006). In a large-scale, longitudinal study examining 66 correlates of juvenile sexual and violent offending, van Wijk and colleagues (van Wijk, Loeber, et al., 2005) found that violent sexual offenders were similar to violent nonsexual offenders with respect to nearly all risk factors relating to family (e.g., poor supervision and communication) and peers (e.g., involvement with delinquent and substance-abusing peers). Similarly, Ronis and Borduin (2007) found that juvenile sexual offenders, like other serious juvenile offenders, had lower bonding to family and school and higher involvement with deviant peers than did nondelinquent youth.

Seto and Lalumière (2010) analyzed results from 59 studies that compared youth with documented sexual offenses to youth with documented nonsexual offenses on 1 or more of 37 factors theoretically linked to juvenile sexual offending. Between groups differences were nonsignificant for the majority (57%) of these factors, including all or most factors that fell under the headings of family problems, interpersonal problems, cognitive problems, and psychopathology. There were more differences on factors falling under the headings of conduct problems, childhood abuse, and sexuality. In terms of conduct problems, youth with sexual offenses had less extensive criminal histories and were less likely to be characterized by substance use and antisocial associations, but were similar to youth with nonsexual offenses with respect to conduct problems, antisocial personal traits, and antisocial beliefs/attitudes. Youth with sexual offenses had more extensive victimization histories and were more likely to have experienced sexual victimization, emotional abuse, physical abuse, and to have families with other members who had been sexually victimized. Groups were equal with respect to consensual sexual experience, although youth with sexual offenses had more exposure to pornography and were more likely to be rated or to self-rate as having atypical sexual interests.

Given that risk factors for nonsexual and sexual conduct problems exist within and across multiple domains of a person's life, Bronfenbrenner's (1979) social ecological model provides a useful organizing framework for MST. According to this model, youth behavior is largely determined by the functioning of the systems (i.e., family, peer, school, and neighborhood) in which the youth is embedded and the reciprocal interplay between these systems. Consistent with this view, MST contends that for treatment to be effective, interventions must have the capacity to target risk factors in multiple domains and between systemic levels (e.g., caregiver interactions with other parents). Factors in the broader ecology (e.g., caregiver work hours, lack of age-appropriate peers in the neighborhood) that create barriers to the effective functioning of proximal systems also must be addressed for positive change to occur.

According to the social ecological perspective, behavior must be considered within its naturally occurring context. This view has direct implications for the design of MST interventions. MST uses a home-based model of service delivery that emphasizes ecological validity in the assessment of behavior and delivery of interventions. Assessments are considered ecologically valid when they solicit information from multiple sources (e.g., caregivers, siblings, extended family, teachers) and gauge the youth's functioning in a variety of real world settings (e.g., at home, in school, during neighborhood activities). Similarly, MST interventions are provided where problems occur (homes, schools, community locations) and, whenever possible, are delivered to the youth by key members of the ecology.

Theory of Change in MST

A central assumption of MST is that caregivers are the key to achieving and sustaining positive long-term outcomes. Thus, interventions focus intensely on empowering caregivers to obtain the resources and skills needed to more effectively parent and manage their children. As caregiver competencies (e.g., ability to provide consistent monitoring and supervision) increase, the therapist guides caregiver efforts to address other factors that might be contributing to a youth's problem behavior, such as excessive unstructured free time and poor school performance. The ultimate goal is to create a context that supports adaptive youth behavior (e.g., relationships with prosocial same-age peers, effective parenting), rather than a context that encourages antisocial or problem sexual behavior. Treatment also aims to surround caregivers with support from family, friends, and members of the community to help sustain the changes achieved during treatment. Importantly, the central emphases of MST on improved parenting and decreased youth association with deviant peers as central vehicles for change have been supported in several studies of both standard

MST and MST-PSB (Henggeler, Letourneau, et al., 2009; Huey, Henggeler, Brondino, & Pickrel, 2000; Schaeffer et al., 2010).

Characteristics of MST Clinical Implementation

Treatment Delivery

MST teams consist of two to four full-time master's level therapists, an advanced master's level or doctoral level supervisor who devotes at least 50% of his or her professional time to the team, and administrative support. Therapists carry caseloads of four to six families each. Members of an MST team usually work for private service provider organizations contracted by public juvenile justice, child welfare, and mental health authorities. Through collaboration with MST team members, therapists provide 24-hour/day and 7-day/week availability, which allows them to work with families at times the family finds convenient and to respond to clinical crises wherever and whenever they emerge. The duration of MST treatment is relatively brief, ranging from 3 to 5 months. However, the intervention process is intensive and often involves a total of 60 or more hours of direct contact with the family and other members of the ecology. As noted previously, there is a strong emphasis on the delivery of MST services in home- and community-based settings, which enhances the ecological validity of assessments and interventions, helps overcome barriers to service access, and facilitates family engagement in the treatment process.

Clinical Procedures

MST is highly individualized and does not follow a rigid manualized plan for treatment. Instead, nine treatment principles provide the underlying structure and framework upon which therapists build their interventions (see Table 2.1). The second treatment principle, for example, emphasizes that all aspects of MST must be strength-based. Therapists communicate an optimistic perspective to the family and other members of the youth's ecology throughout the assessment and treatment process. Therapists look for potential strengths within the contexts of the child (e.g., hobbies and interests, academic skills), family (e.g., problem-solving ability, affective bonds), peers (e.g., prosocial activities, achievement orientation), school (e.g., management practices, after-school activities), and the neighborhood/community (e.g., concerned neighbors, voluntary associations such as Boys and Girls clubs). Identified strengths then are leveraged in interventions. For example, a neighbor or extended family member might be enlisted to assist with monitoring the youth after school until a caregiver gets home from work.

Table 2.1 MST/MST-PSB Nine Treatment Principles

1.	The primary purpose of assessment is to understand the "fit" between the identified problems and their broader systemic context.
2.	Therapeutic contacts should emphasize the positive and use systemic strengths as levers for change.
3.	Interventions should be designed to promote responsible behavior and decrease irresponsible behavior among family members.
4.	Interventions should be present-focused and action-oriented, targeting specific and well-defined problems.
5.	Interventions should target sequences of behavior within and between multiple systems.
6.	Interventions should be developmentally appropriate and fit the developmental needs of the youth.
7.	Interventions should be designed to require daily or weekly effort by family members.
8.	Intervention efficacy should be evaluated continuously from multiple perspectives.
9.	Interventions should be designed to promote treatment generalization and long-term maintenance of therapeutic change.

Importantly, the nine treatment principles are applied using an analytical/decision-making process that structures the treatment plan, its implementation, and the evaluation of its effectiveness. Specific goals for treatment are set at individual, family, peer, and social network levels. Moreover, as noted previously, the adolescent's caregivers are viewed as key to achieving desired outcomes and as crucial for the generalizability and sustainability of treatment gains.

Early in the treatment process, the problem behaviors to be targeted are specified clearly from the perspectives of key stakeholders (e.g., family members, teachers, and juvenile justice authorities), and ecological strengths are identified. Then, based on multiple perspectives, the ecological factors that seem to be driving each problem are organized into a coherent conceptual framework (e.g., the youth's fondling of a younger child in the neighborhood seems to be associated with a lack of caregiver monitoring, no friendships with same-age peers, and truancy). Next, the MST therapist, with support from other team members (other therapists, supervisor, consultant), designs specific intervention strategies to target those "drivers." Strategies incorporate interventions from empirically supported, pragmatic, problem-focused treatments such as structural/strategic and behavioral family therapies, behavioral parent training, cognitive behavioral therapy, and motivational interviewing. Psychopharmacological interventions might also be incorporated into treatment when evidence indicates biological contributors to identified problems (e.g., untreated symptoms of attention deficit disorder). Importantly, these empirically supported interventions are highly integrated and are delivered in conjunction with interventions that address other pertinent ecological drivers of the identified problems (e.g., supporting caregivers in advocating for more appropriate school services, connecting caregivers with the parents of the youth's peers).

As discussed in a subsequent section, intervention effectiveness is monitored continuously from multiple perspectives. For example, MST supervisors review session recordings and client progress notes on a weekly basis and parents provide monthly evaluations of therapist adherence. When interventions are ineffective, identified drivers are reconceptualized, and modifications are made until an effective strategy is developed. This iterative process reinforces two important features of the MST model. First, MST teams strive to never give up on youth and families, doing "whatever it takes" to help families reach treatment goals. Second, when interventions are not successful, the failure is the team's, not the family's. In other words, when the team develops accurate hypotheses of the drivers, identifies barriers to implementation success, and delivers corresponding interventions appropriately, families tend to achieve their goals, and conduct problems among youth usually diminish.

Training, Supervision, and Ongoing Quality Assurance

Training and supervision in the MST model are provided in several ways. First, new therapists participate in a 5-day orientation training that provides initial grounding in MST. The training includes both didactic (instruction in social learning theory, review of research on correlates of conduct problems) and experiential (role plays on engagement, assessment, and intervention strategies) components. Second, as therapists gain experience delivering MST to families, quarterly booster trainings are conducted on site. Third, an on-site clinical supervisor trained in the MST model meets with therapists weekly to review cases, problem solve barriers to successful family engagement, and ensure the multisystemic focus of therapeutic interventions. Fourth, the clinical team discusses cases with an MST expert consultant once a week to obtain additional feedback and direction as needed. This consultant also helps to facilitate adherence to the MST model.

Training, supervision, and consultation take place within a comprehensive quality assurance/quality improvement (QA/QI) system designed to enhance fidelity to the MST treatment model. Considerable resources are devoted to this system because research supports a strong relationship between therapist adherence to MST and positive outcomes, including improved family relations, decreased affiliation with delinquent peers, and reduced long-term rates of arrest and incarceration (Henggeler, Melton, Brondino, Scherer, & Hanley, 1997; Henggeler, Pickrel, & Brondino,

1999; Huey et al., 2000; Schoenwald, Chapman, Sheidow, & Carter, 2009; Schoenwald, Ward, Henggeler, & Rowland, 2000). The process underlying the QA/QI system has been worked out through more than 15 years of experience assisting community-based agencies in developing and maintaining sustainable MST teams. In addition to the well-specified initial and ongoing training, supervision, and consultation protocols, key components of the QA/QI system include validated measures of implementation adherence at all levels (caregivers, therapists, supervisors, and consultants) and a web-based implementation tracking system to provide teams and provider organizations with ongoing specific feedback about adherence and youth outcomes.

In addition to providing weekly support to the clinical team, MST consultants offer organizational support to provider agencies that are interested in establishing MST programs. This support initially involves (a) community assessments to determine whether the needs that prompted stakeholder interest in MST are likely to be met by an MST program; (b) determination of whether an MST program is viable in a specific practice context (e.g., mechanisms are in place to reimburse therapists for mileage used to travel to families' homes); and (c) cultivation of stakeholder buy-in and commitment to the success of the program. After an MST program has been implemented in a community, consultants provide ongoing organizational support in the form of semi-annual program reviews, problem solving of organizational and stakeholder barriers to implementation, and support for program directors.

Interventions Unique to MST-PSB

As noted, MST-PSB is identical to standard MST in its broad focus on the many correlates associated with juvenile offending generally, but goes beyond standard MST by specifically focusing on aspects of the youth's ecology that are functionally related to the youth's sexual delinquency. Specifically, the clinical foci that are unique to MST-PSB include: (a) creating a family safety plan that minimizes the youth's access to potential victims; (b) addressing youth and caregiver denial about the severity of the sexual offense; and (c) improving youth's peer relations so that more age-appropriate and normative sexual experiences can occur with peers. To achieve these goals, MST-PSB tends to place a greater emphasis on structural and strategic family therapy interventions than does standard MST. These clinical adaptations to standard MST are specified in an MST-PSB treatment manual (Borduin, Letourneau, Henggeler, Saldana, & Swenson, 2005) and in 12 hours of supplemental training for MST-PSB therapists and supervisors in addition to those required for standard MST.

Clinical Trials of MST-PSB

Three studies have examined the efficacy and effectiveness of MST-PSB in addressing sexual offending by juveniles. Although modest in scope and size (N = 16), Borduin, Henggeler, et al. (1990) published the first randomized trial with juvenile sexual offenders. Youths and their families were randomly assigned to treatment conditions: MST was delivered by doctoral students in clinical psychology versus outpatient individual therapy (i.e., an eclectic blend of psychodynamic, humanistic, and behavioral approaches) delivered by community-based mental health professionals. Recidivism results at 3-year follow-up were encouraging. Significantly fewer youths in the MST condition were rearrested for sexual crimes (12.5% vs. 75.0%), and the mean frequency of sexual rearrests was considerably lower in the MST condition (0.12 vs. 1.62). Furthermore, the mean frequency of rearrests for nonsexual crimes was lower for the youths who received MST (.62) than for counterparts who received outpatient therapy (2.25).

Borduin, Schaeffer, and Heiblum (2009) evaluated outcomes in aggressive (i.e., sexual assault, rape) and nonaggressive (i.e., molestation of younger children) juvenile sexual offenders (N = 48) who were randomly assigned to MST-PSB or usual services (a combination of cognitive-behavioral group and individual treatment administered in a juvenile court setting). Compared to youths who received usual services, youths who received MST-PSB showed improvements on a range of outcomes immediately following treatment, including fewer behavioral problems, less delinquent behavior (self-reported), improved peer relations (i.e., more emotional bonding with peers, less involvement with deviant peers), improved family relations (i.e., more warmth, less conflict), and better grades in school. A 9-year post-treatment follow-up revealed that MST participants were significantly less likely than their usual services counterparts to be rearrested for sexual (12.5% vs. 41.7%) and nonsexual (29.2% vs. 62.5%) offenses. In terms of frequency of rearrests, MST participants had 83% fewer rearrests for sexual crimes (average 0.13 vs. 0.79 arrests) and 70% fewer rearrests for other crimes (average 1.46 vs. 4.88 arrests) than did those receiving usual services. MST youth also spent on average 75% fewer days in youth (22.50 vs. 97.50 days) and 80% fewer days in adult (365.00 vs. 1842.50 days) detention facilities.

A third randomized clinical trial (Letourneau et al., 2009) used therapists in community practice settings (i.e., effectiveness trial). In this study of 127 participants, MST-PSB was compared to an intervention typical of those provided for juvenile sexual offenders in the United States, namely cognitive-behavioral interventions focused on individual (youth-level) behavioral drivers delivered in weekly group treatment sessions for a year or longer (Letourneau & Borduin, 2008; Walker, McGovern, Poey, &

Otis, 2004). Relative to their comparison condition counterparts, youth who received MST-PSB had significantly greater reductions in problem sexual behavior, delinquent behavior, substance use, and internalizing symptoms over a 12-month postrecruitment follow-up period. In addition, youth who received MST-PSB were significantly less likely to have an out-of-home placement (e.g., in detention or residential facilities) during this time frame than were those who received standard community treatment. These effects did not vary by type of sexual offending (i.e., younger victim vs. not; aggressive or nonaggressive offense).

Case Study

Referral Behavior

"Jared" (a pseudonym) was a 14-year-old boy court-ordered to treatment after adjudication for sexually assaulting his younger female cousin. At the time of the offenses, Jared was 12 years old and his cousin was 9 years old. During an extended visit with his aunt, Jared physically assaulted his cousin, forced her to give him oral sex, and threatened to hurt or kill her if she ever told anyone about the event. He then forced her to give him oral sex on at least two more occasions during the same visit. The girl disclosed the offenses to her mother after about a month of poor sleeping and nightmares. The aunt confronted Jared, who admitted to the offenses. His mother agreed to place Jared in counseling. The aunt contacted the police only after Jared continued to contact her daughter by phone and her daughter continued experiencing nightmares. Jared pled guilty to the charges but subsequently denied sexual involvement with his cousin and instead said that she frequently propositioned him for oral sex. He was convicted of aggravated criminal sexual assault, sentenced to 5 years of probation, and court-ordered to specialized treatment to address the sexual offending behavior.

Desired Outcomes, Strengths, and Needs

At the time of referral, the MST-PSB therapist identified numerous strengths. Jared resided with his mother and younger brother in the home of his maternal grandparents. All family members reported concern for Jared's treatment success. Jared enjoyed school and generally completed assignments, enjoyed sports, and had several prosocial friends. His mother enjoyed significant informal support from her parents and participated in community gatherings. Systemic weaknesses included Jared's disrespectful behavior toward his mother and grandparents and frequent arguments with his younger brother. Jared and his brother had almost no contact with their biological father and there was a lack of structure in the home. Jared's mother was in recovery for drug addiction, had previously been incarcerated, and was unemployed. She was estranged from her siblings, including her sister who had filed the charges against Jared, and an older brother. Jared had relationships with some negative peers in the neighborhood where there also was noticeable drug trafficking and gang presence. He was frequently in trouble at school for unexcused absences and aggressive behavior. As noted above, despite initially acknowledging his offense, Jared subsequently denied his culpability, and the family was bitter toward the victim and her mother.

In collaboration with Jared and his mother, the MST-PSB therapist identified several factors that appeared to be associated with his problem sexual behaviors. These included, at the individual youth level, poor impulse control, poor knowledge of appropriate sexual behavior, and early sexual debut. At the family level, factors included lack of adult supervision, low family cohesion, and low affective bonds. Among these, sexual knowledge and supervision were prioritized immediately, followed by efforts to improve Jared and his mother's affective bond and improve his impulse control.

Treatment goals were obtained from Jared, his mother, his grandparents, his probation officer, and the MST-PSB therapist. These goals tended to focus on (a) elimination of inappropriate sexual behavior; (b) improved respect for adults including parents, grandparents, and teachers; (c) reduced verbal aggression (primarily toward his brother); (d) improved compliance with household rules; and (e) improved academic achievement.

Safety Planning

Because Jared was denying his offense and the family was upset with the victim's mother for pursuing charges, increasing the cousin's and other children's safety from inappropriate sexual acts took priority. Although upset that her sister pursued formal charges, Jared's mother did not deny the abuse and was willing to increase her monitoring of Jared to ensure that he did not have unsupervised access to younger children. Jared's grandparents also agreed to assist with supervision and monitoring. The MST-PSB therapist also facilitated conversations between Jared and his mother regarding expected and appropriate dating and sexual behavior, and establishing clear consequences for violating these expectations.

Intervention for Fit Factors

A supervision plan was developed so that an adult monitored Jared during all after-school and weekend hours. Jared's mother and grandparents provided supervision, and he also was involved in after-school sports during which he was supervised by coaches. The supervision plan appeared to be working, as assessed by unannounced drop-ins by the MST-PSB therapist. However, the increased involvement of Jared's grandparents in his and his brother's care seemed to contribute to increased conflict between Jared's mother and grandparents. After about one month of treatment, Jared's mother departed with both of her children without informing her parents, the MST-PSB thera- pist, or Jared's probation officer in advance. She did, however, remain in touch with the MST-PSB therapist for the 3 weeks they were away and then returned to the city, taking up residence with a friend. The MST-PSB thera- pist tried to assist the family in identifying more permanent housing, but when public housing finally became available, it was far from the mother's family and friends and thus deemed unsuitable by Jared's mother. The therapist also worked with the mother on more effectively addressing conflict and keeping the grandparents involved in Jared's care.

Jared and his brother spent afternoons with their grandparents who con- tinued to provide weekday supervision. Jared's demeanor toward his mother, grandparents, and teachers improved markedly after being targeted in treat- ment. Despite treatment advances, Jared's mother moved a second time with no notice and the MST-PSB therapist became concerned that the mother had returned to abusing substances after 3 years of sobriety. The mother denied substance use and continued to meet regularly with the therapist. The MST- PSB therapist coached the mother for a parent-teacher meeting during which she learned that Jared was doing very well in his classes and with his behavior. The neighbor with whom they lived also became involved in Jared's care and the housing situation seemed stable, with Jared's mother providing instru- mental support to the neighbor in return for housing. However, after a couple of months the neighbor moved, which necessitated the family's third move in 4 months. Also at this time the grandparents withdrew some financial sup- port from the mother, citing their desire for her to become more independent. Shortly thereafter, Jared's mother was arrested and detained for alleged theft and fraud. Jared and his brother then moved in with their maternal uncle and his wife. The MST therapist engaged the uncle and aunt in treatment, and they agreed to keep the boys through the end of the school year to provide stability, but refused to consider keeping the boys longer due to strained rela- tionships with Jared's mother.

After more than 5 months of treatment, there had been no new complaints of inappropriate behavior of any kind. Jared was doing well at school, dem- onstrating respectful behavior toward adults, and was properly supervised. He and his brother appeared to be in reasonably stable housing with their uncle and aunt, and the family seemed ready for discharge. However, Jared's mother was unexpectedly released from custody early, moved back in with her parents, and made clear her intention to retrieve both boys from their uncle. Around this time, Jared was accused of theft involving cash and other items from a teacher, a guidance counselor, and a student at his school. He was suspended from school, punished appropriately by his uncle, and given additional proba- tion requirements. Treatment was extended to ensure that this setback did not spiral into additional behavior problems and also to shore up Jared's uncle's affective bond with Jared. Two months later, Jared's mother did in fact pull the boys from their uncle's care. She was able to move into her own apartment, and her 33-year-old son returned home and moved in to provide support to his mother and his younger brothers. The MST therapist reengaged with Jared's mother and coached her on thanking her brother for his care of her sons, with the aim of strengthening family relations so that Jared and his brother would continue to benefit from extended family involvement.

Jared was successfully discharged from treatment with no accusations or charges for inappropriate or illegal sexual behavior, consistent improvement in school achievement, reduced impulse control problems, and an increased level of respectful behavior toward mother and other family members. He had no new incidents of theft or other school-related behavior problems.

Final Treatment Considerations and Conclusions

As illustrated by the case example, treating youth with problem sexual behaviors often involves addressing factors that, on face value, might appear irrelevant to the goal of reducing a youth's risk for recidivism and increasing his or her likelihood of successfully navigating adolescence. In Jared's case, frequent moves by his mother could have increased his risk for future offending if those moves had been accompanied by reduced supervision and increased opportunities to offend. The MST-PSB therapist exerted considerable effort in helping the mother to ensure that Jared's supervision was maintained with the assistance of family members and friends throughout these moves. He also engaged Jared's probation officer to help ensure that Jared remained in family settings. It is easy to imagine a different scenario, in which a therapist frustrated with a "resistant" parent might collude with a probation officer to remove a youth from parental care and place him in a residential treatment setting to enhance stability and safety. In this alternate and relatively common scenario, the cost of treatment increases, bonds with family members, friends, and schoolteachers are broken, and a multitude of learning opportunities are lost. In those rare cases in which parents or guardians ultimately prove unable to help improve their children's behavior problems, MST therapists look to youths' families and family friends for alternate caregivers, limiting recommendations for residential placement to cases in which such restrictive placement is absolutely required to keep the youth and community safe.

In this case, keeping Jared with family members allowed his mother to establish behavioral expectations with her son, increase her communication with Jared's teachers, and negotiate difficult family situations more effectively. Jared also was able to learn and practice respectful behavior with his brother, mother, and grandparents, and his grandparents and uncle were able to establish better bonds with Jared and increase their role in his care. Involving members of the youth's natural ecology as full collaborators in the youth's care and treatment also helps to ensure that interventions will be culturally appropriate and that treatment gains will be sustained after treatment ends.

Court-ordered treatment presents numerous challenges, including engaging with youth and parents who might perceive treatment as forced upon them. In our experience, a common complaint among therapists is that some parents of delinquent youth are "resistant" to therapists' efforts to intervene. MST therapists and supervisors are trained to evaluate barriers to treatment engagement that extend beyond such simplistic and unhelpful explanations (Henggeler, Schoenwald, et al., 1998, 2009). For example, a common barrier to engagement (though not in the present case) is when parents denied a sexual offense had occurred. In such cases, therapists work to understand the denial (e.g., some parents believed that sex offenses were only committed by "monsters" and their children were not monsters) and then worked to address the barrier (e.g., to help parents understand the context in which a beloved youth with many strengths might commit a sexual offense). When necessary, MST therapists expend considerable effort on initiating and maintaining family engagement and are held responsible for engagement or the lack thereof (Cunningham & Henggeler, 1999). In addition, collaborating effectively with probation officers, lawyers, and other members of the juvenile justice system (which frequently includes other therapists, e.g., for victims) is part of the "art" of effective MST treatment. Although empirical evaluations have not yet tested this hypothesis, we hold that treatment success is partly a matter of aligning all members of the youth's ecology with the treatment goals; consequently, MST therapists are trained to know when to take a "one-down" approach with other professionals to enhance engagement and when to assert control over cases with multiple participants.

Whereas court-ordered treatment can be challenging in general, this is particularly true when the offense involves sexual abuse. The state in which Jared's case was treated has a sex offender management board (SOMB) that had to approve all treatment providers. SOMBs became popular in the 1990s and often are given the authority to develop and enforce state standards regarding sex offender assessment and treatment. In this case, the state SOMB requirements for assessment included polygraph testing, a requirement with numerous troubling qualities. There is no scientific support for the use of polygraphs with adolescents and limited support for its use with adults and only with very narrowly construed questions (National Research Council, 2002). Despite these limits, polygraph test results often inform consequential decisions (e.g., whether to violate a youth's probation) and thus its use seems likely to disrupt therapist–client rapport and engagement and raises serious ethical concerns (Chaffin, 2011). To address these concerns in Jared's case, we successfully petitioned for a waiver of this and other requirements poorly aligned with the MST-PSB treatment model (e.g., a requirement for group treatment, which can increase the risk of delinquency training). MST-PSB therapists routinely engage in such advocacy efforts whenever state or local laws are developmentally inappropriate, not evidence based, and potentially harmful to the youth and families served.

Another consideration is that youth of minority race and ethnicity are often overrepresented in juvenile justice systems (Bishop, 2005). Research has indicated that MST treatment effects can be stronger when therapist and caregiver race or ethnicity match (Halliday-Boykins, Schoenwald, & Letourneau, 2005), possibly due to better appreciation and navigation of cultural factors. Success of MST-PSB in Jared's case might be due, in part, to the fact that Jared's therapist also was African American, as was the MST Supervisor for this MST team. Of note, the relationship between therapist–caregiver match and youth outcomes is partially mediated by therapist adherence to the MST model. Thus, the take-home message is not that therapist and caregiver race and ethnicity must match (an impossible and unnecessary requirement), but that therapist adherence to the MST model should be supervised more closely when race or ethnicity differs between therapists and families. Jared's therapist consistently achieved high adherence ratings and that high adherence to the MST model likely contributed more to treatment success than any other factor.

In summary, strong empirical support for MST as adapted to address problem sexual behaviors (MST-PSB) resulting from three randomized clinical trials indicates that family-based interventions for these types of problems are feasible—even in very difficult family settings and with youth who have engaged in serious sexually abusive behavior. However, more research is needed. No single intervention will ever be sufficient for serving the needs of all youth and their families. There is a strong case to be made for developing less intensive interventions for youth with fewer and less severe behavior problems and an even stronger case for evaluating the effects of treatment delivered in specialized "juvenile sex offender" residential treatment settings which have evaded empirically rigorous evaluation to date. Determining whether common treatment approaches and delivery modalities are effective, ineffective, or harmful is an ethical imperative, given that youth often spend years in these programs (Letourneau & Borduin, 2008).

References

Bishop, D. M. (2005). The role of race and ethnicity in juvenile justice processing. In D. F. Hawkins & K. Kempf-Leonard (Eds.), *Our children, their children: Confronting racial and ethnic differences in American juvenile justice* (pp. 23–82). Chicago, IL: University of Chicago Press.

Borduin, C. M., Henggeler, S. W., Blaske, D. M., & Stein, R. (1990). Multisystemic treatment of adolescent sexual offenders. *International Journal of Offender Therapy and Comparative Criminology, 34*, 105–113.

Borduin, C. M., Letourneau, E. J., Henggeler, S. W., Saldana, L., & Swenson, C. C. (2005). *Treatment manual for multisystemic therapy with juvenile sexual offenders and their families.* Unpublished manual, Department of Psychiatry and Behavioral Sciences, Medical University of South Carolina, Charleston, SC.

Borduin, C. M., & Schaeffer, C. M. (2001). Multisystemic treatment of juvenile sexual offenders: A progress report. *Journal of Psychology and Human Sexuality, 13*, 25–42.

Borduin, C. M., Schaeffer, C. M., & Heiblum, N. (2009). A randomized clinical trial of multisystemic therapy with juvenile sexual offenders: Effects on youth social ecology and criminal activity. *Journal of Consulting and Clinical Psychology, 77*, 26–37.

Bronfenbrenner, U. (1979). *The ecology of human development: Experiments by nature and design.* Cambridge, MA: Harvard University Press.

Chaffin, M. (2011). The case of juvenile polygraphy as a clinical ethics dilemma. *Sexual Abuse: A Journal of Research and Treatment, 23*, 314–328.

Cunningham, P. B., & Henggeler, S. W. (1999). Engaging multiproblem families in treatment: Lessons learned throughout the development of multisystemic therapy. *Family Process, 38*, 265–281.

Deater-Deckard, K., Dodge, K. A., Bates, J. E., & Pettit, G. S. (1998). Multiple risk factors in the development of externalizing behavior problems: Group and individual differences. *Development and Psychopathology, 10*, 469–493.

Elliott, D. S. (1994). Serious violent offenders: Onset, developmental course, and termination. The American Society of Criminology 1993 presidential address. *Criminology, 32*, 1–21.

Eyberg, S. M., Nelson, M. M., & Boggs, S. R. (2008). Evidence-based psychosocial treatments for children and adolescents with disruptive behavior. *Journal of Clinical Child & Adolescent Psychology, 37*, 215–237.

Halliday-Boykins, C. A., Schoenwald, S. K., & Letourneau, E. J. (2005). Caregiver–therapist ethnic similarity predicts youth outcomes from an empirically based treatment. *Journal of Consulting and Clinical Psychology, 73*, 808–818

Henggeler, S. W. (2011). Efficacy studies to large-scale transport: The development and validation of multisystemic therapy programs. *Annual Review of Clinical Psychology, 7*, 351–381.

Henggeler, S. W., Letourneau, E. J., Chapman, J. E., Borduin, C. M., Schewe, P. A., & McCart, M. R. (2009). Mediators of change for multisystemic therapy with juvenile sexual offenders. *Journal of Consulting and Clinical Psychology, 77*, 451–462.

Henggeler, S. W., Melton, G. B., Brondino, M. J., Scherer, D. G., & Hanley, J. H. (1997). Multisystemic therapy with violent and chronic juvenile offenders and their families: The role of treatment fidelity in successful dissemination. *Journal of Consulting and Clinical Psychology, 65*, 821–833.

Henggeler, S. W., Pickrel, S. G., & Brondino, M. J. (1999). Multisystemic treatment of substance abusing and dependent delinquents: Outcomes, treatment fidelity, and transportability. *Mental Health Services Research, 1*, 171–184.

Henggeler, S. W., Schoenwald, S. K., Borduin, C. M., Rowland, M. D., & Cunningham, P. B. (1998). *Multisystemic therapy of antisocial behavior in children and adolescents* (2nd ed.). New York, NY: Guilford.

Henggeler, S. W., Schoenwald, S. K., Borduin, C. M., Rowland, M. D., & Cunningham, P. B. (2009). *Multisystemic therapy of antisocial behavior in children and adolescents* (2nd ed.). New York, NY: Guilford.

Huey, S. J., Henggeler, S. W., Brondino, M. J., & Pickrel, S. G. (2000). Mechanisms of change in multisystemic therapy: Reducing delinquent behavior through therapist adherence and improved family and peer functioning. *Journal of Consulting and Clinical Psychology, 68,* 451–467.

Letourneau, E. J., & Borduin, C. M. (2008). The effective treatment of juveniles who sexually offend: An ethical imperative [Special Issue: Ethics of Treatment and Intervention Research with Children and Adolescents with Behavioral and Mental Disorders]. *Ethics and Behavior, 18,* 286–306.

Letourneau, E. J., Henggeler, S. W., Borduin, C. M., Schewe, P. A., McCart, M. R., Chapman, J. E., & Saldana, L. (2009). Multisystemic therapy for juvenile sexual offenders: 1-year results from a randomized effectiveness trial. *Journal of Family Psychology, 23,* 89–102.

Loeber, R., Farrington, D. P, Stouthamer-Loeber, M., & Van Kammen, W. B. (1998). *Antisocial behavior and mental health problems: Explanatory factors in childhood and adolescence.* Mahwah, NJ: Erlbaum.

National Institute on Drug Abuse. (1999). *Principles of drug addiction treatment: A research-based guide* (NIH Publication No. 99-4180). Rockville, MD: Author.

National Research Council. (2002). *The polygraph and lie detection.* Committee to Review the Scientific Evidence on the Polygraph. Division of Behavioral and Social Sciences and Education. Washington, DC: The National Academies Press.

Reitzel, L. R., & Carbonell, J. L. (2006). The effectiveness of sex offender treatment for juveniles as measured by recidivism: A meta-analysis. *Sexual Abuse: A Journal of Research and Treatment, 18,* 401–421.

Ronis, S. T., & Borduin, C. M. (2007). Individual, family, peer, and academic characteristics of male juvenile sexual offenders. *Journal of Abnormal Child Psychology, 35,* 153–163.

Schaeffer, C. M., Henggeler, S. W., Chapman, J. E., Halliday-Boykins, C. A., Cunningham, P. B., Randall, J., & Shapiro, S. B. (2010). Mechanisms of effectiveness in juvenile drug court: Altering risk processes associated with delinquency and substance abuse. *Drug Court Review, 7,* 57–94.

Schoenwald, S. K., Chapman, J. E., Sheidow, A. J., & Carter, R. E. (2009). Long-term youth criminal outcomes in MST transport: The impact of therapist adherence and organizational climate and structure. *Journal of Clinical Child & Adolescent Psychology, 38,* 91–105.

Schoenwald, S. K., & Rowland, M. D. (2002). Multisystemic therapy. In B. J. Burns & K. Hoagwood (Eds.), *Community treatment for youth: Evidence-based interventions for severe emotional and behavioral disorders* (pp. 91–116). New York, NY: Oxford University Press.

Schoenwald, S. K., Ward, D. M., Henggeler, S. W., & Rowland, M. D. (2000). MST vs. hospitalization for crisis stabilization of youth: Placement outcomes 4 months post-referral. *Mental Health Services Research, 2,* 3–12.

Seto, M. C., & Lalumière, M. L. (2010). What is so special about male adolescent sexual offending? A review and test of explanations through meta-analysis. *Psychological Bulletin, 136,* 526–475.

Thornberry, T. P., & Krohn, M. D. (Eds.). (2003). *Taking stock of delinquency: An overview of findings from contemporary longitudinal studies.* New York, NY: Kluwer/Plenum.

U.S. Public Health Service. (2001). *Youth violence: A report of the Surgeon General.* Washington, DC: Author.

Van Wijk, A., Loeber, R., Vermeiren, R., Pardini, D., Bullens, R., & Doreleijers, T. (2005). Violent juvenile sex offenders compared with violent juvenile nonsex offenders: Explorative findings from the Pittsburgh Youth Study. *Sexual Abuse: A Journal of Research and Treatment, 17*, 335–352.

Van Wijk, A., Vermeiren, R., Loeber, R., Hart-Kerkhoffs, L., Doreleijers, T., & Bullens, R. (2006). Juvenile sex offenders compared to non-sex offenders: A review of the literature 1995–2005. *Trauma, Violence, & Abuse, 7*, 227–243.

Waldron, H. B., & Turner, C. W. (2008). Evidence-based psychosocial treatments for adolescent substance abuse: A review and meta-analyses. *Journal of Clinical Child and Adolescent Psychology, 37*, 1–24.

Walker, D. F., McGovern, S. K., Poey, E. L., & Otis, K. E. (2004). Treatment effectiveness for male adolescent sexual offenders: A meta-analysis and review. *Journal of Child Sexual Abuse, 13*, 281–293.

3

CLINICAL REFLECTIONS ON THE ASSESSMENT AND TREATMENT OF A RAPIST

Lawrence Ellerby

As a forensic psychologist whose practice is primarily clinical in nature, the opportunity to offer a case study of a client and provide reflections related to clinical approaches to assessment and treatment was a welcome invitation. Clinicians need to be informed and guided by the current research and literature related to etiology, theoretical models, assessment, and treatment related to individuals who commit sexual offenses, and clinical interventions should be evidence based. At the same time, the translation and application of research into practice is not always clear, clean, or comprehensive. Clinical realities present challenges that the research literature may not inform on; the literature may identify that a certain tool, theory, model, or intervention is applicable yet not have the research base to actually support this; and at times clinical experiences may not be consistent with existing research findings. The strength of the empirical literature in our field has evolved over the years and provides many important contributions to our knowledge base. Notwithstanding, our ability to operationally define as well as to measure and isolate complex psychological constructs involved in our field is still a challenge and likely impacts the research findings and the direction to which empirical evidence may point. There are times in which good old clinical intuition, founded and grounded in an understanding of the literature and as well as with experience with direct clinical experience contact with clients, can provide direction for clinical assessment and treatment that research has yet to examine or warrantinform. The goal of this chapter is to use a case study to highlight clinical issues important for practitioners to be aware of, as they navigate the challenges of assessing and treating adult males who have committed a sexual offense(s) against adult female victims. The case study will be used to illustrate examples of evidence based assessment and treatment protocols as well as examples of clinical wisdom that may not be reflected in the research literature.

The Case

Lewis is a 36-year-old Caucasian male of Italian descent. At age 33 he sexually assaulted three young women (ages 21, 24, and 26), all of whom were strangers to him, and, at age 35 he was convicted of Sexual Assault, Sexual Assault with a Weapon (x2), Forcible Confinement (x3), Choking to Overcome Resistance, Disguise with Intent, and Break and Enter. He received a 5-year sentence in addition to having spent 1 year of custody in remand prior to being sentenced. On the advice of his defense attorney Lewis entered a guilty plea to the charges against him to acquire this sentence versus going to trial with the prosecution initially looking for an 8-year sentence.

Lewis's offending behavior involved either surprise or manipulation in his approach (e.g., approaching and then immediately attacking, or using a ruse to gain access to the victim). All of the offenses involved violence, including restraining, verbal threats, producing and threatening with a weapon (a knife), and physical assault (e.g., pushing, restraining, choking, holding the knife to their throats). The sexually aggressive behavior in these various offenses included him demanding and forcing the women to masturbate and fellate him, and forced attempted or completed vaginal intercourse. He also directed the women to assume specific poses during two of the assaults to facilitate his arousal, and would masturbate watching them in this position. At the time of his arrest, Lewis was found in the possession of a knife and a form of pepper spray (Bear Spray, which unlike pepper spray is legal to carry in Canada unless it is used to cause "a risk of imminent death or serious bodily harm to another person or harm the environment"). Lewis has a prior history of sexual offending behavior and was on probation at the time he committed the above offenses. At age 29 he was convicted for Criminal Harassment (x7), Possession of Prohibited Weapon, Indecent Telephone Calls (x10), Uttering Threats (x4), and an Indecent Act, and received a 2-year sentence followed by 3 years' probation. These convictions were related to incidents of Lewis following young adult women to their homes, obtaining their addresses, looking up their phone numbers, and then making harassing, threatening, and sexually explicit telephone calls to them. He also made several obscene telephone calls to telephone crisis line workers. The Indecent Act was related to him exposing himself to, and masturbating in front of a young adult woman he followed home.

Lewis was raised by both biological parents and was the youngest child with two older sisters. His father was often absent from the family home, and when home, Lewis described him as passive, avoidant, and emotionally unavailable. He described his mother as being a domineering, controlling, and extremely abusive woman who verbally, physically, and emotionally abused him. Lewis also reported an incident of sexual abuse by a male teacher in elementary school.

Lewis offered having had a number of rather chronic behavioral problems in school (e.g., truancy, fighting) beginning in grade 6 and was average in his academic performance. His marks dropped in grade 10, about the time he began to skip school more frequently and started using marijuana. He described being bored by some subjects, began failing classes, and dropped out in grade 11, prioritizing work over school. He worked as a laborer in construction. Lewis later returned to complete high school as a mature student and attended a community college where he completed a woodworking program. Lewis began working in construction. He later took a course and secured a license that allowed him to drive transport trucks, and drove trucks for a number of years. As a result of incurring criminal charges, which limited his ability to travel, he returned to construction work. Lewis had a relatively stable employment history. Overall, he enjoyed his jobs, had a strong work ethic, and felt competent in his work. He indicated that at the time of his offense he was struggling on the job as he had a new female supervisor whom he described as a "bitch." He claimed she was ineffective and "had it in for me."

Lewis reported a history of casual marijuana use, and regular alcohol consumption, drinking to relieve stress and anger. He acknowledged frequently drinking to the point of intoxication, but denied that his alcohol use had a detrimental impact on his life. He offered that none of his crimes were committed in a state of intoxication, although at the time of arrest for his current offenses he reported telling police he was intoxicated, stating he did this to create a potential mitigating factor for sentencing. Lewis reported a number of "one night stands" and short-term casual sexual encounters (approximately 50) and identified having been involved in three serious relationships in his life. His first was at age 18 with a same aged woman he described being in love with; however she was not as serious about the relationship and ended it after about one year. His next relationship occurred at age 20, and he described not allowing himself to become as emotionally attached to her so he would not be hurt again. This relationship lasted about a year and a half and ended when she relocated. Lewis's next serious relationship began when he was 23 years of age and after 4 years of dating the two married, and within a year had a son. Shortly after this he became involved in his first set of offenses; Lewis was charged, convicted, and incarcerated for almost 2 years. His wife stayed with and supported him; however, she ended the relationship after he re-offended and incurred his most recent charges. Lewis's account of this relationship suggested he felt he was self-sacrificing, unappreciated, used, that his wife contributed little to the relationship and maintenance of the household, and that he was suspicious of her, believing she had been unfaithful during the course of their marriage. He described assuming a passive role, not communicating or dealing with conflict, and acknowledged coping with the stress of the relationship by avoiding home, spending time drinking at the bar, engaging in extramarital affairs, and ruminating about his anger towards women.

Lewis was referred for a risk assessment while he was incarcerated, to assist in case and treatment planning.

Assessment

It is important to use an evidence based approach in conducting forensic/ risk assessments and there are many clinical considerations that can be utilized to optimize the assessment process and provide for a quality evaluation. Assessments are extremely important and can have a significant impact on an individual's life; contributing to the type and length of sentence, restrictions and conditions, the type of facility he or she is detained in, the programming/treatment the person might receive, release to the community, and the possibility of further consequences following the end of the sentence. It is therefore imperative that assessments be conducted with the utmost care, using appropriate and sound practice. A good assessment can serve many roles and should help to provide an understanding of the offending behavior; risk and risk factors; create a baseline from which change may be considered; and offer an opportunity to begin the process of engaging a client into a therapeutic milieu, whether or not the assessing clinicians will be doing follow-up treatment (Barbaree, Peacock, Cortoni, Marshall, & Seto, 1998; Gordon & Hover, 1998; Jones, Winkler, Kacin, Salloway, & Weissman, 1998).

Getting Started

In conducting the assessment on Lewis, the evaluation included a typical series of data-gathering methods including review of background information, clinical interviews, psychological testing and self-report measures, the application of actuarial and guided structured risk assessment tools, and collateral interviews (Ellerby & Ellerby, 2002; Ward, McCormack, Hudson, & Polaschek, 1997). In orienting to and organizing for an assessment, it is important to review and consider the referral question and the background information provided. In Lewis's case, typical of many, the referral agency provided very basic information in their referral request; asking for a risk assessment and information on treatment needs and readiness. It can be helpful to clarify the assessment question(s) with the agency of referral. A brief conversation can clarify their needs and the referral questions, and ensure their expectations are appropriate and realistic, and can be met. In Lewis's case it became evident that, in addition to wanting to know about his risk for sexual recidivism and treatment needs, there were also questions related to his general mental health functioning and his history of substance abuse and current use, and how these may have contributed to his offending, and be related to risk. There were also questions about his treatment amenability as well as his honesty and commitment in therapy, given he re-offended while on probation and in sex offender treatment.

Given that Lewis had a prior history for sexual offending behavior, it was also evident that the background information forwarded at the time of referral was incomplete. It is important to review file information to make sure you have as much of the available material as possible. For example, in Lewis's case, corrections' reports referred to historical reports completed at the time of his past offenses (e.g., psychological report, psychiatric report, treatment and program performance reports); however, copies of these documents were not included. As a result, the agency of referral was tasked by me with securing the additional background information required, and in my initial meeting with Lewis he was asked to sign a consent form authorizing the release of reports that Corrections were uncertain they could acquire. Prior to commencing an assessment it is important to have the requisite background information, and if necessary, to identify limitations in the information reviewed.

The process of starting with the client is of great importance, as it sets the stage for the evaluation process. Lewis's institutional case management officer informed me that although he was willing to participate in the assessment, he was doing this because he felt he "had to" and was not pleased about it. As a result, I anticipated resistance and the possibility of him presenting with a negative and hostile attitude. My goal in starting with Lewis was to attempt to preempt his resistance and respond to any resistance demonstrated in an engaging way. I greeted him in an authentically friendly manner, introduced myself, and extended my hand to shake his, and welcomed him to our meeting. After sitting, having specifically set the seating so we were across from each other versus interviewing him from behind a desk, I let him know I was aware he was not thrilled to be participating in the assessment and was pleased he attended for the interview. The initial focus of my inquiries and our discussion, centered around his concerns about participating in the assessment (i.e., having had a negative past assessment, not trusting the system) and why he had agreed to attend this appointment (i.e., knowing he would not be considered for privileges such as transfer to a lower security institution or an early release through Day Parole if he did not participate). The discussion then shifted to providing him with information about what the assessment process would entail (e.g., reviewing background information, clinical interviews, psychological testing and self-report measures, application of risk assessment tools, collateral interviews), how I, as a clinician, work (e.g., will answer any questions he has, be candid with him about my opinion, assuring him there was no hidden agenda or tricks involved in this process), and discussing how we could attend to his concerns if they arose. We discussed the realities related to the assessment (e.g., the issues of risk in his case) and put this into a context of how the evaluation could be helpful in assisting him begin to better understand the problems that have contributed to his offending and his level of risk. The assessment could also provide recommendations that could assist him in addressing these issues and I hoped assist him to better manage his life, avoid the criminal justice system, and desist from continuing to hurt others and himself. At this point, Lewis appeared much more at ease and his initial negative attitude and posturing subsided.

The next step was to review our Assessment Consent Form with Lewis. The consent form we use is three pages in length, as we want the client to be providing informed consent and be sure he is fully aware of what the assessment will include; the limits of confidentiality; mandatory reporting; when additional consent will be required (e.g., for phallometric testing, for conducting certain collateral interviews); distribution of the report; anonymous use of assessment data for education, training, and research purposes; the potential benefits and risks of participating in the assessment; and his right to withdraw at any time. The client is asked to initial each sub-section of the consent form to ensure he has read, understood, and agreed to that section in addition to signing the overall Assessment Consent Form at the end of the document. The consent form is read and reviewed at the onset of the first clinical interview, after the assessment process and purpose has been verbally explained to the client. Typically, this process occurs between the therapist and the client. On occasion another individual will be a part of the consent process (e.g., if the client has vulnerabilities that impact their ability to read the consent form or provide consent; such as illiteracy, English as a second language, cognitive impairments, or the individual is a young offender). In Canada it is rare that a lawyer would be involved in this process; however, on the infrequent occasions that a client would like to review the consent form with legal counsel, this is respected. Lewis read the Assessment Consent Form and asked some questions. He was concerned about distribution of the report and it was clarified that the report would be released to the Department of Psychology at the institution and that it would be on his psychology file, and would also be read and used by his case management officer. I informed him that we would not release a copy of the report to anyone else without his signed consent. He was also informed that his case management officer would share the report with specific organizations such as the Parole Board of Canada, and if there were concerns about his risk at the time of his release, information from the report or the report itself could potentially be included in the information package provided by the institution to the High Risk Sex Offender Unit and High Risk Prosecutions Unit for determinations related to community notification and seeking a Section 810 Recognizance Order. Section 810 is a provision in the Canadian Criminal Code that allows for a community supervision order of up to 2 years, with extensive conditions, supervised by probation services (in our jurisdiction), and monitored by law enforcement based on the "fear" of being at high risk to re-offend and not requiring further charges. Lewis expressed concern about how the institution might use the report, but indicated he was prepared to participate in the assessment and signed the consent form. With this, we were able to commence the clinical interviews.

These examples of getting the process started are offered to ensure good initial preparation for conducting the report. Focusing on engagement issues, processing client questions and concerns, and preparing for and working through resistance can contribute to a smoother and more effective assessment process.

Clinical Interviews

Clinical interviews represent a central data collection point in the assessment process. There are multiple sources of data that can emerge from the clinical interviews. While we most often consider interview data as including information about the individual's history (e.g., personal history and offense specific information) and how this information is consistent with, contrasts with, or supplements other sources of assessment data, clinical interviews also allow for observing and commenting on the individual's style of presentation, his response to the assessment process, and ability to demonstrate shifts/gains during the assessment process. Gathering this type of process information can be a rich and meaningful source of data. Information about how the individual participates in the assessment (versus the information he provides) can offer illustrations of his style of interacting and coping, defense mechanisms, and level of functioning that can add depth to reporting and interpreting content data. This process information can also offer insight into issues that need to be considered to engage the client and move him forward in treatment and may inform about a potential prognosis. Gathering this type of information should be considered as equally important to gathering content information. In Lewis's case process information of note included: considering and discussing his initial defensive posturing and resistance and ability to decrease these over time; his demonstrated ability to increase his level of self-disclosure and accountability in response to direct, non-judgmental questioning; his overall flat emotional presentation; and his ability to make connections related to insight enhancement.

In commencing the clinical interviews with Lewis, I informed him of all the areas I would be asking him about and would be discussing with him. This included: his family of origin and developmental experiences, religious/spiritual background and orientation, education and employment, relationship history, sexual history (e.g., sexual experiences, interests, arousal, and behaviors), substance use, physical and mental health history, and prior criminal behavior (including past charges, convictions, and behaviors he has engaged in that have not resulted in contact with the criminal justice system—not providing any identifying information). I also informed him that we would be discussing a wide range of offense-specific issues including: the details of his offending behaviors; the factors he believed contributed to his offending; motivational factors related to this behavior, and his awareness of the potential needs he may have been attempting to meet or compensate for through his offending; the role of sexual interests (e.g., paraphilic interests, masturbation practices, use of pornographic and non-pornographic images and materials to stimulate arousal, fantasies). Also under discussion would be his attitudes about his offending behavior and victims; his attitudes toward females, relation-ships, and sex; and offense planning (forethought, deliberation, intention, decision-making, offense preparation). His thoughts and feelings about the impact of his offending behavior on others would be important (e.g., awareness of potential victim impact, experience of empathy); and his use of cognitive defenses (e.g., presence of denial, minimization, rationaliza-tion, justification, projection of responsibility). Finally, I related that we would also be discussing his past response to incarceration, community supervision, and intervention programs. We would discuss his under-standing of what things he must both avoid and actively do in order to manage his risk and risk factors and function in a healthy pro-social way, his identified competencies and strengths, what his current attitude about treatment was, and his ability to identify relevant treatment goals for him-self. These are standard domains included in risk assessments for individu-als who have committed sexual offenses (Dougher, 1995; Hudson, Wales, & Ward, 1998; Krueger & Kaplan, 1997; Ward, McCormack, Hudson, & Polaschek, 1997) and encompass information gathered as part of a Relapse Prevention, Good Lives, and Risk, Need, Responsivity approach (Andrews & Bonta, 2006; Laws, 1989, Yates, Prescott, & Ward, 2010).

In considering the "art" of clinical interviews, one moves from focus-ing on the type of data collected to the process of data collection. This can include an array of issues such as the ordering and pacing of topics discussed, strategies to enhance the level of disclosure and detail being provided, the assessor's communication style (verbal and non-verbal), and strategies and approaches to the management of client responses to the questions (e.g., providing too much or too little information and detail; attempting to divert the discussion; denial, minimization, and projection of reasonability; resistance; attempting to evoke a reaction; becoming emotionally overwhelmed). It is optimal to structure clinical interviews in a way that will optimize the client's engagement and willingness to participate in a forthright manner. This requires determining and attend-ing to responsivity issues (e.g., age, cultural dynamics, cognitive capacity, personality disorder), attempting to eliminate or reduce obstacles that can inhibit and interfere with participation (e.g., anxiety, anger, shame), and avoiding becoming entangled in offender control and resistance issues. There are a number of strategies that can be used to increase the effectiveness of clinical interviewing (see Blanchard, 1995; Jenkins, 1990; McGrath, 1991; Miller & Rollnick, 2002; Prescott, 2009; Yates, 2009). As well, although accounts of therapist qualities most conducive to optimizing client engagement are most often discussed in the context of treatment (Fernandez & Marshall, 2000; Fernandez & Serran, 2002; Kear-Colwell & Pollock, 1997; Marshall, 2005) these qualities can be equally applied and beneficial in conducting assessments.

As noted, Lewis presented as challenging to engage in the assessment process. A constellation of factors contributed to this including an avoidant and defensive style of coping, anti-social personality traits, his prior history with and distrust of the criminal justice system, and him not wanting to face and discuss his sexual offending behavior (likely as a result of embarrassment, shame, fear of being negatively judged, and further negative consequences). He presented with a marked level of mistrust, was initially angry and resistant, and made efforts to control the assessment process. Although gains were made in moderating his overt resistance during the introduction phase of the assessment, he was still defended and his presentation was characterized by a limited and superficial self-disclosure and significant projection of responsibility for his behavior. For example, he was cautious about the level of detail he would share about his offenses, avoided talking about his sexual interests (not answering questions, shifting the topic) and oriented to his own mistreatment (by the criminal justice system, in his relationships). When confronted with this style of presentation the clinician must make a decision about how to move forward. Rather than accept this presentation and use this as the basis of the assessment, the goal with Lewis was to continue to work with his resistance and assist him to enhance his ability to engage and participate meaningfully in the assessment process. In doing this, I used strategies such as allowing him space to vent about the system (while containing how much time this took up), acknowledging how difficult this process is (e.g., facing and discussing painful past life experiences, talking about things you have done wrong in your life, talking about sexual issues), inquiring about his experience of embarrassment and shame, and allowing for discussion of this and focusing on the potential benefits of allowing himself to be more open and disclosing. We discussed his frustration with his lack of success to date (in the system as well as in life), and how participating in the assessment might be helpful in setting some direction to assist him better understand his behavior, manage his risk factors and risk, and offer recommendations that could assist him to reduce his conflict within the system, and move forward in his life goals. This greatly reduced his resistance, and although his self-disclosure was still viewed as underdeveloped, he was much more cooperative and forthcoming about his life history and his offending behaviors. An assessment that simply focused on his resistance and lack of cooperation and participation would have been much less effective than working with and reducing the initially displayed resistance, which resulted in a much richer and more useful assessment.

In my experience, it is optimal to gather interview data over the course of at least two clinical interviews, and to spend 3 to 5 hours interviewing a client. Some circumstances do not allow for this amount of time to be dedicated to assessment interviews; however, it is beneficial to be able to observe and question someone over time, and see the extent to which this results in changes in presentation, consistency in information shared, and the level of depth of the information shared. Lewis was interviewed on two occasions over the course of 2 weeks for a total of 4 hours. At the time of the second interview Lewis was much less defended and provided more detail about his personal history, as well as his sexual interests and offending history. For example, Lewis provided more information about his early experiences of abuse by his mother, was more verbal in discussing his attitudes toward women (venting a number of negative and hostile beliefs about females), and was able to "recall" details he initially identified not remembering (related to the level of threat and aggression used). He was also able to provide more insight into offense precursors. I was also able to elicit further discussion and disclosure by asking questions related to information from the psychological tests and self-report measures that had been administered, scored, interpreted, and reviewed prior to the second interview.

There is always concern with the accuracy of self-report in any clinical interview but this concern is heightened in forensic populations. Thus, it is important to review and contrast the self-report data obtained in clinical interviews across the clinical interviews conducted, with the case background information, and when possible with collateral interviews. Psychological test data may also be helpful in considering the veracity of self-report globally (versus the accuracy of specific details) through review of validity scales, assessing for impression management, and profile interpretations that appear consistent with clinical impressions. Consistency as well as inconsistency between self-report within the assessment and with alternative sources of information can be telling. In considering self-report data oftentimes the focus during assessment, as well as in treatment, is on the individual's level of honesty about the offending behavior. While this is important, of course, it is also necessary to carefully consider the accuracy of other self-reported information such as developmental history, history of abuse, education and work history, relationship history, and use of substances. An offender's explanation for his offending behavior must also be viewed with caution as oftentimes his identified reasons for the offending behavior occurring are either misrepresentations of the truth or a product of distorted perceptions and beliefs. Overall, Lewis's account of his upbringing and personal history presented as credible. In discussing his background there were consistencies in his description of his history across reporting, there was incremental disclosure of traumatic experiences (in that he offered additional details over time: his prior therapist had more information about this than the prior psychological report and this report had more information than the initial psychiatric report; a normative pattern in discussing traumatic life experiences). He did not present as using his abuse history as a mitigating or even contributing factor to his offending (and was resistant and reluctant to discuss his sexual abuse and oftentimes was protective of his mother) and in later treatment it appeared evident that these were emotionally difficult issues for him to face, discuss, and process. In discussing aspects of his personal history, Lewis offered unflattering information that did not present as attempting to portray him in an overly negative light and that further suggested a degree of candor when discussing issues such as his academic functioning and his substance use. One area where it appeared evident that he was not likely to be forthright was in discussing his relationship history and the dynamics of the relationships he had been in. He tended to project responsibility on his partners for all relationship problems and viewed himself as poorly treated, underappreciated, and assumed a "victim" stance. In considering his self-report of his offending behavior it was evident that his account of his offending history (number of victims and type of offenses) was fairly consistent with background information (victim statements, police reports); however, he continued to minimize the level of force used, his use of the weapon, and denied any element of planning (despite indicators of forethought prior to some of his offenses). At the same time he supplemented file information by acknowledging other inappropriate sexual behaviors not previously identified as well as offering information about having maintained inappropriate sexual fantasies.

Psychological and Self-Report Testing

In assessing Lewis, a psychological and self-report test battery was administered as another source of data gathering. In conducting assessments, there are some standard tests I include in most assessments to investigate propensity for socially desirable presentation, screen for psychopathology, and examine coping styles. These are helpful in developing a case conceptualization and provide important information to consider and contrast with the information gathered and clinical impressions formulated over the course of the clinical interviews. Based on the results of these test measures and based on specific presenting issues, additional tests may be added to the battery to explore additional areas of interest (e.g., depression, anger, trauma, psychopathy, intellectual functioning). This allows for an individualized approach to testing based on presenting features. The test battery used in my assessment of Lewis included:

The Paulhus Deception Scale (PDS; Paulhus, 1998). I routinely administer the PDS to assess socially desirable responding, an important factor to consider in forensic evaluations to help conceptualize the client's response style, and how this may impact the validity of the self-report. The PDS can be helpful in developing an understanding of a client's self-report style as it distinguishes between impression management, an intentional effort to present oneself in a favorable manner based on specific situations, and self-deceptive enhancement, a trait-like tendency to provide an unconscious inflated self-description that occurs whenever the individual provides a self-report (for a review of the psychometric properties of the PDS see Lanyon & Carle, 2007). While a client may present in an overly favorable manner in clinical interviews and in responses to psychological testing, there are different implications in terms of case conceptualization and intervention between someone invested in impression management versus someone engaged in self-deceptive enhancement. Lewis's response profile revealed a marked elevation on the Self-Deceptive Enhancement sub-scale in contrast to the Impression Management sub-scale. His profile was characteristic of individuals who are egocentric and demonstrate a rigid overconfidence. Such individuals claim to be more aware and knowledgeable then they are and demonstrate a pervasive lack of insight into themselves. His response profile was consistent with individuals who have a positive sense of self-esteem but potentially demonstrate poor interpersonal adjustment. Although they may make a good early impression, over time they tend to be viewed as arrogant, hostile, and domineering. This profile was consistent with Lewis's presentation, in particular his lack of insight, egocentricity, and experience of anger.

The Personality Assessment Inventory (PAI; Morey, 1991). The PAI is another measure I routinely administer, as it evaluates for symptoms of a broad range of mental disorders, and is a good screening for psychopathology. It also identifies information relevant for clinical diagnosis and treatment planning, and provides validity scales that allow for further evaluation of socially desirable responding (for a review of the psychometric properties of the PAI and its application specific to a forensic population see Douglas, Hart, & Kropp, 2001; Morey, 1991). Lewis's PAI clinical profile was quite consistent with his description of himself and his life, my clinical impressions, and the file information reviewed. His response profile was marked by significant elevations, indicating the presence of clinical features that are likely to be sources of difficulty for him. The configuration of the clinical scales suggested a person with a history of acting-out behavior, including acts of aggression against others, and a personality style that is consistent with a number of anti-social character features. His profile was characteristic of individuals who are likely to be reckless and impulsive, and may engage in risky behaviors that are potentially dangerous to themselves and to those around him. This is certainly consistent with his offending behavior. Lewis's PAI response profile also highlighted significant difficulties in the area of substance abuse, suggesting this has likely led to severe impairment in functioning in adaptive and pro-social ways, has probably alienated people who have been close to him, and that his substance abuse has had significant negative consequences on his life. Although Lewis acknowledged alcohol use during the clinical interviews, his test results suggest he likely minimized the significance of this as a problem and the impact it has had in his life. Lewis's PAI profile also suggested that his interpersonal style is characterized as submissive, conforming, and perhaps naive. Such individuals are likely to find it difficult to assert themselves or display anger in relationships; a difficulty that may be driven by anxiety about potential rejection by others. This description was consistent with his self-report of his involvement in relationships and with my clinical impressions and provided a partial understanding of his avoidant and passive behavior in relationships.

The Psychopathy Checklist Revised (PCL-R; Hare 2003). I do not standardly conduct the PCL-R as part of a test battery; however, I do incorporate this instrument in assessments where the individual's history or presentation style may be indicative of concerns related to traits of psychopathy (for a review of the psychometrics of this scale see Hare, 2003; Hare, Clark, Grann, & Thornton, 2000; Hare & Neumann, 2006). The PCL-R assists in considering the existence of such character traits, and how these may be related to risk for general or violent criminal behavior. This psychological construct measure has been well established as a predictor of general and violent recidivism; however, it does not consider sexual deviance, and as such has not been found to be as effective in evaluating risk for sexual recidivism as sex offense specific tools (Hanson & Morton-Bourgon, 2009). As well, since psychopathy can be considered a responsivity issue, assessing for this can assist in considering issues related to risk management such as compliance with community supervision and treatment responsiveness (Bonta, 2002; Hare et al., 2000). Lewis scored 20 on the PCL-R, placing him in the "Moderate" category in regards to the presence of traits associated with psychopathy. His overall score placed him in the 40th percentile in comparison to a standardized sample of adult male offenders in North America. The PCL-R is made up of two Factors each with two Facets. In reporting the results, considering each of these provides information useful in clinical conceptualization, consideration of risk, and planning for treatment and risk management. Factor 1 measures the callous, selfish, remorseless use of others, and considers the

Interpersonal (Facet 1) and Affective (Facet 2) dimensions of psychopathy. Factor 2 evaluates a chronically unstable and anti-social lifestyle and considers Lifestyle issues (Facet 3) and Anti-Social Behavior (Facet 4). Lewis scored moderately high on Factor 1 (66th percentile), with his highest score related to Facet 1 (78th percentile) while scoring in the 58th percentile for Facet 2. He scored lower on Factor 2 (31st percentile) with a low score on Facet 3 (20th percentile) and a higher score on Facet 4 (55th percentile). The PCL-R results are indicative of Lewis presenting with Moderate traits of psychopathy, with the strongest features being related to the interpersonal dimensions and anti-social behavior. This is consistent with the egocentricity noted in the PDS and PAI, as well as my clinical impressions from the interviews and suggests potential compliance issues.

The Interpersonal Behavior Survey (IBS; Mauger, Adkinson, Zoss, Firestone, & Hook, 1980).   This is a measure I included in this particular assessment because it evaluates excesses and deficits in the domains of aggressive and assertive behavior (for a review of the psychometrics of this scale, see Franzoi, 1985; Hutzell, 1985; Mauger et al., 1980). As clinical interviews revealed Lewis to be markedly passive in his relationships, while acting out anger and aggression against strangers through his sexual offending behavior, I was interested in further exploring the domains of aggression and assertiveness. Lewis's responses on the IBS described him as a passive individual with marked deficits in assertiveness. Lewis's profile indicated significant difficulties in his willingness to communicate his true feelings and opinions, and as being more likely to not express himself, and to hide his feelings and thoughts from others. His profile also indicated that he has great difficulty in saying no to others regardless of whether their demands are reasonable. It was also noted that on the Anger/Aggression domains, Lewis's response profile was indicative of an individual who is prone to show an explosive temper. The IBS test results were consistent with Lewis's described pattern of relating in his relationships (with his ex-wife, family members) as well as with other testing and helped solidify the case conceptualization related to the important role his passivity, lack of assertiveness, and limited communication played in his offending.

The Coping Response Inventory (CRI; Moos, 1993).   This is a measure I routinely administer because it helps to identify an individual's style of coping, specifically looking at various approach and avoidant coping styles (for a review of the psychometric properties of the CRI see Aguilar-Vafaie & Abiari, 2007; Moos, 2004). Understanding an individual's style of coping can assist in developing a case conceptualization related to how the person copes with distress, may offer information relevant to understanding factors contributing to acting out behaviors, and can be important for treatment planning directed at optimizing coping skills that can facilitate risk management and healthy living (a more global treatment target but one I believe bolsters the maintenance of long-term risk management). Interestingly, Lewis's response profile indicated an average proficiency in his approach oriented coping responses. He presented as average in his abilities at logical analysis (attempting to understand and prepare mentally for a stressor and its consequences), positive reappraisal (to construe and restructure a problem in a positive way while still accepting the reality of the situation), seeking guidance and support, and problem solving. Lewis also demonstrated average and above average tendencies toward avoidant styles of coping. Of note, he evidenced above average tendencies toward acceptance or resignation (attempting to react to the problem by accepting it) and emotional discharge (attempts to reduce tension by expressing negative feelings), and was somewhat above average in regards to coping through seeking alternative rewards (attempts to get involved in substitute activities and create new sources of satisfaction). Despite his acknowledgment of not wanting to think about the past and his tendencies toward avoidance, he scored quite low on the sub-scale of cognitive avoidance. In considering this profile, it was my impression that Lewis was more likely to be successful in approach oriented coping skills when it came to task oriented situations (e.g., school, work), and more avoidant in his coping styles when it came to emotionally and inter-personally based issues (e.g., his functioning in relationships). This seems to be consistent with his personal history of demonstrating abilities in school and work, but not coping effectively in his relationships. The avoidant styles of coping noted were consistent with his passivity in his relationships, drinking, casual sexual encounters, and infidelity, as well as his offending.

The Trauma Symptom Inventory (TSI; Briere, 1995; now replaced by the TSI-2). Over years of conducting forensic assessments I have increasingly come to appreciate the importance of assessing for trauma symptomatology amongst forensic clients who have a history of experiencing traumatic events. I have also found that in cases where this is not reported, and the individual presents in some challenging ways during the clinical interviews (e.g., highly defensive and avoidant, highly distorted in their perceptions, emotionally disconnected), that assessing for trauma is often a fruitful endeavor that can help identify deficits in functioning. Assessing for trauma can offer a context for understanding challenging styles of engagement and behavior, and can be of great assistance in case conceptualization, and in developing recommendations for treatment and risk management (for a review of the psychometric properties of the TSI see the manual, Briere, 1995; Briere, Elliott, Harris, & Cotman, 1995).

Lewis's TSI profile identified two major areas of concern, the experience of sexual distress and defensive avoidance. Sexual distress is characterized by excessive, unhealthy sexual behavior that is distressing and potentially harmful to the individual or others. Lewis's responses were indicative of an individual who experiences negative thoughts and feelings during sex, confusion regarding sexual issues, sexual problems in relationships, unwanted sexual preoccupation, and shame about sexual behavior. His responses were characteristic of individuals who have engaged in indiscriminate sexual behavior, sexual risk taking, and unsafe sexual practices that could lead them into trouble. Individuals with this response profile tend to use sexual behavior as a way of achieving non-sexual goals, such as attention, validation, or distraction from internal stress. Some individuals with this response profile report a history of sexual trauma. This interpretation was consistent with Lewis's self-reported sexual history and highlighted further areas for exploration related to his sexual functioning and identified sexuality issues apart from his sexually aggressive interests and sexual offending behavior as treatment targets. Individuals who demonstrate elevations on defensive avoidance tend to have a history of aversive internal experiences that they seek to avoid, and attempt to eliminate painful thoughts or memories from conscious awareness (Briere, 1995). As a result, efforts are made to avoid events or stimuli that might re-stimulate upsetting thoughts or memories in an attempt to neutralize negative feelings about previous traumatic experiences. This pattern of coping was consistent across the other psychological testing (PDS, PAI, IBS, CRI), and also with his self-report of managing stress/distress in his relationships through avoidance and escapism.

Offense Information Questionnaire: Sex Offending Behavior Version (OIQ-SOV; Ellerby, 2004). This self-report measure was developed to gather qualitative data specifically related to an individual's offending behavior. It queries key clinical areas important in evaluating sex offense specific dynamics (e.g., self-disclosure, accountability, memory of offense, sexual fantasy/interests/arousal, cognitive distortions, offense planning, emotional/cognitive/behavioral precursors to offending, victim empathy, risk management strategies). This self-report questionnaire offers individuals an opportunity to increase the information they share, by providing them with a means to respond to very specific and emotionally difficult questions about their sexual interests and behavior in a more private manner (versus telling the clinician interviewing them), and also offers a secondary means of collecting offense specific data that can be contrasted to the information gathered during clinical interviews and identified in background information. Responses to the OIQ: SOV can be quite rich and provide very useful information for case conceptualization, identification of offense precursors and risk factors, and treatment planning. Lewis's responses on the OIQ: SOV were quite detailed. He offered additional information about sexual behaviors he had engaged in (e.g., early engagement in obscene telephone calls, exhibitionism), his sexual interests and arousal (e.g., having become aroused to and masturbated to rape scenes in Hollywood movies), and his awareness of his victims' experience at the time of his offending (e.g., noting the recognition of their fear during the offense). He was also able to provide further information about factors he believed may have contributed to his offending, and identified additional areas he needed to address to support risk management.

Psychophysiological Testing

Our practice has long had a phallometric laboratory and conducted sexual interest testing using penile plethysmography, as well as using our laboratory to work with clients to develop cognitive strategies to inhibit/control inappropriate sexual arousal (arousal to children or to sexualized violence). Many years ago, we did phallometric testing as a standard part of our assessments; however, over the last decade we have been more selective in determining when to utilize this intrusive testing procedure. Currently we rarely conduct phallometric testing during our assessments. We only consider this testing when we have a case where there is information to suggest that an individual has a problem with inappropriate sexual arousal, and he denies this. Lewis acknowledged experiencing sexual arousal to thoughts and images of sexual aggression against women, identifying having masturbated to rape fantasies, and becoming sexually aroused while watching rape depictions in movies. Given his acknowledgment of this arousal and sexual interest, and a history that was consistent with this (having made intimidating obscene phone calls with the intention of causing fear to the women, the use of threats and weapon in his sexual offenses, having multiple stranger victims) inappropriate sexual arousal could reliably be identified, and there was no need to expose Lewis to stimuli (e.g., audiotaped descriptions of sexual aggression) that he could potentially integrate into his fantasy repertoire, and that would likely create arousal, which would then need to be contained and managed following the testing procedure.

Risk Assessment Tools

It is critical that any sex offender risk assessment utilize specialized risk assessment tools. The empirical literature is clear that actuarial risk assessment is superior to clinical judgment, and the use of actuarial risk assessment tools has been identified as appropriate practice (Association for the Treatment of Sexual Abusers, 2005; Hanson & Morton-Bourgon, 2009; Hanson & Thornton, 2000). There are a number of risk assessment tools to choose from. In selecting a risk instrument it is important to be clear on what type of risk you want to assess, to consider the empirical evidence that supports the particular tool as a reliable and valid measure of assessing risk, and being appropriately trained in the use of a particular tool.

The selection of the instrument(s) you use may also be based on your comfort with the measure and the way it conceptualizes and approaches risk assessment. In assessing risk for sexual recidivism in this case I utilized the Static-99 (Hanson & Thornton, 1999; since the time of this assessment I would use the Static-99R, the updated coding form and the most recent normative data for the appropriate normative group, *see Static-99R Workbook*, Phenix, Helmus, & Hanson, 2012; see the manual for an overview of the reliability and validity data). The Static-99 is an actuarial instrument designed to assist in the prediction of sexual and violent recidivism for sexual offenders, primarily through considering static or fixed risk factors associated with recidivism. In a recent survey of sex offender programs, the Static-99 was found to be the most commonly used actuarial risk assessment tool for assessing sexual recidivism (McGrath, Cumming, Burchard, Zeoli, & Ellerby, 2010). Lewis scored 8 on the Static-99 placing him in the High Risk categorization. When formally reporting risk, it is important to offer not only the risk categorization (e.g., low, moderate, high), but the score on your risk assessment tool, the items that resulted in this score (as this allows for transparency and for review), information on the normative data used, and the probability estimates for recidivism and the time frames. It is also important to specify that the data are based on group norms versus being able to identify the specific risk that a particular individual represents (Doren, 2009). In reporting probability statistics for recidivism in a report, I identify the probabilities for recidivism as well as for non-recidivism. In my opinion, this gives a balanced presentation of the data to the reader, and creates a different impression, than only offering the probabilities for recidivism. For example, based on the normative data used for the original Static-99 when Lewis was assessed, the probability estimate indicated that individuals with this score on average sexually re-offend at a rate of 39% over 5 years, and 45% over 10 years. Alternatively, 61% of individuals with this score did not sexually re-offend over 5 years, while 55% did not re-offend sexually over 10 years. This way of reporting is quite striking and provides the reader with a complete account of what the probability estimates mean, and helps to provide a balanced perspective related to the estimates of risk for a client.

In addition to assessing static and primarily fixed historical variables (e.g., criminal history, victim profile), it is critical to also examine and evaluate dynamic risk factors. Dynamic risk factors are particularly important as they inform of areas to be restricted and monitored during community supervision (i.e., acute risk factors), areas that require therapeutic intervention and change (i.e., stable risk factors) and considering dynamic risk factors along with static risk factors increases predictive accuracy (Hanson, 2006). Dynamic risk factors include sexual deviance, anti-social orientation, attitudes, cognitive distortions, intimacy deficits, self-regulation deficits, and compliance issues (Craissati &

Beech, 2003; Hanson & Bussière, 1998; Hanson & Morton-Bourgon, 2005). Dynamic variables are also important to assess as they can be targeted for change through therapeutic intervention and allow for evaluating changes in risk as a result of participation in treatment (Andrews & Bonta, 2006; Hanson, 2006). In evaluating dynamic risk factors, I most often use the Violent Risk Scale: Sex Offender Version (VRS:SO; Wong, Oliver, Nicholaichuk, & Gordon, 2003). This risk assessment tool is appealing because it evaluates both static and dynamic risk factors, and provides a comprehensive review of dynamic variables, clustered in three factors: Sexual Deviance (sexually deviant lifestyle, deviant sexual preference, sexual offending cycle, offense planning, and sexual compulsivity); Criminality (interpersonal aggression, impulsivity, criminal personality, compliance with community supervision, substance abuse, community support, release to high-risk situations); and Attitudes (insight, cognitive distortions, and treatment compliance). Additionally, the VRS:SO is structured to evaluate the client's readiness to change on each of the dynamic risk factors assessed based on the Transtheoretical Change Model (Prochaska, DiClemente, & Norcross, 1992). Post intervention, the client can be re-assessed based on identified progress through the stages of change for each dynamic risk factor to determine if he has made progress in addressing a specific factor, and if these changes result in a modification of his initial assessed level of risk. In considering post-treatment change we are not clear what is being measured; an actual reduction of the individual's originally assessed level of risk or an increased capacity to manage the level of risk associated with the dynamic risk factors (which would be my orientation). However, it is valuable to have a measure that allows for considering mitigation of risk through intervention. For these reasons, this measure is an appealing blend of applying the research literature on risk factors relevant to recidivism, while considering clinical needs of identifying treatment targets and considering treatment readiness and progress.

Lewis's score of 43 on the VRS:SO placed him in the High-Risk category on this risk assessment tool. His static risk rating was elevated based on him commencing inappropriate sexual behavior at an early age (first obscene phone call at age 15, exhibitionism commencing at age 17), the number of prior charges and convictions he has had, and having a number of unrelated victims. Consistent with this, Lewis evidenced the most significant number of dynamic risk factors on the Sexual Deviance Factor; however, he also had a number of risk factors indicated on the Criminality and Attitude factors. Individuals scoring in the risk category range similar to Lewis have been found to sexually re-offend at a rate of 34% over 3 years, 42% over 5 years, and 70% over 10 years. Conversely, 66% do not re-offend over 3 years, 58% do not re-offend over 5 years, and 30% do not re-offend over 10 years.

Collateral Interviews

Collateral interviews offer another avenue to gain further information as well as corroborate self-report. In some cases, collateral interviews are not as pertinent, while in others they are critical. Our Assessment Consent Form includes statements indicating that as part of the assessment process we will discuss this individual's case with representatives from the agency of referral, and in providing their consent to participate in the assessment the client provides consent for this. Because it was Lewis's institutional case manager who referred him, I was able to discuss his case with her as well as other institutional staff. If I felt it necessary to conduct additional collateral interviews outside of this (e.g., a partner, family members, employer, prior psychologist—if not employed by the institution), I would require separate and specific consent to conduct these interviews. In this case, the need for collateral interviews was less pressing, as Lewis provided a high level of self-disclosure during clinical interviews and on testing; there was good background information available; and the key assessment questions could be addressed with the data collected. I was interested, however, in conducting a collateral interview with his family members in an attempt to gain further information about their perceptions of him as well as to identify their willingness to play a role in supporting him once he was released to the community. It is important to note that when considering and identifying potential collateral interviews, particularly with a partner or family member, you want to consider what interviewing this person will add to the assessment data, if the person is likely to be a source of objective information and recognize that interview data from collateral interview subjects must be considered in terms of reliability (e.g., subjects could be overly positive or negative). Lewis would not provide his consent for this to occur (which in and of itself was revealing and became a problematic issue in later treatment) so these interviews were not done. I was also interested in interviewing his prior therapist to gather information about his prior participation in treatment. This would have been particularly relevant as there were no reports outlining his participation and progress in past treatment. Lewis would not provide his consent for this to occur at the time of assessment so this information could not be accessed. Upon his later referral for treatment, part of his acceptance into the treatment program hinged on him providing consent to discuss his case with his past treatment provider.

Interviewing of his case manager revealed that Lewis was challenging to work with as he limited his interactions and contact with his case manager, at times presented in a hostile and resistant manner, and at times had unrealistic expectations about his release planning. The institutional case manager indicated that Lewis received good reports from his work supervisor at the institution and that he was active in recreational (sporting) activities.

Report Writing

Part of the "art" of clinical practice can be found in the writing of assessment reports. It is important that the report is comprehensive and includes the elements identified. The information communicated to the reader is key and often not the subject of discussion in clinical training or the literature. I have found it important to create reports that are consumer friendly as oftentimes our consumers are not mental health practitioners. To be useful the reader must be able to understand the information in the report and how this is pertinent to their decision-making role with the offender. In writing a report it is important to avoid professional jargon, explain psychological concepts, offer a rationale and context for clinical impressions or hypotheses, and provide recommendations that are specific to the individual being assessed (versus generic recommendations) and that are responsive and realistic to the context of that specific individual and his circumstances (e.g., providing recommendations that can actually be put into place). Finally, I have found it important when writing reports to consider how the client will read and experience the report. This can shape the language used and the framing. It does not mean downplaying identification of any problem areas. If the content and tone of a report should act to prompt the client to recognize and acknowledge his deficit areas, see his strengths and capacity for potential, and contribute to the person's motivation to address and build on these; then the report truly serves an important clinical function.

Case Formulation

Clinical formulation is extremely important in providing meaningful treatment and risk management recommendations as well as for guiding and adjusting the course of treatment. I attempt to develop my case formulation while collecting the assessment data and have a good sense of this prior to writing the report, although in some instances the case formulation develops during the writing process or, if already developed, can certainly evolve during the writing. If a report is written without a well-constructed case conceptualization there can be a risk of inconsistencies within a report, too much content, and limited integration of the material. As well, recommendations tend to be more general in nature, rather than specific to the particular case.

In developing a case conceptualization my goal is to attempt to understand and describe, as best as possible, the factors contributing to the individual's offending behavior, the needs the person was attempting to meet or compensate for through the offending, and the experiences relevant in contributing to these unhealthy styles of coping. My case conceptualization also includes consideration of the level of risk, potential obstacles for change, and strategies to address these, responsivity factors to attend to, and identification of client strengths and how these can be harnessed and further developed. In considering these issues I use the frameworks of a few central models including, the Principles of Effective Correctional Programing (Risk, Need, and Responsivity; Andrews & Bonta, 2006), the Relapse Prevention Model (Laws, 1989), and the Self-Regulation and Good Lives Models (Yates et al., 2010). There are aspects of each of these models that inform and guide the development of a comprehensive, thoughtful, and individualized case conceptualization. Client diagnosis may also inform clinical case conceptualization if there is an accurate diagnosis which helps further develop the understanding of a client's unhealthy styles of coping as it directly or indirectly relates to his offending behavior.

In developing Lewis's case conceptualization there were a constellation of factors that appeared relevant to understanding his problematic coping styles and offending behavior. It was my formulation that his early trauma experiences (the abuse by his mother and the sexual abuse by his teacher), the modeling of his parents' relationship dynamic (domineering mother, passive and avoidant father), and difficulties in relationships (feeling abandoned, hurt, unimportant, rejected, controlled) shaped the development of unhealthy styles of coping and personality features that ultimately contributed to his offending behavior. These included: feelings of anger, mistrust, and hatred toward women and a range of distorted attitudes and perceptions about females; a pattern of defensive avoidant coping and inability to assert himself with dominant females in his life (his mother, female partners, his female supervisor); marked feelings of shame in regard to sexuality, and using sex as a means of asserting his masculinity; poor emotional regulation, tending to stuff feelings and then explode; an egocentric orientation focused on meeting his wants and needs and not concerning himself with the consequences and impact of his behavior and challenges in his ability to attach in relationships. Lewis's early sexually offending behaviors (obscene phone calls, exhibitionism) appeared to be attempts to discharge his anger and gain a sense of competency and control by acting out against female strangers because he perceived them as "safe" and he was not threatened or felt endangered by them. This appeared to produce feelings of emotional excitation, which he extended through sexually aggressive thoughts/fantasies often paired with masturbation resulting in a sexual arousal response. His later offending behavior appeared triggered by conflict in his relationships with key females in his life (e.g., his mother, later his wife and his supervisor) and again served as an indirect way of acting out anger and seeking revenge. Based on the distorted views he held and the hurt he carried Lewis felt entitled to engage in sexually aggressive behavior, experienced a release and gratification from the offending, and minimized the inappropriateness and seriousness of his conduct. Lewis also demonstrated strengths in that he was bright and psychologically minded, recognized a need to change his behavior and presented as motivated to do this (even though he still evidenced defended and resistant posturing), had a strong work ethic and desire to find a vocation, had talent as a musician, wished he could have a healthy relationship with a woman he trusted and who cared about him, and wanted to break away from the attitude of the prison subculture. It was also evident that Lewis craved a sense of safety and security in his life, acceptance and nurturing (although feared allowing himself to be emotionally vulnerable in a way that would allow for this), and feeling and being perceived as competent. All these dimensions contributed to understanding his offending and him as a man and to offering recommendations related to risk management and treatment.

Lewis had previously been diagnosed with Anti-Social Personality Disorder (APD) and Sexual Sadism. In assessing Lewis for psychopathy it was clear that he evidenced traits consistent with APD that from a treatment recommendation perspective became a responsivity issue (e.g., finding ways of working with his egocentricity, manipulation, shallow affect) as well as highlighting treatment targets (e.g., addressing his interpersonal skills and style of interaction, building skills at other oriented perspective taking, and considering consequences of his behavior that were meaningful to him, building his ability to be more connected to and experience his emotions). The prior diagnosis of Sexual Sadism was ruled out. While Lewis engaged in intimidation, control, and aggressive behaviors in his offending, his use of violence appeared to be primarily as a means to gain control of his victims, secure victim compliance, and discharge his anger and aggression, in contrast to using violence, domination, and infliction of pain and humiliation as a preferred or required precondition for sexual arousal (Frances & Wollert, 2012). Lewis described experiencing sexual arousal to sexual aggression (e.g., masturbation to sexually aggressive fantasies, arousal to depictions of rape in movies, arousal to women in certain positions—that gave him a heightened sense of power, and arousal during his offending). His arousal experience presented as largely resultant from the themes of control, power, and anger release and the reinforcement of this arousal profile through pairing such images and thoughts with masturbation and orgasm, resulting in a failure to disinhibit to sexually aggressive cues, rather than a sexual preference for sexual aggression. Challenges have been noted in the diagnosis of Sexual Sadism amongst sex offenders, rapists in particular (Frances & Wollert, 2012; Marshall & Kennedy, 2003; Marshall, Kennedy, & Yates, 2002). Care must be used in making such a deleterious diagnosis and an existing diagnosis of Sexual Sadism should be considered with caution.

This clinical conceptualization was derived through the clinical interviews (his account of his personal history, relationship with and attitudes toward women, his experiences of arousal related to sexually aggressive thoughts/fantasies and during his offending); psychological test data (e.g., the results of the PAI, PCL-R, IBS, TSI, and CRI demonstrating patterns of avoidant coping, anti-social traits, and sexual distress and disrupted sexuality); the identification of dynamic risk factors through clinical interviews, a self-report measure (OIQ:SOV), and risk assessment tools (VRS:SO); and collateral information (review of background information, particularly a prior psychological assessment).

Treatment Planning

In developing a treatment plan it is important to consider the principles of effective correctional programming and match the treatment plan to the individual's assessed level of risk, need, and identified responsivity issues (Andrews & Bonta, 2006). As Lewis was assessed at High Risk for sexual recidivism the treatment plan identified him as requiring a more intensive treatment regime, and he was assigned to weekly individual and group therapy. The group he attended was a mixed group of individuals who had offended against both child and adult victims. The number and constellation of clients we have in treatment at our practice at any given time in practical terms does not allow for a homogeneous group for those with adult victims only. Although there may be benefits to this, the composition of sex offender treatment groups does not appear to make a difference to the overall group environment (Harkins & Beech, 2008). It is the group dynamics (e.g., cohesiveness and leader support) versus composition that appears important in an effective group (Beech & Hamilton-Giachritsis, 2005).

A host of psychologically meaningful areas related to his offending behavior (his "need" areas) were identified for therapeutic intervention. These included, but were not restricted to addressing his: victimization experiences and trauma symptomatology; disclosure and accountability related to his sexual offending history; sexual interests and arousal; attitudes toward women and relationships; experience of shame and the impact of this in his life; healthy relationship skills; healthy sexuality and intimacy; substance use and abuse; emotional regulation, specifically related to anger management; and sense of entitlement and egocentricity. The treatment plan also included focusing on identifying, building, and strengthening a host of coping strategies to assist him avoid, manage, or inoculate his vulnerability areas for future risk of sexual offending behavior. The treatment plan also sought to address Lewis's desire and need to feel a great sense of self-worth and competency and develop a positive sense of identity. The key responsivity factors evident were Lewis' egocentric orientation, his emotional disconnectedness, trauma symptomatology (defensive avoidance), and his level of resistance. Based on his assessed level of risk, the identified need areas, and the responsivity issues noted, it was anticipated that therapy would be challenging and long term.

Therapeutic Intervention

The literature on the treatment of sex offenders is largely related to individuals who have committed sexual offenses against children, with little reported on what distinct clinical interventions may be noteworthy for individuals who have offended against adult victims (Ward et al., 1997). Some direction has been offered in this regard (Marshall, Eccles, & Barbaree, 1993; Pithers, 1993; Rada, 1978; Ward et al., 1997), but this is still an underdeveloped area of study. The following highlight the central components of Lewis's treatment, some of which are consistent with what is considered to be "best practice" treatment targets, while others that are not yet evidence based are grounded in the wisdom of clinical experience.

Therapeutic Engagement

In our initial session Lewis presented as quite comfortable, relaxed, and open in spite of the previous assessment having identified him as being high risk. I attributed this encouraging presentation to having moved through the assessment process in a positive way at the time of our first meeting a number of years before. Lewis offered that while he did not like being identified as high risk, he appreciated the assessment process, and believed that the overall conclusions and recommendations were fair and accurate. This was a positive starting place; however, further building and strengthening the therapeutic rapport remained a central treatment goal. A strong therapeutic alliance would assist in reducing potential resistance and help to decrease his defensiveness, a core component of his overall coping repertoire. As well, a healthy therapeutic relationship can be used as a tool for attending to trust issues, attachment deficits, and emotional disconnection. Establishing a strong working alliance should always be an important clinical goal as the therapeutic alliance has been identified as a central component of facilitating change (Beech & Fordham, 1997; Marshall et al., 2006; Rothman, 2007). There has been increasing attention to facilitating client motivation and engagement in sex offender populations and using strategies from other areas of clinical practice and the sex offender-specific literature to guide these processes (Blanchard, 1995; Jenkins, 1990; Miller & Rollnick, 2002). In my work with clients, attending to therapeutic rapport is an ongoing treatment target requiring continuous evaluation, adjustment, and attention over the ebbs and flows of treatment.

Trauma

The role of trauma as it relates to understanding offender vulnerabilities in coping, and as a relevant risk factor, is an under-evaluated area in our field (Maschi & Gibson, 2012). In this case, as in many others, attending to trauma was both a responsivity issue (as the coping styles symptomatic of trauma can impact participation in treatment) as well as a relevant target for risk management: His core feelings of rage, resentment, hate, and desire for revenge against women, as well as his distortions in perceptions about women was grounded in his abuse by his mother. This historical factor would continue to be a trigger and unless addressed it would result in an exacerbated reaction to current day conflicts with females. Intervention included helping Lewis to process the feelings associated with his victimization experiences; review, challenge, and replace his perceptions about these experiences (e.g., "I should have been strong enough to protect myself, if I had resisted the abuse would not have persisted, I will never be okay because of this"); consider the factors that contributed to his mother and teacher abusing him (their own dysfunction and the experiences that could have created this); and focusing on how him holding these feelings has negatively impacted his life. This work also focused heavily on addressing issues related to shame and reviewing and helping Lewis consider and challenge his perceptions of the world and himself and focus on positive identity development beyond his sense of himself as a damaged victim or a monstrous offender.

Self-Disclosure and Accountability

Focusing on enhancing self-disclosure and increasing Lewis's ability to discuss and describe his sexual development, including the evolution of his sexually aggressive thoughts, fantasies, arousal, and his sexual acting out was an important treatment goal. Although questions have been raised about the utility of this pursuit given findings that denial is not related to future risk (Hanson & Bussière, 1998; Hanson, & Morton-Bourgon, 2004, 2005), there are a number of clinical rationales for this being included as a relevant treatment target. Enhanced information allows for more detailed exploration and understanding of the motivation and intentions related to the offending behavior and the needs the person is attempting to meet. This allows for a more precise and comprehensive case conceptualization, development of a more complete offense pathway, and a more refined and effective treatment and risk management plan. In Lewis's case, he was able to disclose the early use of fantasy as a response to his victimization experiences (to gain a sense of control, release anger, and exact revenge, and heighten his sense of masculinity) and disclosed early acting out including making obscene phone calls and exhibitionism. He also provided an enhanced account of his ongoing and more current use of sexually aggressive fantasies (the content and themes). This enhanced level of disclosure and acceptance of responsibility contributed to a better understanding of his offending behavior, risk and risk factors, and strategies required for treatment and risk management. The intervention and risk management plan and process would have been severely compromised without having gained this information.

Facilitating an enhanced level of self-disclosure and responsibility can also contribute to addressing shame. Offenders often experience shame, both in relation to their own personal histories as well as for their own behavior. Shame can serve to perpetuate a negative sense of self that can inhibit positive change and perpetuate, if not exacerbate, the vulnerabilities related to future risk. Although not often considered, an individual's proneness to shame has been found to be positively related to a number of poor outcomes such as low self-control, high stimulus seeking, substance abuse, impulsivity, criminogenic patterns of thinking, and a host of psychological problems (Tangney, Stuewig, Mashek, & Hastings, 2011). Maintaining secrets of undesirable experiences, thoughts, fantasies, and behaviors can retain a shame-based identity. The process of disclosing, processing, and releasing allows for a shift away from this. Although it was very difficult and took considerable time in treatment, Lewis's eventual disclosure of more specific details of his victimization, his early exhibitionism, and the content of his sexual fantasies, not only allowed for these to be addressed from a risk management perspective, but to also explore the impact experiences, thoughts, and behaviors had on his sense of self and identity and begin to address this. His work in this area marked a significant turning point in his treatment, his commitment to the process of change, and his increased stabilization in the community.

I have also found that, at times, the disclosure of thoughts/fantasies can be useful in helping individuals interrupt behavior. For example, Lewis talked more explicitly about a fantasy related to the abduction of a victim and his thoughts about what he could do if he had a woman captive for a period of time. He related that disclosing this fantasy and having someone else know of its existence significantly decreased its potency and his interest in the fantasy. Hearing himself describe it out loud revealed to him the seriousness, distorted nature, and implications of engaging in such behavior and appeared to result in the fantasy losing its power and attractiveness for him.

The process of enhancing self-disclosure can be a complex one and is most effectively done at the client's pace and with a clear understanding of the therapeutic intent and value of this treatment target. It is important to note that attempting to secure "full" responsibility and complete consistency with "official" versions of the offending behavior and using confrontational approaches to do so, in my opinion, is not the desired or required goal. Such an approach is unlikely to lead to enhanced accountability, will likely take the treatment process off course, and can result in client resistance, therapist–client control battles, or the client's response based on therapist-created demand characteristics, and the client acting in a compliant but ungenuine manner to placate the therapist.

Offense Pathways

A central component of sex offender treatment includes the client disclosing his offending behavior and the circumstances and events preceding it in order to understand, monitor, address, and manage the contributory factors. There have been different conceptualizations of organizing the information detailing offense precursors including offense cycles, chains, pathways, and progressions. As treatment progressed Lewis's offense pathway evolved, which led to identified historical and situational precursors to his offending behavior; contributory emotional, cognitive, and behavioral factors; and identification of the role of sexual thoughts and fantasy, cognitive distortions, and forethought/planning in his offenses; as well as a listing of the evolution of and details regarding his offending behaviors. These domains were not described as necessarily cyclical in nature and were considered along with phases of the self-regulation model (Yates et al., 2010). I have found, however, that often clients' understanding of their offense precursors and risk factors is advanced and retained through use of simple and concrete exemplars versus the more complex theoretical models preferred by researchers and theorists. As such, I tend to work with clients still using simple and clear conceptions and illustrations of offense cycles/ pathways (e.g., Ellerby, Bedard, & Chartrand, 2000). Lewis was able to develop a very thorough offense cycle/pathway that was quite detailed and lengthy. Over time we focused on refining it, highlighting the most significant contributing/risk factors so he was more likely to remember, monitor, and attend to these versus being overwhelmed with too much information that he might be less likely to utilize. Lewis was also willing and able to share this information with others who were involved in his life to support his risk management and healthy living (his parole officer, partner, and support people).

Attitudes and Beliefs

Lewis held many hostile and negative attitudes toward women. He had little trust, respect, or regard for women and believed that interactions with women would ultimately result in him being hurt, used, disrespected, and unappreciated. This belief system resulted in him justifying his aggression toward women and feeling entitled to act out and punish women for the mistreatment and pain he felt he had endured. These types of attitudes and beliefs are consistent with the literature on rapists (Mann & Hollin, 2001; Marshall & Moulden, 2001; Myers, 2000; Scott & Tetreault, 1987; Serran, Looman, & Dickie, 2004) and the direction that these be a target area for therapeutic intervention. Over time in individual and group therapy these perceptions were challenged in supportive ways, recognizing the difficult experiences he has had with pivotal women in his life, encouraging him to consider the range of contacts he has had with females (with him being able to identify women who did not fit this perspective, including the female co-facilitator of his therapy group), considering and coming to accept how his behavior contributed to a number of his negative experiences with women (e.g., drinking, avoidance, lack of communication, limited emotional availability, infidelity, offending), and flagging his own use and abuse of women (through indiscriminate sexual contacts, offending). His negative belief system weakened as he worked on altering other more general aspects of his distorted cognitive processing (e.g., his tendency to personalize, rigid/black and white thinking).

In terms of offense specific distortions, many of these were challenged simply through Lewis verbalizing these beliefs and hearing how distorted they were (e.g., believing that if he made an obscene phone call or exposed himself to a woman they would "want me") and through developing an understanding of the factors contributing to his offending behavior. For example, he came to realize that a stranger victim in no way deserves to be attacked because of her gender; he came to recognize that he was taking his pain and rage out on an innocent person versus dealing with his own issues; and he came to view acting out on a "safe" target versus dealing with the source as a sign of weakness versus the strength he was looking to achieve. His participation in group therapy also assisted him in recognizing how many of his beliefs were not grounded in reality by hearing others with similar experiences and different beliefs, and by being a part of a group of others working toward a healthy and non-distorted way of perceiving the world, women, men, and their victims.

Emotional Regulation

Another key treatment target for Lewis was attending to emotional regulation. As noted, he presented as being extremely vulnerable to perceiving rejection and quickly escalated from feeling hurt to being enraged, with his thinking becoming distorted. He would become anchored in thoughts of revenge and act out impulsively; not thinking about the implications and consequences of his behavior. Lewis had a limited ability to recognize and identify his various emotional states, orienting mostly to "feeling shitty" or "feeling pissed." In focusing on emotional regulation and impulse management a range of cognitive-behavioral, relaxation, and mindfulness techniques were reviewed. Sessions focused on discussing and naming feelings, practiced recognizing his varied emotions, and becoming aware of the physiological response evident for different emotional states. In addition, we attended to his self-talk and how the messages he gives himself impact his emotional state and his decision making, and we focused on strategies for taking a time-out, challenging his perceptions, considering alternative perspectives, and looking for the core emotion at play and dealing with this (e.g., focusing on addressing the feelings of rejection and hurt versus acting on the feeling of rage).

Sexual Interests and Arousal

Addressing sexual interests and arousal can be a critical goal in sex offender treatment, yet despite the importance of this as a treatment target to support risk management, it appears to be often neglected (McGrath et al., 2010). In my experience with men who have committed sexual offenses against adult victims, most often deviant arousal is not present (consistent with Baxter, Barbaree, & Marshall, 1986; Looman & Marshall, 2005), as the offenses are typically emotionally (e.g., anger, power, control) versus sexually driven. In a smaller proportion of cases, I have worked with men who have described, evidenced (through crime scene behaviors), or demonstrated (during phallometric testing) a sexual arousal response to sexual violence cues. Amongst this group I have noted two sub-groups of offenders. There appear to be individuals who have a sexual interest/arousal to sexual violent cues (and at times to non-sexual violence cues). These individuals describe sexually aggressive fantasies; evidence crime scene behavior indicative of marked aggression and excitation to control, dominate, cause suffering to the victim, and violence; and demonstrate sexual arousal to sexually aggressive cues in response to psychophysiological testing. These individuals are most likely to meet the diagnostic criteria for Sexual Sadism (Barbaree, Seto, Serin, Amos, & Preston, 1994; Marshall & Kennedy, 2003). More often, I have found that offenders who experience arousal to sexual violence cues are not sexual sadists aroused by these cues, but are individuals who are unable to separate the violence cues from the sexual cues in their arousal response. With these offenders it is not that they are becoming sexually aroused by the sexual violence, rather they are not disinhibiting their sexual arousal response to the inclusion of violence cues occurring simultaneously with sexual cues. This appeared to be the case for Lewis. As a result, treatment focused on helping him distinguish between violence and sexual cues, and to explore the reasons these appeared intertwined for him. Treatment also focused on discussing what healthy sexuality and intimacy looked like and introduced behavioral techniques to help him shape his fantasy and masturbation practices to shift from incorporating aggressive and control cues, to orienting to non-aggressive, non-controlling cues.

Therapy also explored the themes of his sexual fantasies and offending behavior, spending more time discussing this than the actual content. I have found this to be a very useful clinical technique as at times offenders will demonstrate some excitement or pleasure in discussing the inappropriate sexual content of their fantasies or actions; however, they do not seem to like to hear the need areas this content appears to be attempting to address (i.e., themes). For example, in Lewis's fantasies and offending behavior, power, control, and humiliation were central themes (in the things he said to the woman in his fantasy, the sexual positions and behaviors engaged in, the aggression introduced, in posing his victims). While he could talk about these things in a cavalier manner, he did not like to discuss how the themes of power, control, and humiliation seemed to suggest his own sense of helplessness, lack of control, inadequacy, and shame. This helped in orienting him toward seeing his fantasies and behavior differently, to be more motivated to change and wanting to have a fantasy life and sexual experiences that were oriented to meeting intimacy, connection, and nurturing needs (the needs he identified as really wanting to achieve).

All of Lewis's sexual fantasies included either control or aggression and needed to be altered. In evolving a healthy sexual fantasy life, explicit discussion was required to formulate what consenting, mutual, and healthy sexuality would look like for him. In the initial phases he related not being able to arouse to intimate sexual imagery and when queried further about his attempts he offered masturbating to the thoughts of going on a date with a beautiful woman, picking her up at her home, and the excitement about the date, going out to a nice restaurant, and sitting at the table together and enjoying a wonderful steak dinner. At this I interrupted, suggesting it was not likely he would become sexually aroused to a steak dinner (no matter how good the steak might be) and re-oriented him to specific images and cues he could use that were of an explicit sexual nature and did not contain control or aggression cues (e.g., a female's body, caressing/fondling, sexual positions such as the woman on top, the physical sensations of his own body). The goal, consistent with orgasmic reconditioning (Cook, 1978; McGrath, 2001), was that Lewis experience sexual gratification and orgasms to appropriate fantasy images and begin the process of reinforcing these. Over time Lewis was able to describe an increased ability to masturbate to fantasies where he was able to shift away from control and aggressive cues and experience orgasm to a non-control/non-aggressive sexual thoughts/images. This led to greater ease at removing these unhealthy cues from his fantasy almost completely.

Healthy Sexuality

Addressing healthy sexual behavior was an important treatment goal on a number of levels for Lewis. As noted, he did not have a reference point for consenting, mutual, and intimate sexual contact and addressing healthy sexuality was required to help him manage and replace his inappropriate sexual fantasy. In discussing his sexual behavior and preferences in his relationships it became evident that Lewis primarily engaged in sexual behaviors that although non-criminal and consenting in nature, reinforced the themes of control, dominance, power, and also minimized intimate connection. Thus, sessions focused on how he could alter his sexual behavior to be more intimate and connective so as not to perpetuate the themes he was attempting to change in his sexually aggressive fantasy life and to support his efforts to desist from offending. The exploration of non-offending sexual behavior can be important to clarify how sexual and emotional needs are being met in consenting sexual relationships and if these practices are in any way connected with inappropriate sexual interests and offending. Attending to healthy sexuality with Lewis also involved and was connected to the therapeutic work being done in addressing his attitudes and beliefs about women, with his capacity for healthy sexual relationships becoming possible as hostile and distorted attitudes were challenged and replaced. As well, his capacity to have healthy and satisfying sexual relationships was connected to the work of addressing his sexual victimization and the confusion and shame he experienced around sexuality and his experiences of having intrusive memories of his abuse triggered during sex. Therapy related to healthy sexuality also was connected to the work being done to help Lewis to build his level of self-confidence and healthy identity development. Having a positive and secure sense of self was key in moving from intentionally remaining disconnected in relationships so as not to get hurt and using females as a means to achieve sexual release, to not being fearful about the possibility of letting a woman get close to him or of being emotionally vulnerable so he could participate in a sexually intimate relationship.

Relationships Skills

Intimacy deficits, problems in relationships, and disruptions in attachment styles have been found to be relevant dynamic risk factors and treatment targets in sex offender treatment (Hanson & Morton-Bourgon, 2004; Hudson & Ward, 1997). Lewis's relationship history contributed to him feeling hurt, used, abandoned, and unappreciated by his female partners. He quickly closed himself off emotionally in relationships to protect himself, distorted his perceptions to view his partner in negative terms, and when triggered by conflict in a relationship perseverated on anger and revenge oriented fantasies or behaviors. A significant component of treatment was discussing healthy relationship skills (e.g., perceptions of women/partners, communication, listening, assertiveness, being attentive to his partner and her needs, compromise, conflict resolution, managing his tendency to personalize and project, allowing himself to be vulnerable in a safe way). When Lewis became involved in a relationship, much time was devoted to processing experiences he had, discussing healthy coping strategies, and him working on building and practicing intimacy skills. Once it was apparent that this relationship was serious, Lewis was invited to bring his partner to a session. Although initially resistant to this idea, at the urging of his partner, he did bring her to his sessions on a couple of occasions. During these sessions we discussed issues related to his offending behavior and risk management, as well as issues related to relationship functioning. While it is important to be cautious about setting yourself up in the role of providing individual therapy to your client and couple therapy (which ideally if required should be done by another therapist), there can be significant advantages to including the partner into the treatment process and helping her or him to become an informed support person. A partner can provide further information about the client's real level of functioning, can offer enhanced monitoring of how he is managing his risk factors, and can facilitate enhanced engagement and motivation in treatment (or in some cases the opposite).

Victim Empathy

Attending to empathy as part of treatment is another area in which research has questioned efficacy (Marshall, Anderson, & Fernandez, 1999; Hanson & Morton-Bourgon, 2005), nevertheless many treatment programs have persisted in continuing to address this as a key treatment target (McGrath et al., 2010). It has recently been noted that the complexities of conceptualizing and measuring empathy may impact research findings in this area and the efficacy of this treatment target has yet to be determined (Barnett & Mann, 2013). Attending to victim impact and empathy issues was determined to be an important treatment target for Lewis. His deficits in these areas were connected to other treatment targets (e.g., cognitive distortions about and hostility toward women, egocentricity, emotional disconnection, tendency to cope through defensive avoidance). Each of these areas was attended to as part of the overall treatment plan and later facilitated exploration of victim impact issues (insight at a knowledge base level) and the development of appreciation for the harm done by his offending behavior (insight at an emotional level). Given his egocentricity, defended nature, and emotional restrictedness, Lewis was not oriented to thinking about others or attuned to feelings so this was very challenging work for him. While he made gains in becoming aware of how his actions affect others, including his victims and others impacted by his crimes (the victims' families and friends, his family, professionals working with the victims—nurses and physicians, law enforcement, prosecution, mental health professionals, journalists covering the story) it took longer for him to gain an emotional awareness of the harm done and required much work in other areas (egocentricity, defensive avoidance, emotional awareness) to make this progress. There are multiple strategies that can be employed to facilitate gains in this area (see Polaschek, 2003); however, it is important that the objective and the process be oriented to helping the client have a realistic perspective of the harm caused and the people affected, versus using victim empathy training to shame the offender.

Substance Abuse

Lewis's substance use/abuse did not appear directly connected to his sexual offending behavior, as none of his offenses appeared to have been committed while intoxicated, and he did not identify alcohol use prior to his offending. Of concern, was that he turned to drinking during times of distress and this behavior appeared indicative of his avoidance and attempt to escape stress/distress versus dealing with problems in his life. Attending to his alcohol misuse was viewed as a relevant treatment target because avoidance and escape styles of coping were part of his pathway to offending and it was deemed important to address these styles of coping in all aspects of his life (offense and non-offense specific areas), to facilitate long-term stability and risk management. Attending to alcohol use amongst individuals who have engaged in sexual aggression against women has been identified as a relevant treatment target (Marshall, 2005).

Practical Life Skill Interventions

I am a strong believer in the importance of attending to practical life skills within the treatment of offenders and see this as a vital component of long-term risk management. Humans present with a hierarchy of needs (Maslow, 1943) and if basic needs are not being attended to, it is naive to believe that clients will be capable of attending to higher level psychological functioning (e.g., clear and reality based thinking and perceptions, healthy emotional regulation). While typically, such skill building has tended to be conceptualized as being in non-criminogenic need areas, attention to these types of treatment goals has been considered to be relevant within the constructs of the Good Lives Model (Ward & Gannon, 2006; Yates et al., 2010). Our practice employs a number of community integration managers (CIMs) a position that works with our clients in real time in the community, assisting them in implementing the skills being developed in individual and group treatment, monitoring their use of healthy coping skills and risk management strategies, providing assistance with practical life skills, and being available for crisis intervention. In addition to his individual and group therapy Lewis worked with a CIM. Lewis showed competency in many areas related to practical life skills (e.g., employment, financial management); however, he wanted to improve his work skills and his CIM worked with him to find training program opportunities and funding for the program in which he was interested. Lewis also had limited experience with pro-social recreational activities so his CIM worked with him in this regard. Lewis had a keen interest in music (he played guitar, sang, and wrote songs). His CIM was able to support him in building on this interest and developing healthy community connections through connecting him with other musicians to play with, and was also able to facilitate a group of clients with musical skills to perform and record a compact disk. The CIM also assisted and supported Lewis to become involved in a recreational hockey league where he was able to participate in a sport he loved and further increase his network of friends, build pro-social relationships, and further his integration to the community. This support is consistent with facilitating client involvement in what is described in the Good Lives Model as secondary or instrumental goods in an effort to assist in fulfilling primary human goods (e.g., see Yates et al., 2010). Assisting and supporting Lewis in these various endeavors greatly contributed to his positive sense of identity development and sense of competency based on healthy activities. It facilitated him making positive connections with others, building healthy relationships, andcreating exposure to environments where he could observe the modeling of healthy pro-social interpersonal and coping behaviors from peers, and where such behaviors were expected of him and ultimately contributed to him feeling a part of the community. Additionally, the positive experiences produced by these activities contributed to his commitment and motivation to participate in his overall treatment and enhanced his motivation and desire to lead an offense free lifestyle.

Wellness Planning

In the mid-1990s we moved from developing relapse prevention plans outlining the areas the individual must avoid in order to manage his risk, to developing wellness plans (Ellerby et al., 2000), which provided a positive framing of this exercise that clients appeared to embrace. The focus is on identifying a range of approach oriented strategies, as well as relevant avoidance strategies, that are unique and specific to that individual and that the individual actually has the interest and capacity to utilize. Lewis's wellness plan focused on identifying a host of things he needed to remain aware of and coping strategies he needed to proactively integrate into his life. Examples of this included: practicing being real (not pretending things are better than they really are), communicating, listening, being patient, considering other peoples' feelings and how his behavior may affect others. He was encouraged to focus on strategies for perspective taking, practice being aware of his feeling states, and identify core emotions under feelings such as anger. Also stressed were the importance of avoiding material that could activate inappropriate sexual fantasy and arousal, practicing the use of positive self-talk strategies and using cognitive restructuring skills, checking his motivation prior to acting, being attentive to his body and physical cues of emotion rising, the identification of a range of self-care and self-nurturing strategies (e.g., proper diet and sleep, exercise, time for self). He was reminded to use affirmations about remaining hopeful, ensuring he remains active (work, hobbies), taking time to be creative (music), and maintaining his spiritual life to feel a sense of strength and comfort. He also noted the need to access his supports and allow them to help him and to never lose sight of the consequences of his offending behavior. Near the end of treatment Lewis attended a session eager to present a plan he had developed that condensed and highlighted the key components of his wellness plan. He titled his plan STOP & ACT with the acronym cuing him for the following:

S—*STEP BACK* from what has caused me to feel threatened.
T—*TAKE A TIME-OUT* to consider what has happened and what I am feeling.
O—*KEEP AN OPEN MIND* about what has happened so every possibility can be considered. Be honest.
P—*PONDER* the situation and think about all the possibilities that could exist in it.
&
A—*ASSESS* what I am feeling, what are my emotions? Am I using anger to cover up deeper feelings?
C—*CHALLENGE* my emotions. Where are they coming from? Am I blowing them up?
T—*TALK* to someone to gain an outside perspective. Listen to what is being said to me.

What is important is that Lewis's wellness plan was not generic. It addressed his key risk factors, included approach oriented strategies that he was interested in doing and able to do, and considered healthy coping skills that not only contributed to risk management but healthy living. As well, he was invested in the process and was able to condense his wellness plan so he had a short, easy to refer to, and easy to remember list of core risk management and healthy living strategies. It is vital that a wellness plan is client generated so it is meaningful to the individual and will be utilized.

The Risk Management Team

Interventions and risk management are most effective when there is a team approach and collaboration. In working with Lewis there was both an internal team approach within our practice, as well as a larger team approach including agencies and individuals outside our practice. Within our practice there was ongoing case discussion, consultation, and problem solving that occurred between the group co-facilitators, the CIM attached to the case, and myself. Outside of our practice, regular case discussion occurred between the parole officer and myself. Additionally, as part of our practice protocol, we regularly use team meetings (varying in frequency based on the client's level of risk and stability) as a means of reviewing cases and sharing information. For Lewis, team meeting attendees included the treatment team (one of the group facilitators, his CIM, myself), his parole officer, a halfway house staff member, a police officer from the high risk offender unit, his volunteer support people (through a faith based organization that was involved with him while he was incarcerated and after his release), Lewis, and, on occasion, his girlfriend. As well, there were times we had smaller team meetings with just the clinical team or with the clinical team and the parole officer. This was an important component of the treatment plan as it allowed for bringing all the systems together and discussing and clarifying roles; sharing information; and participating in collaborative problem solving and decision-making (Ellerby, 2007). Team meetings also reduced the possibility of splitting and ensured all the key people involved had similar information about the case. This was particularly useful at times when Lewis was struggling and following behaviors that resulted in him being suspended.

Reduction of Treatment Intensity and Termination

In providing clinical services to Lewis the goal was to reduce the intensity of treatment over time and work toward termination of treatment 2 months prior to the end of his sentence so he had a period of time under supervision without therapeutic supports. The intensity of treatment was reduced in response to Lewis demonstrating gains and consistently using the knowledge and skills learned; stability in the community (e.g., successfully managing risk factors and actively involved in pro-social and productive activities, such as school, work, recreation, stability in his relationship); and as he assumed increased responsibility taking and independence (e.g., following a period of successful independent living after being released from a halfway house). Individual sessions were reduced over time from weekly, to bi-weekly, to monthly, and then ended 3 months prior to the end of his parole. The CIM supports also reduced from weekly, to bi-weekly, and then terminated 4 months prior to the end of his parole. Lewis attended group up until 2 months prior to his parole ending.

The focus of termination sessions involved reviewing what he had come to learn about his personal vulnerability areas and offense specific risk factors and the what he must do to avoid and manage these as well as to keep himself balanced, healthy, and coping in positive ways. Termination sessions also reviewed Lewis's sense of who he was and wanted to be as a man, and reflected on his accomplishments and his pride in the changes he was able to make in his life. Lewis's partner also joined one of the termination sessions so she could be a part of sharing and hearing about the gains he had made and his plan for continuing to move forward post sentence and treatment.

Complications in Treatment

Treatment with Lewis, as with all clients, was not without complications. The primary challenges with Lewis involved his initial resistance and the time it took for him to be willing to explore his inappropriate sexual interests and the origin of these at a deeper level. Also problematic was his persistence in drinking, despite abstinence being a condition of his parole. This resulted in two suspensions of his parole and return to custody.

It is not uncommon for there to be ebbs and flows in long-term therapy. At times, in my work with Lewis, the treatment plan was on track and we were advancing, as I would hope. Other times the treatment plan was altered, as there were relevant presenting issues or a crisis that would require attention. There were also periods where there was a lull, as Lewis was resistant to return to discussing areas not fully addressed. During these times it was important to re-review my case conceptualization, revisit, and if necessary revise the treatment plan, and discuss the treatment process, challenges, direction, and goals with Lewis.

As well, at times complications resulted from things not related to Lewis, such as a change in team members (e.g., being transferred to a new parole officer, a new police officer, assigned to the high-risk unit) and needing to manage less then optimal attitudes and behavior by some of the professionals involved in the case.

Things to Avoid

In the provision of clinical services to sex offender clients probably the biggest pitfall to avoid is "biting"! Often clients will present with control and resistance issues that are tempting to react to. It is important to stay focused and remind oneself that the client's job is to be challenging, and our job is to work with and through the presenting resistance to engage the client in the therapeutic process. With Lewis, there were several points of resistance, at the initial time of assessment, upon the commencement of therapy, and following his release after having been suspended. At each of these times it would have been easy to get caught up in control issues that could have resulted in sabotaging the treatment process.

It is also important to avoid taking your client's words or behaviors personally, to manage transference and countertransference, to be warm, empathic, and supportive but maintain appropriate and professional boundaries. It is important to be client centered but not allow the client to shift the focus of sessions onto irrelevant issues, to not over- or under-prescribe treatment, and to not forget that therapy is a process and takes time. In this work it can be about "baby steps" (Dr. Leo Marvin, as played by Richard Dreyfuss in *What About Bob*, 1991), and to avoid getting disheartened and giving up on clients when they struggle, progress slowly, or have multiple set-backs. Failures on the client's part do not necessarily mean therapy, or you as a therapist, is not effective. When working with this population, lapses and even relapses are to be expected.

The Art of Therapy

The literature on sex offender assessment and treatment informed by theoretical writings and research is important to guide clinical practice so that our approaches are evidence based. Notwithstanding, the implementation of the theory and science will always remain an art. It is important to acknowledge the art of therapy and to recognize the power of the human connection and the relational dynamics between the client and the therapist in facilitating change. We are in an age of manualized interventions and modulized, psycho-educational short-term interventions, often attempting to remove the art of therapy in the name of consistency, efficiency, and cost effectiveness. As we continue to learn more about how best to assess and treat sexual offending behavior, it will always require individuals to take this information and find ways of applying it in a manner that will optimally engage the client and facilitate the process of change and risk management. It is important to recognize, value, and promote the importance of process-oriented therapeutic interventions and provide opportunities for training, professional development, and support for treatment providers to learn and practice the art of therapy.

References

Aguilar-Vafaie, M., & Abiari, M. (2007). Coping Response Inventory: Assessing coping among Iranian college students and introductory development of an adapted Iranian Coping Response Inventory (CRI). *Mental Health, Religion, and Culture, 10,* 489–513.

Andrews, D. A., & Bonta, J. (2006). *The psychology of criminal conduct* (4th ed.). Newark, NJ: LexisNexis/Anderson.

Association for the Treatment of Sexual Abusers. (2005). *Practice standards and guidelines for the evaluation, treatment, and management of adult male sexual offenders.* Beaverton, OR: Author.

Barbaree, H., E., Peacock, E. J., Cortoni, F., Marshall, W. L., & Seto, M. (1998). Ontario Penitentiaries' Program. In W. L. Marshall, Y. M. Fernandez, S. M. Hudson, & T. Ward (Eds.), *Sourcebook of treatment programs for sexual offenders* (pp. 59–77). New York, NY: Plenum.

Barbaree, H. E., Seto, M. C., Serin, R. C., Amos, N. L., & Preston, D. L. (1994). Comparisons between sexual and nonsexual rapist subtypes: Sexual arousal to rape, offense precursors, and offense characteristics. *Criminal Justice and Behavior, 21,* 95–114.

Barnett, G. D., & Mann, R. E. (2013). Cognition, empathy, and sexual offending. *Trauma, Violence, & Abuse, 14,* 22–33.

Baxter, D. G., Barbaree, H. E., & Marshall, W. L. (1986). Sexual responses to consenting and forced sex in a large sample of rapists and non-rapists. *Behavior Research and Therapy, 24,* 513–520.

Beech, A. R., & Hamilton-Giachritsis, C. E. (2005). Relationship between therapeutic climate and treatment outcome in a group-based sexual offender program. *Sexual Abuse: A Journal of Research and Treatment, 17,* 127–140.

Beech, T., & Fordham, A. S. (1997). Therapeutic climate of sexual offender treatment programs. *Sexual Abuse: A Journal of Research and Treatment, 9,* 219–237.

Blanchard, G. T. (1995). *The difficult connection: The therapeutic relationship in sex offender treatment.* Brandon, VT: Safer Society Press.

Bonta, J. (2002). Offender risk assessment: Guidelines for selection and use. *Criminal Justice and Behavior, 29,* 355–379.

Briere, J. (1995). *Trauma Symptom Inventory professional manual.* Odessa, FL: Psychological Assessment Resources.

Briere, J., Elliott, D. M., Harris, K., & Cotman, A. (1995). Trauma Symptom Inventory: Psychometrics and association with childhood and adult trauma in clinical samples. *Journal of Interpersonal Violence, 10,* 387–401.

Cook, G. (1978). The behavioral treatment of the rapist. *The Prison Journal, 58,* 47–52.

Craissati, J., & Beech, A. R. (2003). A review of dynamic variables and their relationship to risk prediction in sex offenders. *Journal of Sexual Aggression, 9,* 41–55.

Doren, D. M. (2009). Actuarial risk assessments in US court rooms. In A. Beech, L. Craig, & K. Brown (Eds.), *Assessment and treatment of sex offenders: A handbook* (pp. 551–556). Chichester, UK: Wiley.

Dougher, M. J. (1995). Clinical assessment of sex offenders. In B. K. Schwartz & H. R. Cellini (Eds.), *The sex offender: Corrections, treatment and legal practice* (pp. 8.1–8.18). Kingston, NJ: Civic Research Institute.

Douglas, K. S., Hart, S. D., & Kropp, P. R. (2001). Validity of the Personality Assessment Inventory for forensic assessments. *International Journal of Offender Therapy and Comparative Criminology, 45,* 183–197.

Ellerby, L. (2004). *Offence Information Questionnaire—Sex offender version (OIQ-SOV).* Unpublished Self-Report Measure.

Ellerby, L. (2007). *Cats and dogs living together: A multi-systemic approach to risk management.* Paper presented at the 26th Annual Research & Treatment Conference, Association for the Treatment of Sexual Abusers. San Diego, CA.

Ellerby, L., Bedard, J., & Chartrand, S. (2000). Holism, wellness and spirituality: Moving from relapse prevention to healing. In D. R. Laws, S. M. Hudson, & T. Ward (Eds.), *Remaking relapse prevention with sex offenders: A sourcebook* (pp. 427–452). New York, NY: Sage.

Ellerby, L., & Ellerby, B. (2002). Specialized sex offender assessments: What child welfare workers should know. *Envision: The Manitoba Journal of Child Welfare, 1*, 1–12.

Fernandez, Y. M., & Marshall, W. L. (2000). Contextual issues in relapse prevention treatment. In W. L. Marshall, Y. M. Fernandez, S. M. Hudson, & T. Ward (Eds.), *Sourcebook of treatment programs for sexual offenders* (pp. 225–234). New York, NY: Plenum.

Fernandez, Y. M., & Marshall, W. L. (2003). Victim empathy, social self-esteem, and psychopathy in rapists. *Sexual Abuse: A Journal of Research and Treatment, 15*, 11–26.

Fernandez, Y. M., & Serran, G. (2002). Characteristics of an effective sex offender therapist. In B. A. Schwartz & C. Cellini (Eds.), *The sex offender* (Vol. 4, pp. 9-1–9-17). Kingston, NJ: Civic Research Institute.

Frances, A., & Wollert, R. (2012). Sexual sadism: Avoiding its misuse in sexually violent predator evaluations. *Journal of the American Academy of Psychiatry and the Law, 40*, 409–416.

Franzoi, S. L. (1985). Review of the interpersonal behavior survey. In J. V. Mitchell, Jr. (Ed.), *The ninth mental measurements yearbook* (Vol. 1, pp. 699–700). Lincoln, NE: University of Nebraska Press.

Gordon, A., & Hover, G. (1998). The Twin Rivers sex offender treatment program. In W. L. Marshall, Y. M. Fernandez, S. M. Hudson, & T. Ward (Eds.), *Sourcebook of treatment programs for sexual offenders* (pp. 3–15). New York, NY: Plenum.

Hanson, R. K. (2006). Stability and change: Dynamic risk factors for sexual offenders. In W. L. Marshall, Y. M. Fernandez, L. M. Marshall, & G. A Serran (Eds.), *Sexual offender treatment: Controversial issues* (pp. 17–31). Chichester, UK: Wiley.

Hanson, R. K., & Bussière, M. T. (1998). Predicting relapse: A meta-analysis of sexual offender recidivism studies. *Journal of Consulting and Clinical Psychology, 66*, 348–362.

Hanson, R. K., & Morton-Bourgon, K. (2004). *Predictors of sexual recidivism: An updated meta-analysis* (User Report 2004-02). Ottawa, ON, Canada: Public Safety and Emergency Preparedness Canada.

Hanson, R. K., & Morton-Bourgon, K. (2005). The characteristics of persistent sexual offenders: A meta-analysis of recidivism studies. *Journal of Consulting and Clinical Psychology, 73*, 1154–1163.

Hanson, R. K., & Morton-Bourgon, K. E. (2009). The accuracy of recidivism risk assessments for sexual offenders: A meta-analysis. *Psychological Assessment, 21*, 1–21.

Hanson, R. K., & Thornton, D. (1999). *Static-99: Improving actuarial risk assessments for sex offenders* (User Rep. 1999-02). Ottawa, ON, Canada: Department of the Solicitor General of Canada.

Hanson, R. K., & Thornton, D. (2000). Improving risk assessments for sex offenders: A comparison of three actuarial scales. *Law and Human Behavior, 24*, 119–136.

Hare, R. D. (2003). *The Hare Psychopathy Checklist–Revised* (2nd ed.). Toronto, Ontario, Canada: Multi-Health Systems.

Hare, R. D., Clark, D., Grann, M., & Thornton, D. (2000). Psychopathy and the predictive validity of the PCL-R: An international perspective. *Behavioral Sciences and the Law, 18*, 623–645.

Hare, R. D., & Neumann, C. N. (2006). The PCL-R assessment of psychopathy: Development, structural properties, and new directions. In C. Patrick (Ed.), *Handbook of psychopathy* (pp. 58–88). New York, NY: Guilford.

Harkins, L., & Beech, A.R. (2008). Examining the impact of mixing child molesters and rapists in group-based cognitive-behavioral treatment for sexual offenders. *International Journal of Offender Therapy and Comparative Criminology, 52,* 31–45.

Hudson, S. M., Wales, D. S., & Ward, T. (1998). Kia Marama: A treatment program for child molesters in New Zealand. In W. L. Marshall, Y. M. Fernandez, S. M. Hudson, & T. Ward (Eds.), *Sourcebook of treatment programs for sexual offenders* (pp. 17–28). New York, NY: Plenum.

Hudson, S. M., & Ward, T. (1997). Intimacy, loneliness, and attachment style in sexual offenders. *Journal of Interpersonal Violence, 12,* 323–339.

Hutzell, R. R. (1985). Review of the interpersonal behavior survey. In J. V. Mitchell, Jr. (Ed.), *The ninth mental measurements yearbook* (Vol. 1, pp. 700–702). Lincoln, NE: University of Nebraska Press.

Jenkins, A. (1990). *Invitations to responsibility: The therapeutic engagement of men who are violent and abusive.* Adelaide, South Australia: Dulwich Centre Publications.

Jones, R., Winkler, M. X., Kacin, E., Salloway, W. N. & Weissman, M. (1998). Community-based sexual offender treatment for inner-city African-American and Latino youth. In W. L. Marshall, Y. M. Fernandez, S. M. Hudson, & T. Ward (Eds.), *Sourcebook of treatment programs for sexual offenders* (pp. 457–476). New York, NY: Plenum Press.

Kear-Colwell, J., & Pollack, P. (1997). Motivation and confrontation: Which approach to the child sex offender? *Criminal Justice and Behavior, 24,* 20–33.

Krueger, R. B., & Kaplan, M. S. (1997). Frotteurism: Assessment and treatment. In D. R. Laws & W. T. O'Donohue (Eds.), *Sexual deviance: Theory, assessment, and treatment* (pp. 131–151). New York, NY: Guilford.

Lanyon, R. I., & Carle, A. C. (2007). Internal and external validity of scores on the balanced inventory of desirable responding and the Paulhus Deception Scales. *Educational and Psychological Measurement, 67,* 859–876.

Laws, D. R. (1989). *Relapse prevention with sex offenders.* New York, NY: Guilford.

Looman, J., & Marshall, W. L (2005). Sexual arousal in rapists. *Criminal Justice and Behavior, 32,* 367–389.

McGrath, R. J. (1991). Sex-offender risk assessment and disposition planning: A review of empirical and clinical findings. *International Journal of Offender Therapy and Comparative Criminology, 35,* 329–351.

McGrath, R. J. (2001). Utilizing behavioral techniques to control sexual arousal. In M. S. Carich & S. E. Mussack (Eds.), *Handbook for sexual abuser assessment and treatment* (pp. 105–116). Brandon, VT: Safer Society Press.

McGrath, R. J., Cumming, G. F., Burchard, B. L., Zeoli, S., & Ellerby, L. (2010). *Current practices and emerging trends in sexual abuser management: The Safer Society 2009 North American Survey.* Brandon VT: Safer Society Press.

Mann, R. E., Hanson, R. K., & Thornton, D. (2010). Assessing risk for sexual recidivism: Some proposals on the nature of psychologically meaningful risk factors. *Sex Abuse, 22,* 191–217.

Mann, R. E., & Hollin, C. R. (2001, November). *Schemas: A model for understanding cognition in sexual offending.* Paper presented at the 20th Annual Research and Treatment Conference of the Association for the Treatment of Sexual Abusers. San Antonio, TX.

Marshall, W. L. (2005). Therapist style in sexual offender treatment: Influence on indices of change. *Sexual Abuse: A Journal of Research and Treatment, 17*, 109–116.

Marshall, W. L., Anderson, D., & Fernandez, Y. M. (1999). *Cognitive behavioral treatment of sexual offenders.* Chichester, UK: John Wiley & Sons.

Marshall, W. L., Eccles, A.. Barbaree, H. E. (1993). A three-tiered approach to the rehabilitation of incarcerated sex offenders. *Behavioral Sciences and the Law, 11*, 441–455.

Marshall, W. L., & Kennedy, P. (2003). Sexual sadism in sexual offenders: An elusive diagnosis. *Aggressive and Violent Behavior, 8*, 1–22.

Marshall W. M., Kennedy, P., & Yates, P. (2002). Issues concerning the reliability and validity of the diagnosis of Sexual Sadism applied in prison settings. *Sex Abuse, 14*, 301–311.

Marshall, W. L, Marshall, L. E., Serran, G. A., & Fernandez, Y. M. (2006). *Treating sexual offenders: An integrated approach.* New York, NY: Routledge.

Marshall, W. L., & Moulden, H. (2001). Hostility toward women and victim empathy in rapists. *Sex Abuse: A Journal of Research and Treatment, 13*, 249–255.

Maschi, T., & Gibson, S. (2012). Schema behind bars: Trauma, age, ethnicity, and offenders' world assumptions. *Traumatology, 18*, 8–19.

Maslow, A. (1943). A theory of human motivation. *Psychological Review, 50*, 370–396.

Mauger, P. A., Adkinson, D. R., Zoss, S. K., Firestone, K., & Hook, D. (1980). *The Interpersonal Behavior Survey professional manual.* Los Angeles, CA: Western Psychological Services.

Miller, W. R., & Rollnick, S. (2002). *Motivational interviewing: Preparing people to change addictive behavior* (2nd ed.). New York, NY: Guilford.

Moos, R. H. (1993). *Coping Response Inventory: Adult form professional manual.* Odessa, FL: Psychological Assessment Resources.

Moos, R. H. (2004). *Coping Response Inventory: An update on research applications and validity: Manual supplement.* Lutz, FL: Psychological Assessment Resources.

Morey, L. C. (1991). *Personality Assessment Inventory: Professional manual.* Tampa, FL: Psychological Assessment Resources.

Myers, R. (2000). *Identifying schemas in child and adult sex offenders and violent offenders.* (Unpublished Masters thesis). University of Leicester, England.

Paulhus, D. L. (1998). *Paulhus Deception Scale (PDS). The Balanced Inventory of Desirable Responding–7.* North Tonawanda, NY: Multi Health System.

Phenix, A., Helmus, L., & Hanson, R. K. (2012). *Static-99 Revaluator's workbook.* Retrieved from http://www.static99.org/pdfdocs/Static-99RandStatic2002REvaluatorsWorkbook 2012-01-09.pdf.

Pithers, W. D. (1993). Treatment of rapists: Reinterpretation of early outcome data exploratory constructs to enhance therapeutic efficacy. In G. C. N. Hall, R. Hirschman, J. R. Graham, & M. S. Zaragoza (Eds.), *Sexual aggression: Issues in etiology, assessment, and treatment* (pp. 167–196). Washington, DC: Taylor and Francis.

Polaschek, D. L. L. (2003). Empathy and victim empathy. In T. Ward, D. R. Laws, & S. M. Hudson (Eds.), *Sexual deviance: Issues and controversies* (pp. 172–189). Thousand Oaks, CA: Sage.

Prescott, D. S. (2009). *Building motivation to change in sexual offenders.* Brandon, VT: Safer Society Press.

Prochaska, J. O., DiClemente, C. C., & Norcross, J. C. (1992). In search of how people change: Applications to addictive behaviors. *American Psychologist, 47*, 1102–1114.

Rada, R. T. (1978). *Clinical aspects of the rapist.* New York, NY: Grune & Stratton.

Rothman, D. B. (2007). *The role of the therapeutic alliance in psychotherapy with sexual offenders* (Unpublished doctoral dissertation). University of Manitoba, Winnipeg, Manitoba, Canada.

Scott, R. L., & Tetreault, L. A. (1987). Attitudes of rapists and other violent offenders toward women. *Journal of Social Psychology, 127*, 375–380.

Serran, G.A., Looman, J., & Dickie, I. (2004, October). *The role of schemas in sexual offending.* Paper presented at the 23rd Annual Research and Treatment Conference of the Association for the Treatment of Sexual Abusers. Albuquerque, NM.

Tangney, J. P., Stuewig, J., Mashek, D., & Hastings, M. (2011). Assessing jail inmates' proneness to shame and guilt: Feeling bad about the behavior or the self? *Criminal Justice and Behavior, 38*(7), 710–734.

Ward, T., & Gannon, T. (2006). Rehabilitation, etiology, and self-regulation: The Good Lives Model of sexual offender treatment. *Aggression and Violent Behavior, 11*, 77–94.

Ward, T., McCormack, J., Hudson, S. M., & Polaschek, D. (1997). Rape: Assessment and treatment. In D. R. Laws & W. O'Donohue (Eds.), *Sexual deviance: Theory, assessment and treatment* (pp. 356–393). New York, NY: Sage.

Wong, S. C. P., Olver, M. E., Nicholaichuk, T. P., & Gordon, A. E. (2003). The Violence Risk Scale-Sexual Offender Version (VRS-SO). Saskatoon, Saskatchewan, Canada: Regional Psychiatric Centre and University of Saskatchewan.

Yates, P. M. (2009). Using the Good Lives Model to motivate sexual offenders to participate in treatment. In D. S. Prescott (Ed.), *Building motivation to change in sexual offenders.* Brandon, VT: Safer Society Press.

Yates, P. M., Prescott, D., & Ward, T. (2010). *Applying the Good Lives and self-regulation models to sex offender treatment: A practical guide for clinicians.* Brandon, VT: Safer Society Press.

4

THE GOOD LIVES MODEL OF OFFENDER REHABILITATION

A Case Study

Jo Thakker, Tony Ward, and Chi Meng Chu

Introduction

The purpose of this chapter is to demonstrate how the Good Lives Model (GLM) can be applied in each stage of the clinical assessment and treatment process in the case of a child sexual offender. As stated below, in order to protect the clients' confidentiality, the case used is a composite, drawn from several different individuals. However, all of the details that are described (such as psychometric tests) are those that were used in one or other of the cases. It is the view of the authors that using a composite does not detract from the purpose of this chapter, which is primarily to show how the good lives model may be applied to a clinical case. All three authors are qualified clinical psychologists who have experience working with sexual offenders.

The chapter begins with a brief overview of the GLM. Due to the focus of the chapter it was not possible to provide an in-depth discussion of the model. Readers are referred to Ward and Stewart (2003) for a detailed early exposition of the model and to Laws and Ward (2011), and Ward, Yates, and Willis (2012) for more recent discussions that respond to some of the criticisms of the model that have emerged in the recent literature. Following this, the case begins with a description of the client's background, including important familial and cultural factors. The next section looks at the assessment process, including assessment of both general factors and risk factors for sexual reoffending. The case is then formulated, using the GLM as a framework for the case conceptualization. Following this, the treatment process is outlined, including, the treatment components, treatment rationale, and the client's response to each treatment component.

Once these core aspects of the case have been covered the chapter then discusses a range of peripheral issues, including challenges in the case, ethical considerations, and cultural factors, and then concludes with a brief overview of the key learning points in the case.

A Brief Overview of the Good Lives Model

The GLM was developed by one of us (Tony Ward) about 10 years ago and over the last decade it has been further elaborated and applied in a number of areas of rehabilitation. It has been explicated in relation to a variety of offense types (Ward & Maruna, 2007), including sexual offending (e.g., Laws & Ward, 2011; Willis & Ward, 2011) and violent offending (e.g., Langlands, Ward, & Gilchrist, 2009), as well as other psychological problems, such as substance abuse (e.g., Thakker & Ward, 2010). While the model has been criticized for not having any substantive advantages over the more widely accepted risk need responsivity (RNR) model (see Andrews, Bonta, & Wormith, 2011), in our view it provides a comprehensive and systematic guide to offender rehabilitation and is unique in the way in integrates well-being enhancement and risk reduction elements of forensic practice.

The GLM is a strengths-based model which has the dual objectives of encouraging offenders to work toward their goals while also managing their risks for reoffending (Barnao, Robertson, & Ward, 2010; Ward & Maruna, 2007). It is strength based because it (a) takes offenders' personal value commitments and areas of expertise seriously, and (b) seeks to equip them with the internal and external resources to promote these interests in ways that are socially acceptable and personally fulfilling (Laws & Ward, 2011). The model proposes that in order to fully understand an individual's motivation for offending it is important to understand the basic functions that the offending serves. Furthermore, the GLM suggests that, accordingly, rehabilitation needs to include a component that encourages offenders to meet their basic needs in more prosocial ways (Ward, Mann, & Gannon, 2007). Thus, rather than simply instructing offenders to avoid certain risks, according to the GLM, it is also important to assist offenders to identify, and work toward, their personal commitments and associated goals. As summarized by Barnao et al. (2010): "individual patients are seen as self-determining agents rather than disembodied carriers of risk" (p. 217).

The GLM proposes that all human endeavor centers on the desire to fulfill basic human needs and to seek the primary human goods toward which these needs are directed. For example, a person might meet the primary human need for intimacy by securing the good of relatedness. Similarly, consuming healthy food and exercising regularly might contribute to the basic good of physical and mental well-being, while playing a musical instrument may fulfill the basic good of creativity. Ward argues that the motivation to attain these "goods" is inherent in human nature and that therefore we all naturally strive to attain them in our lives. However, for many offenders, the *way* that they go about attaining these goods is problematic. Ward and colleagues write: "both sexual and non-sexual offenders are naturally disposed to seek a range of primary human goods that if secured will result in greater self-fulfillment and sense of purpose" (Ward, Collie, & Bourke, 2009, p. 304). In other words, the primary goods that an offender wishes to attain are no different from those of a nonoffender; however, the process is problematic in that it involves illegal activity.

In describing the GLM, Ward distinguishes between primary and secondary goods. While primary goods are essentially ends in themselves, secondary goods relate to the means of attaining primary goods. For example, as shown below, friendship is conceptualized as a primary good, thus secondary goods would be any activities which contributed to this primary good, such as a stable intimate relationship or a positive relationship with a parent. Drawing on theoretical work from a range of disciplines, including anthropology and evolutionary psychology, Ward and Stewart (2003) propose that there are at least 10 primary human goods, namely:

> Life (including healthy living and functioning), knowledge, excellence in play and work (including mastery experiences), excellence in agency (i.e., autonomy and self-directedness), inner peace (i.e., freedom from emotional turmoil and stress), friendship (including intimate, romantic and family relationships), community, spirituality (in the broad sense of finding meaning and purpose in life), happiness, and creativity. (p. 356)

Purvis, Ward, and Willis (2011) have made a distinction between play and work and argued for 11 primary goods.

Ward suggests that all human beings naturally desire these primary goods and that accordingly, offenders engage in activities, which are aimed at attaining them. However, offenders use *inappropriate means* (i.e., goods are sought in ways that are inappropriate or counterproductive); demonstrate a *lack of scope* (i.e., only some goods are sought); display *conflict or lack of coherence* (i.e., the ways some goods are sought directly reduces the chances of others being secured); and typically possess *a lack of capacity* (i.e., individuals lack the skills, opportunities, and resources to achieve a certain good in specific ways). It is important to note that the process of striving to attain primary goods is not conceptualized as conscious. Rather, Ward proposes that the process is natural and not typically part of an explicit, organized plan. Most people in everyday life do not make a list of goods and then develop a plan of how to attain them. However, one of the goals of treatment is to sharpen offenders' awareness of their most heavily weighted primary goods and to orient any subsequent intervention plans around these core commitments. Within the GLM framework, criminogenic needs (i.e., dynamic risk factors associated with the continuation of offending behavior) are internal and external obstacles that hinder or prevent the acquisition of primary human goods in prosocial ways, or represent secondary goods in and of themselves (e.g., relying on antisocial peers to fulfill the primary good of friendship).

As illustrated in the case outlined below, according to the GLM, a sexual offender such as John used *inappropriate means* to attain the good of relatedness. He sought sexual intimacy (and there is nothing wrong with that in itself) by having sex with individuals under the age of consent. Thus, the way in which he attempted to realize this good was ethically unacceptable and also likely to be ultimately unfulfilling. There was also *conflict and a lack of coherence* in terms of his sexual offending as his offending behavior probably made it more likely that he would not form an appropriate relationship with an adult woman. For example, he would have needed freedom and secrecy in order to maintain the offending behavior and these would have been more difficult to attain if he was in a long-term intimate relationship. Furthermore, in the case of John, a *lack of capacity* (in terms of his ability to relate to adult women and his problems with emotional regulation) may have also played a role in his offending.

As outlined by Ward, a GLM approach to offender rehabilitation needs to include a thorough assessment of the relationship between offending reacted actions and the goods that were associated with the offending. In other words, the therapist needs to ask the question: What primary goods was the offender attempting to obtain in committing the offense? In the case of John, it would appear that the most important goods (there might also be others) were relatedness and community. Once the primary and secondary goods have been identified then a good lives plan is developed with the aim of assisting the offender to develop the knowledge and skills necessary to attain his goods in a more prosocial manner. Thus, in line with the GLM, treatment should recognize the importance of basic human needs and normalize the desire for these. But, it should demonstrate to offenders how they have attempted to attend to these needs in problematic ways and support them in finding new prosocial ways of attending to them.

The Case

As mentioned above, this case study has been created from several different individual cases, which have a common thread. All of the details are real, insofar as they occurred in one or other individual; however, they do not all exist in one person. It was decided to approach the case study in this manner in order to protect the confidentiality of all clients. All of the individuals concerned were clients of the authors of this chapter and they were all seen in the context of the Prison Service in New Zealand or Australia.

John Tan is a 40-year-old man of Chinese descent, who was charged with five counts of child molestation. Specifically, he had sexually offended against his 12-year-old niece and two 13-year-old females over a period of 3 months. John was convicted of a total of 5 sexual offenses and he was sentenced to 18 months' imprisonment. Furthermore, he was directed to attend relevant offender rehabilitation programs (including specialized therapy to address his sexual offending behavior). John had no previous convictions.

Background Information

With regard to his personal and family history, John reported that he is a first generation New Zealander; he was born in New Zealand while his parents were born in China. Furthermore, he said that his real name is Jiang, but that he preferred to be called John. He described his parents as conservative and strict and said that they did not easily adapt to life in New Zealand. For example, he stated that they wanted all of the children to marry individuals of Chinese descent. John is the youngest in the family; he has two older sisters.

John reported an unremarkable childhood history, and shared that he maintained cordial relationships with his family members. Although he had attended family gatherings frequently, John did not confide in his family members about his problems and did not perceive them to be a source of social support. However, he explained that this is typical in Chinese society, as stoicism and emotional fortitude are valued and it is frowned upon to show weakness. He provided an example of this, explaining that his father had some sort of "breakdown" when John was about 14 years old. He said that his father had some financial difficulties at the time and was worried that he was going to be declared bankrupt. He recalled that his father "went away" for about a month while he was having some sort of treatment for this. However, John said that his family never discussed it and his father returned and continued as if nothing had happened.

With regard to his peer relationships, it appeared that John had only engaged in structured interactions with his peers and did not easily make friends. For instance, he said that he learned the violin at the local School of Music from when he was 5 to 15 years of age and was a member of an orchestra for much of this time. He said that he got to know many of his fellow orchestra members quite well but never socialized with them outside of rehearsals or performances. According to John, he did not experience harsh discipline or peer victimization during his childhood or youth. However, John reported that an unknown male had molested him on a public bus when he was 12 years old. John said that he did not tell anyone about this incident at the time.

With regard to his education, John had generally performed well in his studies and had completed his Bachelor of Science qualification in Mathematics with honors. In addition, he completed a Postgraduate Diploma of Education and joined the Education Service as a high school teacher. John had worked as a teacher before he was convicted and incarcerated for his current sexual offenses. His work performance had been satisfactory and his colleagues had remarked that he had been a "dedicated and responsible teacher" even if he appeared rather reserved. John did, however, remark that he was under a lot of pressure at work to deliver outstanding results. As a result of his conviction, John was retrenched from his job and he was no longer allowed to teach.

Outside of work, John was an avid photographer who had enjoyed taking pictures of nature since his undergraduate education. He was also actively involved in the photographic society during his university days. Although photography was a pastime for John, he had won several local awards for some of his pictures in the past. In addition, John had a talent for graphic designing, and his parents and school were supportive of this interest during his high school education, which had helped him to hone his skills. John was grateful for this support and had shared that his graphic designing skills were complementary to his photography interest. Nevertheless, he had stopped these interests in recent years due to his preoccupation with child pornography and young females. Pertaining to substance use, John informed that he had consumed alcohol in moderate amounts, but had never abused alcohol or other substances.

According to John, he became aware of sexual matters when he was about 14 years old. Citing self-exploration as his initial means of discovery, John shared that he had begun masturbating at about that time. In addition, John began using pornography; initially just magazines from a local book store. He said that the magazines always showed pictures of topless adult women, but nothing more revealing than that. He recalled that he regularly masturbated whilst looking at these images. John explained that over time he began looking at pornography on the Internet and eventually developed a preference for increasingly younger females. John reported that when he was in his early 30s he began visiting prostitutes after he had come across a pornography website that had links to a local brothel. John's description of his use of pornography and prostitutes suggested that he used these activities as a means of coping during times when he felt stressed.

John reported that he had traveled to Thailand on three occasions, during the 5 years prior to his incarceration, to engage the services of female prostitutes aged between 13 and 15 years. He justified his actions with the belief that he was helping the girls' families to "break free from a wretched life of poverty," as well as "teaching the girls about love and sexuality." Furthermore, John appeared to have developed distorted views about female sexuality from his use of pornography. For instance, he appeared convinced that the young prostitutes enjoyed having sex with him and loved him. Moreover, he believed that teenage girls with pet dogs were likely to be interested in acts of bestiality, having watched pornographic scenes depicting females having sex with animals. He added that he had been sexually aroused whenever he saw young teenage girls rollerblading in the park near his residence or dressed in their swimsuits at the swimming pool. John reported that his longest intimate relationship lasted about 4 months and ended when his girlfriend suggested that they live together. John explained that he was nervous about this as he had not told his parents about the relationship and he believed that they would not approve because his girlfriend was not of Chinese descent. He said he was 22 years old at the time.

John admitted that he was preoccupied with thinking about young girls, and had difficulties managing his urges to engage in sexual activities with them. His current offenses occurred in the context of him taking care of his niece who was staying with him when his sister (a single mother) was out of the country for work, as well as during the course of his work in his high school. John shared that he had groped his niece's breasts and genitalia on the pretext of tickling her and playing a wrestling game. In addition, he had groomed her by sharing tips about "boy-girl" relationships, and also by piquing her interest in topics about sexuality. With regard to the sexual offenses that were committed against his students, John revealed that he had asked his female students to stay back for remedial classes with him. Specifically, John had brushed against the breasts of his students whilst he sat close to them during the class. According to John, he had later masturbated to his recollections of these offenses in the school toilet and fantasized that he was having sexual intercourse with them. John admitted that he had hoped to engage in sexual intercourse with them in due course if he had not been discovered and arrested. He added that although he had engaged paid sexual services of young teenage females, John was getting more and more preoccupied with having sexual intercourse with young females and could not resist offending against his students. In particular, he felt that his life was spinning out of control given his sexual preoccupations. John appeared regretful, but he seemed to be unaware of the full severity of his actions and could not fully empathize with the impact of his actions on his victims. Nevertheless, he expressed a willingness to engage in psychological treatment for his sexual offending behavior. As a result of his sexual offenses, his family had cut off all contact with him.

Clinical Assessment

General Assessment

Psychological assessment of John consisted of three separate interviews, review of file information (including the Judge's sentencing notes, the Police summaries of fact, and the Probation Service presentence report), and administration of several psychometric tools. John was quite reticent and shy during the first interview but was increasingly forthcoming in the second and third interviews, and a good level of rapport was established. It was not possible to interview any members of John's family as John did not give his permission for this; in denying permission he cited the fact that his family has ceased all contact with him.

The following psychometric tools were used to assess John:

- The Psychopathy Checklist-Revised (PCL-R; Hare, 2003): This was used to determine the presence of psychopathic traits.
- The Beck Depression Inventory—Second Edition (BDI-II; Beck, Steer, & Brown, 1996): This was used to screen for the presence of depression. This was considered useful because John stated that he did not like to discuss his feelings, thus it was reasoned that he may be more likely to respond honestly to a questionnaire. Furthermore, the results on the BDI-II were used as starting points for discussion in talking to John about his mood and his thoughts and feelings as pertaining to his future.
- The Personality Assessment Inventory (PAI; Morey, 2007): This was used to assess the presence of problems in the areas of personality and psychopathology.

John's scores on the PAI all fell within the normal range apart from his scores on the Stress (Str) Scale. On this scale his scores were significantly elevated indicating that he was experiencing a great deal of stress in many areas of his life. As outlined in the PAI manual, individuals who score highly on this scale typically feel quite overwhelmed by the perceived stressors in their lives and often feel that they are unable to control the situation. It is interesting to note also that usually people with this amount of stress are vulnerable to developing various forms of psychopathology. John's scores on the four validity scales indicated that he had answered questions honestly.

When questioned about his stress levels, John said that he was unsure how to proceed in his life as he had lost his job and had been "excommunicated" from his family. He explained that he could not easily see a way forward from his present situation. This was reflected in his scores on the BDI-II; while he did not evidence depression on this measure, he did appear to be feeling quite hopeless about his future. However, he acknowledged that his offending had contributed to his current difficulties. John was questioned about his stress at the time of his offending and he explained that (as mentioned above) he was under pressure at work. On elaboration, he stated that due to falling enrolment at the school where he taught, restructuring was taking place and he felt that his job was at risk. He believed that in order to keep his position at the school, he needed to achieve excellent results, which meant that his students needed to perform at a very high level.

John's results on the PCL-R suggested that he does not have psychopathic traits; there were no elevations on either Factor 1 or 2; however, he was elevated on the trait of "Promiscuous Sexual Behavior." This is one of four traits on the scale that is not associated with either of the factors.

It is interesting to note that John did not display a lack of empathy on the PCL-R even though he presented as lacking empathy for his victims. Thus, he did not appear to have more general empathy deficits.

Risk Assessment

John's risk of sexual reoffending was assessed by examining both static and dynamic factors. Static factors are characteristics that are historical and unchangeable (such as criminal history and number of victims) while dynamic factors are those that may change over time (such as impulsivity and antisocial beliefs). The risk assessment measures that were used in this instance were:

- Level of Service/Case Inventory (LS/CMI; Andrews, Bonta, & Wormith, 2004): This broad assessment tool was used to measure the presence of both static and dynamic risk factors for general recidivism. Note that it is not specifically designed for use with sexual offenders.
- The Risk for Sexual Violence Protocol (RSVP; Hart et al., 2003): This was used to gain further information about the various risk factors that contributed to John's sexual offending. As stated by Laws (2010) this tool is designed for "*risk formulation*, not risk prediction" (p. 2). Note that the RSVP includes both static and dynamic risk factors for sexual recidivism.
- The Static-2002R (Hanson, Lloyd, Helmus, & Thornton, 2012): This was used to assess the presence of static risk factors for sexual reoffending.
- The Stable-2007 (Hanson, Harris, Scott, & Helmus, 2007): This was used to assess the presence of dynamic risk factors for sexual reoffending. Note that it covers some of the same ground as the RSVP (such as mental health and relationships) but also includes some other areas (such as social supports and sexual self-regulation).

John did not exhibit significant antisocial antecedents or a criminal history. He also did not have significant difficulties pertaining to his education or employment, family circumstances, procriminal attitudes/ orientation, or display any indications of substance abuse. Relative to other adult offenders, John's risk of *general reoffending* was assessed as Low using the LS/CMI, and his risk for *sexual reoffending* was Low based on his score on the Static-2002R. However, John's risk of future *sexual offending* was assessed as Moderate using the RSVP and the Stable-2007. Although he did not condone an offending lifestyle, he had a chronic history of engaging in inappropriate sexual activities with underaged females, and was sexually preoccupied with young females. In addition, it was clear that John had endorsed significant sexually deviant and sexual-offense-supportive attitudes. It should also be noted that John had difficulties controlling his urges to engage in inappropriate sexual activities with young females.

Notwithstanding that John did not exhibit other significant antisocial features, his sexual preoccupation with young females, cognitive distortions about females, sexual-offense-supportive attitudes, lack of empathy toward his young female victims, lack of effective coping and preventative strategies, and chronic inappropriate sexual behavior toward young females were serious concerns. Another possible area of concern was John's lack of prosocial support from his peers and family; specifically, he did not appear to have any stable and long-term friendships and intimate relationships with adults, even though he did not associate with antisocial peers.

Case Formulation

In terms of John's early life, there are a number of factors that may be important in explaining his behavior as an adult. His discussion of his familial relationship points to possible attachment problems: his parents provided him with a stable home, but it appears that there was little by way of love and affection. Thus, he might have developed a pattern of insecure attachment. Furthermore, he was molested on a public bus when he was 12 years old and this could have had a range of effects on him, including the development of feelings of guilt and shame in relation to the incident and the manifestation of beliefs endorsing sexual interactions between children and adults. The fact that John never told anybody about the incident would have made it more likely that any maladaptive cognitive and emotional responses continued unchecked.

It seems likely that John's self-regulation deficits in the form of impulsivity may have predisposed him to his sexual offending. Importantly, John's use of pornography and sexual preoccupation toward young females were key factors that predisposed him to his current sexual offenses. Furthermore, it was likely that his preference for young females developed over time as he viewed images of increasingly younger individuals. Thus, a conditioning process was probably at play, in which successive approximations were reinforced. John's family modeled a maladaptive approach to dealing with emotional difficulties. Specifically, they tended to hide their emotions and not discuss their difficulties. This might have contributed to John's tendency to conceal his emotions from others. This family tendency might also have its roots in their cultural background.

John did not appear to have readily available prosocial support from his family members as well as peers, which could be partially attributed to his limited ability to build and maintain relationships with his peers. John's personality traits (e.g., being guarded and untrusting in relationships, and being suspicious of the motives of others), as well as his oversensitivity to perceived criticism and rejection might have affected how he related to and confided in others, which could have led to further emotional isolation. It was likely that John's parents' rejection of his first long-term intimate partner contributed to his tendency to isolate himself and avoid long-term romantic relationships with adult women.

Notably, the lack of readily available prosocial support could also have led John to develop deeply entrenched coping scripts involving pornography, such that in times of high stress, pornography (and sex with young females) was used as a coping strategy and viewed as possessing key stress-reduction properties. These together with his sexual-offense-supportive attitudes, and frequent sexual encounters with young prostitutes (which not only assuaged his feelings of stress and loneliness but also reinforced his sexual attraction for young females) served to maintain his inappropriate sexual behavior as well as sexual offending behavior. However, it was noted that John did not have significant antisocial cognitions and behavior, and crucially, he has not engaged in substance use behavior that might have further contributed to his potential to engage in further criminal offending behavior.

Although John did not appear to fully appreciate the impact of his offending on others, he was regretful of his actions. With regard to his primary human goods, John appeared to seek pleasure (e.g., feelings of happiness), relationships (e.g., family and romantic relationships), creativity (i.e., photography and graphic designing), inner peace (i.e., freedom from stress and feelings of isolation), excellence in work (i.e., being a responsible teacher), as well as excellence in play (i.e., his photography hobby). His sexual offending behavior arguably represented a misguided way to obtain his goods of pleasure, inner peace, and relatedness. A lack of effective social skills and perceived social support, sexual-offense-supportive attitudes, and his sexual preoccupation with young females were criminogenic needs that blocked the attainment of his primary human goods in a prosocial manner (see Table 4.1 for a summary of John's offending according to the GLM framework). As such, future interventions should aim to help John to achieve these goods and live a satisfying life without harming others or putting others' lives in danger. In addition, John's perception of himself might have constituted a core value commitment and thus any future treatment plan should incorporate this aspect of his practical identity. This primary good was associated with the good of community.

Treatment Plan and Rationale

Following the assessment process outlined above, John engaged in individual therapy with the same correctional psychologist who had conducted his assessment. Given the importance of maintaining rapport in the therapeutic process, continuity from assessment to treatment is

Table 4.1 The GLM Mapping Table (from Purvis, Ward, & Willis, 2011)

Name: John
Person ID:

Table Number: ____ / ___ / ___
Date table commenced:

| GOODS | WEIGHTING (preferences/ most valued good/s) | CAPACITY | | | | MEANS Appropriate vs. Inappropriate | RELATIONSHIP TO OFFENDING Direct or Indirect Pathway Protective or No Relationship |
		Internal Capabilities (strengths)	Internal Obstacles (deficits)	External Capabilities	External Obstacles		
Community							
Creativity	✓	Talented at photography & graphic designing	Sexually preoccupied with young females; impulsivity	Professional recognition for photography	Incarceration	Appropriate	Protective
Excellence in Agency							
Excellence in Play	✓	Talented at photography	Sexually preoccupied with young females; impulsivity	Professional recognition for photography	Incarceration	Appropriate	Protective
Excellence in Work	✓	Responsible teacher	Sexually preoccupied with young females; impulsivity	Respected by colleagues	Banned from teaching children; offended against his students	Inappropriate	Direct (misused trust, & opportunity, to offend against his students)

Inner Peace	✓	Willingness to go for therapy; recognized need to address issues	Ineffective & deviant coping style; distrustfulness	Therapy	Lacked perceived social support; ostracized by family	Inappropriate	Direct
Knowledge							
Life							
Pleasure	✓	Willingness to go for therapy; recognized need to address issues; talented at photography	Sexual preoccupied with young females; distrustfulness; impulsivity;	Therapy	Family blamed him for offences; lacked perceived social support	Inappropriate	Direct
Relatedness	✓	Capacity for caring	Lacked social skills; distrustful; impulsivity; sought sexual intimacy through paid sexual services	Therapy	Family blamed him for offences; lacked perceived social support	Inappropriate	Direct (had sexual intercourse with underage prostitutes)
Spirituality							

encouraged; thus if possible, the offender should have the same clinician for both. Therapy involved 25 one hour sessions which were conducted either weekly or every 2 weeks over a period of 30 weeks. Note that most sexual offenders within the prison system are treated in group settings; however, John's relatively short sentence did not provide sufficient time for him to complete a specialist sex offender program. Thus, he was referred for individual treatment.

1. *Assess John's readiness for treatment and establish a strong therapeutic alliance.* According to the GLM, it is beneficial for the practitioner to adopt a patient and supportive (rather than a strongly confrontational) approach to establishing a good therapeutic relationship with the client before the commencement of the treatment. This is consistent with the literature, which indicates that a good therapeutic alliance is fundamental to treatment efficacy (e.g., Kozar & Day, 2012). This was considered to be especially important given that John did not trust others easily. Moreover, it was important to build up his self-efficacy and communication skills given that he was sensitive to criticism and rejection so that he was equipped to engage in treatment and complete treatment tasks. This type of positive approach is central to the GLM and is consistent with other widely used approaches such as motivational interviewing (MI) (e.g., as outlined by Prescott & Porter, 2011). Furthermore, structuring intervention and treatment plans around individuals' personal priorities and core commitments makes it much easier to motivate them to engage in the process of change.

2. *Assess John's own goals, priorities in life, and also the goals of treatment.* This aspect of treatment was important to the process of developing a good lives plan (see Table 4.2 for a summary of John's good lives plan). Obviously, in order for the plan to be successful, it needed to be consistent with what he wanted in life. More broadly, treatment (according to the GLM) needs to be collaborative. The implementation of a good lives plan can reduce dynamic risk factors (criminogenic needs) in two ways. First, the establishment of internal and external capacities can directly reduce risk factors because the building of skills necessarily weakens their influence. For example, in the case of John, assisting him to achieve the primary good of inner peace (e.g., emotional equilibrium) meant it was less likely he would resort to the use of pornography to soothe himself. Second, basing treatment around an offender's personal priorities may increase his motivation to work on his overall treatment plan, and thereby indirectly function to eliminate or weaken his array of dynamic risk factors.

3. *Introduce John to the key concepts and ideas of the GLM.* This aspect of treatment was used to help John to envisage a different life for himself (i.e., the "new me"). This component involved a thorough examination

Table 4.2 John's Good Life Plan

OODS	GOALS ASSOCIATED WITH GOODS	STEPS TO GOALS
*Community	Re-establish a connection with his local community	Join a photography club Join the local amateur orchestra Join a local gym
*Creativity	Engage in a creative activity	Join a photography club Join the local amateur orchestra
Excellence in Agency	Engage in activities that will give him a sense of self-efficacy	Join a photography club Join the local amateur orchestra
Excellence in Play	Engage in leisure activities that will give him a sense of self-efficacy	Practice playing his violin and get lessons occasionally Develop his knowledge of photographic software so that he can extend his skills
Excellence in Work	Find satisfactory employment	Consider his work options given his offence history Retrain if necessary Find some part-time employment to support himself in the meantime
*Inner Peace	Manage stress effectively	Practice relaxation and mindfulness skills Go for regular walks
Knowledge	Continue to learn about himself (in particular, his weaknesses, risks, and strengths Learn about his cultural background	Continue to engage in follow-up treatment in the community (with the SAFE Network) Find out about Chinese cultural groups in his local community Take a trip to China
Life	Maintain good physical health	Have a good diet Get regular exercise
Pleasure	Engage in pleasurable pro-social activities	Watch movies Go for regular walks
Relatedness	Develop his social connections	Make opportunities to meet an appropriate intimate partner Join a club or orchestra (as suggested above) Try and re-establish connections with his family
Spirituality	Find meaning in his life experiences so that he can move forward in a positive way	Read Chinese philosophy, in particular the Tao Te Ching Learn about the meditation tradition that underlies mindfulness

of each primary human good that John sought along with an understanding of how secondary goods (the means of achieving primary human goods) were attaining (or not attaining) the primary human goods. The ultimate aim was to begin establishing a new personal or practical identity as a nonoffender, capitalizing on John's overarching primary human goods (see Maruna, 2001). Because offenders often find it difficult to reflect on their lives and associated core values, it is important that clinicians translate the rather abstract primary goods into examples of specific activities and qualities. For example, the good of relatedness can be unpacked in terms of relationships with particular people and participating in concrete activities.

4. *Assist John to recognize his strengths.* It was considered important that John had realized that he also possessed a number of strengths that could be used to structure the desistance process despite encountering difficulties. In addition, it was paramount to help John understand that the identified approach goals were not, in themselves, always directly criminogenic, and consistently adopting prosocial means to achieve them would most likely lead to a reduction or elimination of his array of criminogenic needs (see Tables 4.1 and 4.2). Therefore, these approach goals were utilized to increase his responsivity to attending to the risk management interventions. Note that strength-based approaches have gained popularity in the mental health field in the last decade or so and are arguably now the status quo (for a discussion of the approach in the mental health field see Wong, 2006; for a comprehensive look at its application to sexual offenders see Marshall, Marshall, Serran, & O'Brien, 2011).

5. *Encourage John to consider his approach goals and their implications.* John was encouraged to consider his approach goals and think about how attaining these could have a positive impact on him and others. Also, the relationship between these goals and his criminogenic needs (either directly or indirectly) was clarified. The practitioner and John needed to understand the relationship or linkage between his criminogenic needs and his desired approach goals in order for treatment to be meaningful. Thus a good lives plan should clearly identify the most highly weighted primary goods, specific in a graded way how goals are intended to achieve these goods, and either through directly building specific internal or external capacities, or indirectly through motivational effects, demonstrate how dynamic risk factors will be targeted. This aspect of treatment brings together the GLM and the RNR model in that it focuses on the link between dynamic risk factors and the goals associated with attaining a good life. In order for the goals to be attainable dynamic risk factors need to be addressed.

6. *Teach John emotional regulation skills: Relaxation and mindfulness skills.* John was taught relaxation and mindfulness skills to help him

manage his stressors and negative emotions. This was considered to be an essential element of treatment because assessment showed that he was experiencing significant stress at the time of his offending and after, when he was serving his sentence. Furthermore, inclusion of this component is consistent with the literature, which indicates that most sex offender treatment programs have an emotional regulation component which includes the acquisition of coping skills for dealing with stress (Thakker, in press). Along with the more traditional relaxation component, mindfulness skills are also now being included in many offender treatment programs. Analysis of John's offending revealed that he tended to use sex as a way of soothing himself when experiencing distressing emotions or encountering difficult interpersonal situations.

7. *Increase John's involvement in positive activities.* John was encouraged to engage in constructive, prosocial, and personally fulfilling activities within the prison (e.g., community service, religious activities, and hobbies [photography]) and to plan how he would continue with these upon his release. All of these activities were clearly connected to his good lives intervention plan and the primary and secondary human goods (see below). It was reasoned that these activities would help him establish a prosocial support network whilst also helping him to relax. Importantly, it was thought that some of these activities would also help him achieve his primary goods of relatedness and mastery whilst also managing his risk of reoffending. Further, it is noted that social skills training is an established component of sex offender treatment programs (Thakker, in press).

8. *Address John's sexual deviancy.* It was important to address John's deviant sexuality, including his sexual preoccupation with young females, sexual-offense-supportive attitudes, and cognitive distortions toward females. Pleasure and relatedness were two primary goods associated with his deviant sexual preferences and activities. John's deviant sexual preferences and fantasies were treated by masturbatory reconditioning, along with other mainstream methods such as covert desensitization (for further reading in this area, refer to Marshall, O'Brien, & Marshall, 2009). Given that John was uncomfortable discussing his sexual activity, this aspect of treatment took place once a strong therapeutic alliance had been established.

John's offense-related attitudes and beliefs were addressed using cognitive restructuring. In line with the GLM it was important to identify and challenge the beliefs that were placing limitations on John's ability to establish intimate relationships with adult females. For example, one problematic belief that was identified was that "relationships are difficult and stressful." Approach goals were then set that specify exactly what particular relationships and activities would be sought, and internal and external capacities required to achieve them were identified.

9. *Help John to develop a good lives plan.* The therapist assisted John to identify his core practical identities and their associated primary human goods or values (i.e., good lives formulation) to assist with the development of a good lives plan. The key point of this component was to establish what John really wanted in life and to begin this by asking questions such as: "What do you want to be? In an ideal world, what would you be doing?" Once these ideals are determined then the approach usually involves working backwards to identify the steps required to achieve the ideals and goals (see Tables 4.1 and 4.2). It is important that the goals are both prosocial and realistic. In other words, if the goals appear to be unattainable then they should not be encouraged as it would not be considered to be constructive to encourage an offender to strive for something and fail. Thus, there should be a discussion about how goals can be achieved and goals should be changed (via negotiation with the offender) if they do not appear to be realistic. Of course the therapist can only determine if the goals are realistic if he or she has a firm understanding of the offender's strengths and weaknesses.

10. *Assist John to develop a support network.* John was asked to identify a list of contact persons that he could turn to for help and advice whenever he might contemplate engaging in sexually deviant acts again. From a GLM perspective, such networks should follow naturally from the type of primary goods sought. For example, given John's interests in learning more about his Chinese heritage, community groups and volunteers could be recruited to help John obtain a greater understanding of Chinese culture, language, and practices. Similarly, pursuing his interest in photography (the primary good of creativity) would involve joining a club and thus extending his social and support network. It could be possible that John would be open about his offending in such groups. If not, then it would still be possible that they will provide general levels of social support and activity.

11. *Maintenance of treatment gains and relapse prevention.* This aspect of treatment involved developing a plan for maintaining treatment gains and preventing relapse. While traditional relapse prevention (RP) approaches tend to focus on risk avoidance, the GLM approach places equal importance on approach goal setting (Thakker & Ward, 2010). Thus, the approach taken here was to increase John's awareness of his risks but also to encourage him to work toward his goals in order to lessen the appeal of antisocial options. For example, it was reasoned that if he could maintain a stable intimate relationship he would be less likely to be drawn to the idea of sexual interaction with a minor.

12. *Treatment termination.* This component of treatment focused on terminating treatment in a manner that was comfortable for John and which did not heighten his risk in any way. Treatment ended once all of the treatment areas had been covered and it was considered that there was nothing further for John to gain from ongoing therapy. The point at which treatment was to be terminated was discussed with John so that he was able to contribute to the decision, and he was kept aware of how many sessions remained when the final sessions were being held.

In line with GLM, the final sessions of treatment need to have the dual foci of clarifying the way that risks are to be managed and revising the steps to goals. The objectives of this approach are to increase the likelihood that clients will be able to (a) recognize risky situations, (b) prevent or manage those situations, and (c) carry out the tasks required to achieve their goals.

Treatment Response

As mentioned above, John was initially quite reserved during the assessment phase; however, by the time that treatment was started, he was quite relaxed and a good level of rapport was maintained throughout the treatment process. John was consistently friendly and cooperative during treatment sessions and he completed all treatment-related tasks, including homework. While he initially struggled to discuss his sexual activities, he became more comfortable with this over time, such that by the end of treatment, he was able to discuss a range of topics, including his sexual fantasies.

John responded well to treatment and showed significant treatment gains in a number of areas. This appeared to be, at least in part, due to his level of intellectual functioning; he demonstrated an excellent understanding of treatment concepts and of the principles that underpinned the treatment approach. Furthermore, he was able to easily recall the content from previous sessions, which again showed that he has understood it. John eventually showed some insight into his offending; by the conclusion of treatment he appeared to have a reasonable understanding of the various factors that had contributed to his sexual offending. For example, he could see how his lack of skills in intimate relationships had contributed to his decision to target young females.

John was at times resistant to the idea of using support people. Although, he responded well to the relaxation skills training, he did not like the idea of sharing his problems with others. He insisted that he has always coped well on his own and did not need to rely on other people. John referred to his cultural background at this point, and stated that it was normal in Chinese culture for individuals to cope with problems on their own, without relying on others or seeking counsel from others. This issue was discussed at length with John and a compromise was reached. Essentially, he agreed that he would make contact with various support services if need be, such as the SAFE Network (which is a community-based network for sexual abusers). He said that he was more comfortable talking to strangers about his difficulties than to individuals he knows well. However, John agreed that he would engage in activities that would assist him in developing his relationship skills and which would provide him with opportunities to meet adult women, and that he would work on being more open with an intimate partner in future.

Challenges in Treatment

One of the key challenges in treating John was finding a balance between accepting his cultural background and challenging his maladaptive coping strategies. John referred to his parents' approach to life and his upbringing frequently when discussing his own life and at times he seemed to use his cultural background as a justification for his behavior. For example, he said that his parents did not allow him to express his feelings and that they rejected his girlfriend. He also stated that he had never learned how to deal with difficult emotions or with stress and he saw this as having its roots in his cultural background. These were good insights for John to have; however, at the same time that he expressed these ideas he also indicated a desire to maintain the status quo because he saw this as part of his identity. Thus, he seemed stuck in a particular way of being.

This was a challenge in treatment because it seemed important to acknowledge and respect his cultural point of view but it was also necessary to encourage him to try new things and to establish a new prosocial approach to life and relationships. Earlier in treatment it appeared that John was using his culture as a smokescreen to detract attention away from the issues, and indicating a degree of sensitivity in relation to his culture. However, over time, it became clear that he was less rigid about his cultural practices than he had initially indicated and he was more upfront and honest about the issue. In fact, it was apparent that he was keen to learn more about his Chinese background and culture. Furthermore, he eventually acknowledged that he has used his stoicism and emotional guarding as a defense and a justification. Once this process was discussed openly in treatment, it was possible to move forward more effectively.

Another challenge in treatment was John's belief that his sexual interaction with his young female victims was not harmful to them. Even toward the end of treatment he continued to make comments that indicated the presence of pro-offense beliefs. For example, he said that his victims were willing participants, that they enjoyed the activity, and that it was educational. Accordingly, he held the position that his behavior was only problematic because the girls' parents had become involved and because society imposed strict and unreasonable rules upon him.

At one point in treatment, John began to make more appropriate comments and it appeared that he had learned that individuals of that age and in that context were not able to provide their consent because of their youth and their lack of understanding, and because of the imbalance of power in the context of a school. However, later he reverted to expressing his earlier held beliefs and it appeared that he had made no progress in this area. In supporting his position he said that Western culture is contradictory and confusing because on the one hand it promotes sexual freedom and on the other it enforces strict rules and laws in relation to who can have sex with whom. In making this comment John seemed to be implying that his cultural background made it more difficult for him to understand the local laws in relation to sexual activity. It was anticipated that one of the benefits of fleshing out his identity as a Chinese New Zealander was that he would be exposed to more adaptive views about females and what constituted appropriate sexuality.

Conclusion

In this chapter we have outlined the application of the GLM to an individual who had committed sexual offenses against children. One of the unique characteristics of the GLM approach to treatment is the way it integrates attention to risk management with the enhancement of individuals' level of well-being. In the case of John, this required the therapists to capitalize on a number of his strengths such as creativity and knowledge to create a possible good lives plan concerned with establishing stronger levels of community connection and relatedness. John's practical identity was largely focused around his perception of being Chinese, relatedness, and the importance of creativity to his sense of personal worth. Therefore, his intervention and subsequent desistance plan revolved around these overarching primary goods. Despite continued difficulties with some of his beliefs concerning sex with children, increasing John's degree of social involvement provided a natural forum for these to be naturally challenged in the future and also offered a powerful resource to help him to modulate his negative emotions and social isolation.

References

Andrews, D. A., Bonta, J., & Wormith, J. S. (2004). *The Level of Service/Case Management Inventory* (LS/CMI). Toronto, ON, Canada: Multi-Health Systems.

Andrews, D. A., Bonta, J., & Wormith, J. S. (2011). The risk-need-responsivity (RNR) model: Does adding the good lives model contribute to effective crime prevention? *Criminal Justice and Behavior, 38*, 735–755.

Barnao, M., Robertson, P., & Ward, T. (2010). Good lives model applied to a forensic population. *Psychiatry, Psychology, & Law, 17*, 202–217.

Beck, A. T., Steer, R. A., & Brown, G. K. (1996). *Manual for the Beck depression inventory-II.* San Antonio, TX: Psychological Corporation.

Hanson, R. K., Harris, A. J. R, Scott, T.-L., & Helmus, L. (2007). *Assessing the risk of sexual offenders on community supervision: The Dynamic Supervision Project* (Corrections Research User Report 2007-5). Ottawa, ON, Canada: Public Safety Canada.

Hanson, R. K., Lloyd, C. D., Helmus, L., & Thornton, D. (2012). Developing non-arbitrary metrics for risk communication: Percentile ranks for the Static-99/R and Static-2002/R sexual offender risk tools. *International Journal of Forensic Mental Health, 11*, 9–23.

Hare, R. D. (2003). *Hare Psychopathy Checklist Revised* (2nd ed.). Toronto, ON, Canada: Multi-Health Systems.

Hart, S., Kropp, P. R., Laws, D. R., Klaver, J., Logan, C., & Watt, K. A. (2003). *The Risk for Sexual Violence Protocol* (RSVP): *Structured professional guidelines for assessing risk of sexual violence.* Vancouver, BC, Canada: The Institute against Family Violence.

Kozar, C. J., & Day, A. (2012). The therapeutic alliance in offending behavior programs: A necessary and sufficient condition for change? *Aggression and Violent Behavior, 17*, 482–487.

Langlands, R. L., Ward, T., & Gilchrist, E. (2009). Applying the good lives model to male perpetrators of domestic violence. *Behavior Change, 26*, 113–129.

Laws, R. (2010). *The Risk for Sexual Violence Protocol (RSVP).* Retrieved from http://pacific-psych.com/wp-content/uploads/2010/04/Pacific-Psych_RSVP-ppt.pdf

Laws, D. R., & Ward, T. (2011). *Desistance from sex offending: Alternatives to throwing away the keys.* New York, NY: Guilford.

Marshall, W. L., Marshall, L. E., Serran, G.A., & O'Brien, M. D. (2011). *Rehabilitating sexual offenders: A strength-based approach.* Washington, DC: American Psychological Association.

Marshall, W. L., O'Brien, M. D., & Marshall, L. E. (2009). Modifying sexual preferences. In A. R. Beech, L. A. Craig, & K. D. Browne (Eds.), *Assessment and treatment of sex offenders: A handbook* (pp. 311–327). Chichester, UK: John Wiley and Sons.

Maruna, S. (2001). *Making good: How ex-convicts reform and rebuild their lives.* Washington, DC: American Psychological Association.

Morey, L. C. (2007). *The personality assessment Inventory professional manual.* Lutz, FL: Psychological Assessment Resources.

Prescott, D. S., & Porter, J. (2011). Motivational interviewing in the treatment of offenders. In D. Boer, R. Eher, L. Craig, M. Miner, & F. Pfäfflin (Eds.), *International perspectives on the assessment and treatment of sexual offenders: Theory, practice and research* (pp. 373–396). Chichester, UK: Wiley-Blackwell.

Purvis, M., Ward, T., & Willis, G. M. (2011). The good lives model in practice: Offence pathways and case management. *European Journal of Probation, 3*, 4–28.

Thakker, J. (in press). Sex offender treatment. In *The Encyclopedia of Criminology and Criminal Justice.* New York, NY: Springer.

Thakker, J., & Ward, T. (2010). Relapse prevention: A critique and proposed reconceptualisation. *Behavior Change, 27*, 154–175.

Ward, T., Collie, R. M., & Bourke, P. (2009). Models of offender rehabilitation: The good lives model and the risk-need-responsivity model. In A. R. Beech, L. A. Craig, &

K. D. Browne (Eds.), *Assessment and treatment of sex offenders* (pp. 293–310). Chichester UK: John Wiley and Sons.

Ward, T., Mann, R., & Gannon, T.A. (2007). The good lives model of offender rehabilitation: Clinical implications. *Aggression and Violent Behavior, 12,* 87–107.

Ward, T., & Maruna, S. (2007). *Rehabilitation: Beyond the risk paradigm.* London, England: Routledge.

Ward, T., & Stewart, C. (2003). The treatment of sex offenders: Risk management and good lives. *Professional Psychology Research and Practice, 34,* 353–360.

Ward, T., Yates, P., & Willis, G. M. (2012). The good lives model and the risk need responsivity model: A critical response to Andrews, Bonta, and Wormith (2011). *Criminal Justice and Behavior, 39,* 94–110.

Willis, G. M. & Ward, T. (2011). Striving for a good life: The good lives model applied to released child molesters, *Journal of Sexual Aggression, 17,* 290–303.

Wong, Y. J. (2006). Strength-centred therapy: A social constructionist, virtues-based psychotherapy. *Psychotherapy: Theory, Research, Practice, Training, 2,* 133–146. doi:10.1037/0033-3204.43.2.133

5

TREATMENT OF SEXUAL MASOCHISM

Amy Lykins and Stephen J. Hucker

As currently defined by the *DSM-IV-TR* (American Psychiatric Association, 2000), sexual masochism is diagnosed when a person experiences "recurrent, intense, sexually arousing fantasies, sexual urges, or behaviors involving the act (real, not simulated) of being humiliated, beaten, bound, or otherwise made to suffer" for a period of at least 6 months. For a diagnosis to be made, the fantasies, urges, or behaviors must also cause clinically significant distress or impairment in social, occupational, or other important areas of functioning for the presenting individual. Large-scale studies on sexual interests in the general populations of the United States and Australia have suggested that approximately 2 to 5% report experiencing sexual pleasure from receiving pain or involvement in bondage/dominance/sadism/masochism (BDSM) activities (Hunt, 1974; Richters, Grulich, de Visser, Smith, & Rissel, 2003). Disagreement exists over whether sexual masochism should be classified as a mental disorder, with opponents arguing that its inclusion is unnecessary and pathologizes groups that consensually engage in alternative sexual practices (see Krueger, 2010a). Indeed, a number of studies have indicated a relative lack of associated pathology in individuals who engage in sexually masochistic behaviors (e.g., Connolly, 2006; Moser & Levitt, 1987; Sandnabba, Santtila, & Nordling, 1999; Santilla, Sandnabba, Alison, & Nordling, 2002; Williams, 2006). However, it is likely to be retained in *DSM-V*, with arguments supporting its inclusion highlighting the potential for severe harm or even death to occur in some sexual masochists (e.g., Blanchard & Hucker, 1991; Hucker & Blanchard, 1992; Sandnabba et al., 1999), as well as the fact that the diagnostic criteria, if used correctly, would not apply to the vast majority of individuals who practice these behaviors. This distinction has important implications for the treatment of persons presenting with sexual masochism, as it will help inform treatment options and directions.

While acknowledging the literature that has shown that most practitioners of sexually masochistic behaviors seem to be relatively well-adjusted, it is important to note that other research has shown persons with diagnosed paraphilias to have higher than expected rates of co-morbid Attention-Deficit/Hyperactivity Disorder, as well as affective, anxiety, and substance use disorders (Kafka & Hennen, 2002; Lehne, Thomas, & Berlin, 2000). Though these studies did not examine sexual masochists apart from other persons with paraphilias, the treatment of mental disorders can often be impacted by co-morbid psychopathology, and thus it is important to screen for other difficulties in addition to the presenting pathology in case additional issues need to be addressed.

Further, paraphilias tend to cluster amongst themselves (Kafka & Hennen, 2002; Kafka & Prentky, 1994), and both clinical experience and research have shown sexual masochism often to be co-morbid with transvestic fetishism and sexual sadism (Blanchard & Hucker, 1991; Freund, Seto, & Kuban, 1995; Hucker & Blanchard, 1992). In fact, 37% of the 54 patients included in the Freund et al. study were fetishistic transvestites. Less commonly associated paraphilias co-occurring with sexual masochism include preoccupation with one's own anal/rectal region, urination, and defecation (Freund et al., 1995), and vorarephilia (i.e., sexual arousal associated with the desire to consume or be consumed by another being; Lykins & Cantor, under review). Although not considered a disorder separate from sexual masochism (Hucker, 2011), asphyxiophilia so often co-occurs with sexual masochism that the *DSM-V* workgroup has recommended that it be listed as a specifier in the upcoming version of the *DSM* (Krueger, 2010b). Asphyxiophilia is defined as sexual arousal associated with asphyxiation (often by ligatures or the inhalation of gases or vapors), and can be acted out either with a partner or alone ("autoerotic asphyxiophilia"). It remains one of the most dangerous yet not uncommon presentations of sexual masochism, with "accidental autoerotic deaths" occurring frequently enough to warrant consistent mention in textbooks on forensic medicine and pathology (e.g., Dolinak, Matshes, & Lew, 2005; Saukko & Knight, 2004). The mortality rate associated with this behavior is significantly higher than that of most other paraphilias, and it therefore warrants specific and targeted intervention.

Review of the Treatment Literature

A search of the treatment literature on sexual masochism shows it to be quite sparse, particularly in comparison to other mental disorders and even relative to the extant literature on many of the other paraphilias. This is perhaps not especially surprising because many researchers and clinicians have noted that persons with sexual masochism rarely present for treatment (Freund et al., 1995; Moser & Levitt, 1987; Spengler, 1977). Gudjonsson (1986) suggested that persons with paraphilias typically present for treatment if: (a) their sexual behavior is disturbing to them or affects their functioning; (b) their behavior is considered to be unacceptable by their partner or family; or (c) their behavior is illegal. Most sexual masochists generally appear not to be particularly bothered by their behavior. They infrequently pursue treatment even at a center specifically targeting sexological problems (Freund et al., 1995), rarely get into legal trouble (Krueger, 2010b), and appear to be much more likely to seek the support of others who share their interests rather than professional intervention (Lehne et al., 2000). One other potential concern in evaluating the overall literature in this area is that most reports on the treatment of paraphilias are case reports or series (Thibaut et al., 2010); this is particularly true when considering those reporting on the treatment of sexual masochism. Further, many of the reports that included persons with sexual masochism were published quite some time ago, which seems to suggest that either they are not often accessing clinical services for help, or clinical interest in trying to modify these behaviors has waned.

Psychological Treatment

Historically, the first treatments were psychoanalytic and even today there are therapists practicing in this type of therapy who make use of traditional psychoanalytic concepts, though the focus is usually on what Freud termed "moral masochism" rather than the type of sexual behavior under consideration in this chapter (but see e.g., Gavin, 2010 for a readable account of this type of approach).

More often treatment methods of choice have been behavioral, typically aversive methods such as use of shock or nausea, under the premise that sexual preferences are conditioned and thus can be deconditioned. Early studies applying conditioned aversion showed positive results (Abel, Levis, & Clancy, 1970; Bancroft & Marks, 1968; Brownell, Hays, & Barlow, 1977; Pinard & Lamontagne, 1976). There has been some concern about whether aversive stimuli such as electric shock would even be experienced as such by sexual masochists, given that some of these stimuli are used specifically to induce sexual arousal (Feldman, 1966). Marks, Rachman, and Gelder (1965) explored this issue in their treatment of a masochistic male, who did experience the shocks as aversive, and it was reported that his longstanding masochistic desires and fantasies had ceased after only two sessions. Thus, Marks et al. (1965) concluded that masochism did not necessarily contraindicate aversion treatment. However, it must be emphasized that this was a case study of one male, and thus how representative this particular case is of the typical sexual masochist is unknown.

Further problems exist in the interpretation of the aforementioned studies that may limit their conclusions. Most of these studies included only a handful of subjects with sexual masochism, did not identify if the subjects were in the primary aversion treatment group or the alternate treatment, and had relatively short follow-up periods (if any). Additionally, most studies collapsed sexual sadism and masochism into sadomasochism, thus any potential differences between the two presentations were lost in data analyses. Further, the studies relied on self-report of sexual preference and behavior change, which may contribute to unreliability as these patients were likely motivated to report significant change in their preferences even if they did not actually experience it.

More recent efforts have focused less on strictly behavioral therapies and more on cognitive-behavioral therapies (CBT). One somewhat recent case study reported on a female engaging in autoerotic asphyxiation, with treatment taking a two-pronged approach of desensitization to her sexual fantasies combined with cognitive-behavioral therapy (CBT) and interpersonal process therapy (IPT) to target her depression and social avoidance (Martz, 2003). The author reported success in eliminating the autoerotic asphyxiation behaviors following this treatment. Shiwach and Prosser (1998) reported a case study of a man who was sexually aroused by being burned or crushed, which had contributed to his engagement in dangerous and potentially lethal behaviors. Treatment included psycho-dynamic therapy, sex education and social skills training, aversive behavior therapy, and rounds of anti-androgen and antidepressant medication. The authors reported that anti-androgens and aversive behavior therapy were most effective in the short-term, but at follow-up the subject had resumed his masochistic activities.

Kilmann, Sabalis, Gearing, Bukstel, and Scovern (1982) reviewed the paraphilia treatment outcome literature at that point in time and concluded that almost all studies had found at least some positive treatment effects, recommending a "multiple behavioral treatment package" tailored specifically to the presenting client's preferences. However, most authors argue that the paraphilias tend to be relatively resistant to treatment and are pessimistic about expected outcomes (Thomas-Peter & Humphreys, 1997). The pessimism surrounding paraphilia treatment outcome, including sexual masochism, seems to mirror the difficulties seen in attempting to change any type of sexual preference (e.g., sexual orientation). Different directions in treatment, including pharmacotherapy, have started to focus less on changing the preferences themselves and more on managing behavior and risk.

Pharmacological Treatment

The pharmacological treatment of paraphilias is not intended to be "treatment" so much as assistance in the management of behavior. Researchers have not looked to pharmacotherapy as a method of changing sexual preferences; rather, various classes of medications have been used in an attempt to lower sexual urges to a point that clients feel they have more control over whether or not they act out on them. Most of these studies have targeted patients (primarily men) who engage in illegal sexual behavior, such as sexual offenses against children associated with pedophilia or sexual assault related to sexual sadism. However, a handful of studies have included one to three men each who likely would have been diagnosed with sexual masochism (e.g., Czerny, Briken, & Berner, 2002; Gottesman & Schubert, 1993; Meyer, Walker, Emory, & Smith, 1985; Money, Bennett, & Cameron, 1981). In a review of this literature, Thibaut et al. (2010) argued for the utility of antilibido medication combined with CBT as the ideal treatment to control sexual urges and decrease distress in the paraphilic subject. Krueger and Kaplan (2001) explored the use of depot-leuprolide acetate in 12 paraphilic men, one of whom was diagnosed with sadomasochism. They concluded that the overall effects were good in reducing sexual interest, although negative effects (e.g., decreased bone density) were noted in long-term treatment. The patient diagnosed with sadomasochism pursued treatment because his sexual preferences were severely interfering with his marital relationship. Treatment was effective for this patient as well in that there was a complete cessation of all deviant sexual interest and behavior; however, he lapsed into a depressive episode following treatment (a result not uncommon with this type of medication). With regard to selective serotonin reuptake inhibitors (SSRIs), which have been used as a milder medication known to dampen sexual interest and arousal, Balon (1998) reported that sadomasochism in particular did not seem to respond well to fluoxetine. Gottesman and Schubert (1993) suggested that a low-dose of medroxyprogesterone acetate (MPA) might be useful for treatment compliant patients not at risk for contact offenses.

Ultimately what we can conclude about the pharmacological treatment of sexual masochism is that there is very little known about it, and any medical intervention should be approached with significant caution. Most studies have targeted paraphilic presentations that pose more danger to persons other than the patient presenting for treatment, with sexually masochistic patients grouped in with all the others. It is our opinion that pharmacological treatment of sexual masochism should only be considered for those individuals who pose the highest risk of harm to themselves and who report experiencing difficulty controlling their urges to act out on these types of behaviors.

Treatment Recommendations

Based on the reviewed literature, we make the following treatment recommendations for what are likely to be the most commonly presenting types of clients engaging in sexually masochistic behaviors. These are: (a) non-partnered client sexually aroused by masochistic behaviors but disturbed by this; (b) partnered client whose masochistic interests or behaviors are interfering with the current relationship; or (c) client engaging in behaviors with high potential for severe harm or even death.

If a client is presenting with "ego-dystonic" sexual masochism but not engaging in behaviors that are potentially very harmful or lethal, treatment should focus on changing the client's thoughts about his or her sexual interests. Cognitive-behavioral therapy is likely to be most effective in these situations. These clients often present with significant guilt and shame (Thomas-Peter & Humphreys, 1997). Acceptance and commitment therapy (ACT; Hayes, Luoma, Bard, Masuda, & Lillis, 2006) specifically targets acknowledgment and acceptance of "private events" that can contribute to anxiety and self-judgment, followed by committed action toward moving on with one's life. ACT has not yet been directly applied to individuals with sexual masochism (to our knowledge), but it may be a therapeutic regimen worth pursuing with this type of client. Further, it may be useful to guide these clients toward groups for people with shared sexual interests so that they are able to explore their sexual preferences in a safe environment.

Case Example 1

The patient was a single, female postgraduate student in her mid-20s who was living with her parents at the time she sought help. Her presenting complaints included depression, anxiety, bulimia/anorexia, and "addiction to uncontrollable" sexual behavior. An antidepressant had been prescribed by her family physician but she was unsure that this had helped. Both her sister and her mother had also received treatment for depression.

Her problematic sexual behavior centered on masochistic fantasies and activities which she remembers experiencing continuously since childhood. These involved dominance/submission and subjection to pain. However, she had never acted out these fantasies until about a year before she sought psychiatric help. This occurred after she broke up with her partner of nearly 5 years. Then she began exploring her masochistic interests with several men. Her sexual orientation was generally heterosexual but her fantasies involved vampirism, being kidnapped and forced into sexual activities. She experienced no orgasm during conventional intercourse.

Clinical interview revealed depressive symptoms for several months at the time of the initial interview, along with loss of pleasure, and reduced interest in activities that normally interested her. Her appetite had increased and she was sleeping more than usual. She felt tired all day and felt guilty about things she had done. She had negative thoughts and felt like a failure, had difficulty concentrating, and thought of dying in passive ways, wishing she was dead and having thoughts of suicide though she lacked a strong wish to attempt it. For several weeks she had experienced the feeling that she was unable to control her eating, went on binges followed by feelings of disgust, and she tried to prevent weight gain by dieting strictly and exercising. She noted that her weight and body shape were the most important things that affected her opinion of herself. She also experienced episodes of panic for no apparent reason but also had specific phobias such as going far away from home, being in crowded places, standing in long lines, traveling by public transport, or riding in a car. In addition she experienced social anxiety. Finally, she expressed concern that her drinking and consumption of marijuana were excessive.

The patient's presentation and history also suggested borderline and histrionic personality traits with expressed feelings of inner emptiness, a history of attempts at suicide and self-harmful behavior, fear of abandonment, feeling misunderstood, many short term relationships, use of drugs, and regularly getting drunk.

She agreed to complete the Multiphasic Sex Inventory-II (female version) and the responses were consistent with her self-report during the interviews. The reliability and validity scales suggested the results were valid. She reported that her father was very strict with her and she was a loner as a child. She was not the victim of any physical or sexual abuse. Her responses indicated that she had attempted suicide in the past and had an elevated score on the suicide index indicating also some depression at the time she took the test. Drug use had been a problem for her. Her elevation on the Cognitive Distortion and Immaturity Scales suggested she likely spent most of her life feeling she is a victim of circumstances and other people and that she had never been in control of events in her life. She indicated that she was addicted to pornography and referred to concerns about her masochistic behaviors involving affairs and cybersex. She was very disclosing of her obsession with sex and her interest in bondage/ discipline behaviors (both submissive and dominant). She was clearly masochistically inclined and felt a desire to be raped. Her fantasies were reported as about being raped, aggression and anger against her being sexually arousing, being restrained, physically hurt, whipped/paddled being sexually arousing, and possibly engaging in hypoxyphilia and playing with death during sex. She presented as hypersexual and had concerns about her sexual functioning. She appeared to have serious concerns about her body image and viewed herself as physically unattractive (though to others she appeared the opposite). She had deep seated fears of loneliness and need for affection which she associated with her sexual impulses and desires. She appeared to be embarrassed about sex and lacked confidence in her social interaction with her peers. She also disclosed a fetish for urine and feces. She reported being bisexual and there was some indication that she feels like a male, which she expressed through cross-dressing. Her knowledge of sexual anatomy and physiology was accurate.

The patient's main practical concern stemmed from her more recent exploration of her masochistic interests and having come close to being harmed during her encounters with men about whom she knew little or nothing. The possibility of finding social and personal satisfaction through contacts at a local BDSM club was discussed with her. She agreed to explore this and quite quickly joined such a group. Medication in the form of a selective serotonergic reuptake inhibitor (SSRI) anti-depressant was continued with improvement in her mood. She was lost to follow-up after about 6 months because she moved to another city, but during that time found she enjoyed the social contacts and her sexual life considerably improved as she got to know her sexual partners better than her previous one night stand encounters and the culture of the club was in keeping with a "safe, sane, and consensual" approach.

The second type of client typically presents because his or her masochistic interests/activities are significantly interfering with the primary romantic relationship. De Silva (1993) discussed how a sexual fetish may be successfully incorporated into a couple's sex life, with recommendations that may also be useful in treating clients with sexual masochism. Treatment is thus not targeted at eliminating masochistic behaviors, but rather directed toward a successful integration of these interests into the couple's sexual relationship. As such, this is likely to be administered in the form of couple's therapy as opposed to individual therapy (as with the first type of client). The aim of treatment in this case is to reduce the interference of the paraphilia in the relationship. De Silva (1993) recommends attempting to incorporate the paraphilic behavior into sex in a limited and controlled way if it is acceptable to the client's partner. He also suggests timetabling of the paraphilic activity, such that it may be acted out on some days but not on others so that the overall pressure on the relationship is reduced. He also recommends assisting the client in gradually reducing his or her reliance on the paraphilic activity, though the degree to which this is likely to be successful will depend on the client. Sandnabba et al. (1999) reported that approximately 27% of their sample stated that only S/M sex could satisfy them, so although a significant proportion of this population can still be satisfied by "ordinary sex," a significant proportion feel that they cannot, and thus may be more treatment resistant. Pharmacological treatment is unlikely to be indicated for persons in this group.

The previous two types of clients differ from the third in the relative amount of potential harm the masochistic behavior is likely to cause. These first two types are likely to be low-risk clients; their treatment goals are more related to adjustment to masochistic interests. The third type, however, is engaging in potentially harmful behavior with a greater likelihood of serious physical consequences, including death. Therefore, specific targeted treatment addressing the acting out of masochistic behaviors and risk management is warranted. Depending on the behavior the client is engaging in (e.g., autoerotic asphyxiation), complete cessation may be the goal, as the risks of continuing the behavior are very high. It may be that the behavior can be modified in some meaningful way such that risk is significantly reduced (e.g., introduction of failsafe mechanisms on ligatures, only engaging in the behavior with another trusted partner), but this needs to be evaluated on a case-by-case basis. If the client is not able to cease engaging in these behaviors, pharmacotherapy may be warranted. Thibaut et al. (2010) recommends that SSRIs might be first line treatment in these types of higher risk cases, particularly when depression or anxiety-type features are present. It is recommended that clinicians follow the Belgian Advisory Committee on Bioethics 2006, which states that medication is indicated only if the condition represents significant risk of serious harm and no less intrusive means of treatment is available or efficacious (Thibaut et al., 2010).

Case History 2

This patient presented at about age 45 years with a history of cross-dressing and a desire to be female. As far as he could recall this began around puberty and he had used his sister's and mother's clothes for this purpose for masturbation on occasions. During his masturbatory rituals he would imagine himself as a woman being humiliated or hurt in some way by men. By the time he was referred to the Clinic he had elaborated these rituals over a number of years. He had been married since age 20 and his wife had become aware of his transvestism but was repulsed by it. He therefore carried out the activities in private. He would often cross-dress completely in a woman's clothes and then carry out a series of masochistic maneuvers including striking his testicles with a hard object such as the heel of a shoe, tying his genitals tightly with a string ligature, surrounding his genitals in ice cubes, or blowing hot air from a hair dryer on to them. He also inserted objects such as hairbrush handles or ice into his rectum. As well, he considered applying electricity to his nipples but had not yet done so. After such masochistic behavior had aroused him sufficiently he would then suffocate himself by placing his head in a plastic bag or wrap himself in a garment bag. However, more typically he would hang or strangle himself with ropes, belts, towels, or sometimes his bare hands. Several times he barely managed to avert losing consciousness completely before being able to extricate himself.

During these activities he would fantasize about being a woman subjected to various acts of humiliation and torture. Thus he would imagine being incarcerated in a women's prison, being stripped and forced to wear a metal brassiere and corset and then assume uncomfortable positions. He also fantasized such scenes as being captured by sadistic women who trained him to dress up as a woman, undergo a sex change operation, and then work for them as a prostitute. He would be beaten and whipped if he failed in this task.

The patient had presented initially to a Gender Identity Clinic as he had confided to his family doctor that he sometimes dressed in female clothing. He had been prompted to seek help when the family physician (who was also his wife's physician) frankly breached their confidential relationship by suggesting that problems in their marriage were due to the fact that, in his view, her husband was gay! When the couple were interviewed together it became clear that although in some ways they were devoted to each other, there were some longstanding difficulties in communication and differences in sexual needs. Moreover, the patient tended to consume alcohol regularly, though not excessively, and his wife disapproved of this.

The patient disclosed the extent of his masochistic fantasies when his transvestism was explored in more detail. He explained that he had often thought that he was "going crazy" as he considered the fantasies to be bizarre and he had no idea that others experienced similar desires as he had never discussed them with anyone before. As the patient disclosed more about his sexual activities it became clear that he regularly came close to death as a result of repetitive self-hangings and strangulations. He was concerned himself that one day he would miscalculate and his death would ensue. He therefore accepted treatment with the sex drive reducing drug medroxyprogesterone acetate (Provera) in an oral dose of 200 mg a day. Over the course of the next year he took the medication regularly and his blood testosterone was lowered to prepubertal levels. He noted a gradual reduction in his sexual fantasies and his self-hanging episodes diminished completely. However, although his wife had been a party to discussions regarding the treatment and its effects she protested that her husband no longer showed any sexual interest in her. This was approached during conjoint counseling to some benefit when her husband explained how close he came to killing himself.

After approximately a year it became necessary to explore alternative treatment approaches. The patient began to report that the medication was losing its efficacy and initially the dose of Provera was increased, eventually reaching 500 mg per day by mouth. This was not a desirable situation as the risk of adverse effects increases at such a high dose.

At the time of this development Provera and Androcur (cyproterone acetate) were the only sex drive reducing medications available. If the problem were to present today then the almost complete testosterone suppression produced by drugs such as leuprolide acetate (Lupron), a gonadotrophin releasing hormone agonist, would have been an appropriate substitute. However, the only alternative that could be offered at that time was the possibility of surgical castration. This was discussed with the patient and members of his family over the next several months and the patient after written, fully informed consent was referred for orchidectomy.

This procedure was carried out uneventfully and, over the course of about 12 months, the patient was completely relieved of his desire to hang or strangle himself for sexual gratification. All other sexual activity eventually ceased also. The patient's wife continued to have difficulties accepting the fact that her husband no longer wished to have sexual relations despite all the explanation and discussion that had preceded the operation.

A number of years after the surgery the patient had by that time retired and moved to another city but maintained contact with the author. He reported an episode when he consulted his new doctor because of urinary frequency. Examination revealed a small hard prostate which the patient, out of embarrassment, did not explain was due to the removal of his testes a number of years previously (soft plastic implants are inserted in the scrotum to preserve the semblance of normal testes for "cosmetic reasons." Testosterone supplements were prescribed and within 24 hours all the masochistic fantasies and behaviors that had been absent for years returned. After initial reluctance the patient allowed the author to write to the doctor explaining his medical and psychiatric history, the testosterone was withheld, and the fantasies again subsided and have not returned.

The patient has now been followed intermittently for nearly 30 years. His wife died several years ago but he continues to lead a full life with hobbies, friends, and his family. He has never regretted having the orchidectomy and often thanks the author for having saved his life.

Other Considerations

Unlike most paraphilias, sexual masochism is likely to present in both males and females. In fact, an estimated 13 to 30% of sadism/masochism practitioners are female (Hucker, 2008). Baumeister (1988) wrote about sex differences in masochistic scripts, suggesting that males and females may vary in what types of masochistic behaviors they prefer. Potential variation between men and women should be taken into account in treatment.

As noted earlier, paraphilias have been found to cluster among themselves and to be co-morbid with a variety of other psychopathology, including ADHD and affective, anxiety, and substance use disorders (Kafka & Hennen, 2002; Lehne et al., 2000). These should be addressed in treatment as well, either with the clinician responsible for management of sexual masochism or another clinician. Some research has shown sadism/masochism practitioners to have higher than average histories of sexual abuse, about 8% of males and 23% of females in one study (Sandnabba et al., 1999), and this should be addressed in treatment if deemed relevant. It is important to remember the ethical responsibilities we have as treating clinicians to keep clients safe. Thus, the number one priority should always be harm reduction and risk management for those clients engaging in potentially dangerous sexual activities.

Finally, mention must be made of recent developments in the treatment of sexual masochism that have been the result of greater openness in Western societies generally. It has even been proposed that professional dominatrices sometimes view their work as a form of therapy for their clients (Lindemann, 2011).

As already noted, patients/clients with problems involving this type of sexual practice have traditionally not come to the attention of mental health professionals very often. Those who have done so often felt discouraged by the attitudes of those to whom they turned for help. Thus, Hoff and Sprott (2009) reported that of 32 heterosexual couples who practiced consensual bondage/discipline, dominance/submission, sadism/masochism (BDSM) found some therapists terminated the therapeutic relationship when the BDSM interests were disclosed, others showed frank prejudice and the clients were exposed to pejorative comments about their sexual practices, though others knew something of these and adopted a supportive stance. Others still did not disclose their sexual interests, fearing that the revelation would have a negative effect on the therapy. Participants in this study recommended that therapists consider the sexual masochism as only one aspect of their situation and treat other issues as equally important. They also recommended that the practitioner needs to be able to determine when the BDSM practices are not "safe, sane, and consensual." Nichols (2011) similarly raised issues of counter-transference and differentiation of problem behaviors from those that are merely unusual. Lawrence and Love-Crowell (2008) had noted how little the issues of treatment of sexual masochism had been studied and conducted structured interviews with 14 therapists who worked with BDSM clients. They emphasized the need to adopt a nonjudgmental attitude and to become aware of BDSM practices and cultural values. BDSM was rarely the central issue in therapy but rather general relationship issues. It was cautioned that therapists who practiced BDSM themselves often developed boundary problems with their clients, though perhaps this should be best seen in the context of the vulnerability of therapists involved with all types of patients in regular psychotherapy (Perlman, 2009).

References

Abel, G. G., Levis, D. J., & Clancy, J. (1970). Aversion therapy applied to taped sequences of deviant behavior in exhibitionism and other sexual deviations: A preliminary report. *Journal of Behavioral Therapy and Experimental Psychiatry, 1,* 59–66.

American Psychiatric Association. (2000). *Diagnostic and statistical manual of mental disorders* (4th ed., text rev.). Washington, DC: Author.

American Psychiatric Association. (2013). *Diagnostic and statistical manual of mental disorders* (5th ed.). Washington, DC: Author.

Balon, R. (1998). Pharmacological treatment of paraphilias with a focus on antidepressants. *Journal of Sex & Marital Therapy, 24,* 241–254.

Bancroft, J., & Marks, I. (1968). Electric aversion therapy of sexual deviations. *Proceedings of the Royal Society of Medicine, 61,* 30–33.

Baumeister, R. F. (1988). Gender differences in masochistic scripts. *Journal of Sex Research, 25,* 478–499.

Blanchard, R., & Hucker, S. J. (1991). Age, transvestism, bondage, and concurrent paraphilic activities in 117 fatal cases of autoerotic asphyxia. *British Journal of Psychiatry, 159,* 371–377.

Brownell, K. D., Hays, S. C., & Barlow, D. H. (1977). Patterns of appropriate and deviant sexual arousal: The behavioral treatment of multiple sexual deviations. *Journal of Consulting and Clinical Psychology, 45,* 1144–1155.

Connolly, P. H. (2006). Psychological functioning of bondage/domination/sado-masochism (BDSM) practitioners. *Journal of Psychology & Human Sexuality, 18,* 79–120.

Czerny, J. P., Briken, P., & Berner, W. (2002). Antihormonal treatment of paraphilic patients in German forensic psychiatric clinics. *European Psychiatry, 17,* 104–106.

De Silva, P. (1993). Fetishism and sexual dysfunction: Clinical presentation and management. *Sexual and Marital Therapy, 8,* 147–155.

Dolinak, D., Matshes, E., & Lew, E. (2005). *Forensic pathology: Principles and practice.* Amsterdam, the Netherlands: Elsevier Academic Press.

Feldman, M. P. (1966). Aversion therapy for sexual deviations: A critical review. *Psychological Bulletin, 65,* 65–79.

Freund, K., Seto, M. C., & Kuban, M. (1995). Masochism: A multiple case study. *Sexuologie, 4,* 313–324.

Gavin, B. (2010). No pain, no gain: Masochism as a response to early trauma and implications for therapy. *Psychodynamic Practice, 16*(2), 183–200.

Gottesman, H. G., & Schubert, D. S. (1993). Low-dose oral medroxyprogesterone acetate in the management of the paraphilias. *Journal of Clinical Psychiatry, 54,* 182–188.

Gudjonsson, G. H. (1986). Sexual variations: Assessment and treatment in clinical practice. *Sexual and Marital Therapy, 1,* 191–214.

Hayes, S. C., Luoma, J. B., Bond, F. W., Masuda, A., & Lillis, J. (2006). Acceptance and commitment therapy: Model, processes and outcomes. *Behavior Research and Therapy, 44,* 1–25.

Hoff, G., & Sprott, R. A. (2009, September 30). Therapy experiences of clients with BDSM sexualities: Listening to stigmatized sexuality. *Electronic Journal of Human Sexuality, 12,* 1–12.

Hucker, S. J. (2008). Sexual masochism: Psychopathology and theory. In D. R. Laws & W. T. O'Donohue (Eds.), *Sexual deviance: Theory, assessment, and treatment* (2nd ed., pp. 250–263). New York, NY: Guilford.

Hucker, S. J. (2011). Hypoxyphilia. *Archives of Sexual Behavior, 40,* 1323–1326.

Hucker, S. J., & Blanchard, R. (1992). Death scene characteristics in 118 fatal cases of autoerotic asphyxia compared with suicidal asphyxia. *Behavioral Sciences and the Law, 10,* 509–523.

Hunt, M. (1974). *Sexual behavior in the 1970s.* Chicago, IL: Playboy Press.

Kafka, M. P., & Hennen, J. (2002). A *DSM-IV* Axis I comorbidity study of males (n = 120) with paraphilias and paraphilia-related disorders. *Sexual Abuse: A Journal of Research and Treatment, 14,* 349–356.

Kafka, M. P., & Prentky, R. A. (1994). Preliminary observations of *DSM-III-R* Axis 1 comorbidity in men with paraphilias and paraphilia-related disorders. *Journal of Clinical Psychiatry, 55*(11), 481–487.

Kilmann, P. R., Sabalis, R. F., Gearing, M. L., Bukstel, L. H., & Scovern, A. W. (1982). The treatment of sexual paraphilias: A review of the outcome research. *Journal of Sex Research, 18,* 193–252.

Krueger, R. B. (2010a). The *DSM* diagnostic criteria for sexual sadism. *Archives of Sexual Behavior, 39,* 325–345.

Krueger, R. B. (2010b). The *DSM* diagnostic criteria for sexual masochism. *Archives of Sexual Behavior, 39,* 346–356.

Krueger, R. B., & Kaplan, M. S. (2001). Depot-leuprolide acetate for treatment of paraphilias: A report of twelve cases. *Archives of Sexual Behavior, 30,* 409–422.

Lawrence, A. A., & Love-Crowell, J. (2008). Psychotherapists' experience with clients who engage in consensual sadomasochism: A qualitative study. *Journal of Sex & Marital Therapy, 34,* 67–85.

Lehne, G., Thomas, K., & Berlin, F. (2000). Treatment of sexual paraphilias: A review of the 1999–2000 literature. *Current Opinion in Psychiatry, 13,* 569–573.

Lindemann, D. (2011). BDSM as therapy? *Sexualities, 14*(2), 151–172.

Lykins, A. D., & Cantor, J. M. (under review). *Vorarephilia: A case study in masochism and erotic consumption.*

Marks, I. M., Rachman, S., & Gelder, M. G. (1965). Methods for assessment of aversion treatment in fetishism with masochism. *Behavior Research and Therapy, 3,* 253–258.

Martz, D. (2003). Behavioral treatment for a female engaging in autoerotic asphyxiation. *Clinical Case Studies, 2,* 236–242.

Meyer, W. J., Walker, P. A., Emory, L. E., & Smith, E. R. (1985). Physical, metabolic, and hormonal effects on men of long-term therapy with medroxyprogesterone acetate. *Fertility and Sterility, 43,* 102–109.

Money, J., Bennett, R. G., & Cameron, W. R. (1981). Postadolescent paraphiliac sex offenders: Hormonal and counseling therapy follow-up. *International Journal of Mental Health, 6,* 25–45.

Moser, C., & Levitt, E. E. (1987). An exploratory-descriptive study of a sadomasochistically oriented sample. *Journal of Sex Research, 23,* 322–337.

Nichols, M. (2011, Spring). Couples and kinky sexuality: The need for a new therapeutic approach. In J. Malpas & A. Leu (Eds.), *At the edge: Exploring gender and sexuality in couples and families* (pp. 25–33). (AFTA Monograph Series, 7). Washington, DC: American Family Therapy Academy.

Perlman, S. D. (2009). Falling into sexuality: Sexual boundary violations in psychotherapy. *Psychoanalytic Review, 96,* 917–941.

Pinard, G., & Lamontagne, Y. (1976). Electrical aversion, aversion relief and sexual retraining in treatment of fetishism with masochism. *Journal of Behavioral Therapy and Experimental Psychiatry, 7,* 71–74.

Richters, J., Grulich, A. E., de Visser, R. O., Smith, A. M. A., & Rissel, C. E. (2003). Sex in Australia: Autoerotic, esoteric, and other sexual practices engaged in by a representative sample of adults. *Australian and New Zealand Journal of Public Health, 27,* 180–190.

Sandnabba, N. K., Santtila, P., & Nordling, N. (1999). Sexual behavior and social adaptation among sadomasochistically-oriented males. *Journal of Sex Research, 36,* 273–282.

Santtila, P., Sandnabba, N. K., Alison, L., & Nordling, N. (2002). Demographics, sexual behaviour, family background and abuse experiences of practitioners of sadomasochistic sex: A review of current research. *Sexual and Relationship Therapy, 17,* 39–55.

Saukko, P., & Knight, B. (2004). *Knight's forensic pathology* (3rd ed.). London, England: Hodder Arnold.

Shiwach, R. S., & Prosser, J. (1998). Treatment of an unusual case of masochism. *Journal of Sex & Marital Therapy, 24,* 303–307.

Spengler, A. (1977). Manifest sadomasochism of males: Results of an empirical study. *Archives of Sexual Behavior, 6,* 441–456.

Thibaut, F., de la Barra, F., Gordon, H., Cosyns, P., Bardford, J. M. W., & WFSBP Task Force on Sexual Disorders. (2010). The World Federation of Societies of Biological

Psychiatry (WFSBP) guidelines for the biological treatment of paraphilias. *The World Journal of Biological Psychiatry, 11*, 604–655.

Thomas-Peter, B., & Humphreys, M. (1997). Masochism: Assessment, treatment and the quality of consent to injurious behaviour. *Journal of Forensic Psychiatry & Psychology, 8*, 669–677.

Williams, D. J. (2006). Different (painful!) strokes for different folks: A general overview of sexual sadomasochism (SM) and its diversity. *Sexual Addiction & Compulsivity, 13*, 333–346.

6

VOYEURISM

A Case Study

Robert P. Stuyvesant, Diane G. Mercier, and Ashley Haidle

With the explosion of reality television shows, pornographic websites, and advances in technologies which create the opportunity to remotely observe and record others with or without their knowledge, voyeuristic behaviors are more acceptable and commonplace than ever before in our culture. Voyeuristic behaviors, however, can become both pathological and criminal in nature.

From a clinical perspective, for an individual's voyeuristic behavior to be classified as a sexual disorder, or a paraphilia, the American Psychiatric Association's *Diagnostic and Statistical Manual of Mental Disorders* (*DSM-IV-TR*; American Psychiatric Association, 2000) outlines two criteria which must be present:

> A. Over a period of at least 6 months, recurrent, intense sexually arousing fantasies, sexual urges, or behaviors involving the act of observing an unsuspecting person who is naked, in the process of disrobing, or engaging in sexual activity.

> B. The person has acted on these sexual urges, or the sexual urges or fantasies cause marked distress or interpersonal difficulty. (p. 575)

Up until the last decade or so, from a legal perspective, the "Peeping Tom" offense was most typical of a voyeuristic behavior resulting in legal ramifications, because jurisdictions primarily had addressed only the loitering or trespass component of voyeurism (*Voyeurism as a Criminal Offence: A Consultation Paper*, 2003/2012). In such cases, the individual would approach the residence of another person and attempt to peer in a window to surreptitiously observe her or him in some form of a private act. If the particular jurisdiction did not have a specific statute addressing voyeurism, the individual engaged in such behavior might be charged with trespass, disorderly conduct, or indecent exposure, if caught while masturbating. Voyeurism is often a behavior which occurs in the context of an offender committing other types of sexual offenses, such as incest, exhibitionism, child molestation, and stalking (Kaplan & Krueger, 1997). In these cases, the other offenses typically precipitate the offender's entrance into the criminal justice system. The individual may only be charged with what is considered the more serious crime and voyeurism may not always be charged as a separate offense. At the time of arrest or conviction there may be no knowledge that voyeuristic behaviors also occurred. Being subsumed in other sexual offense charges or charged as a nonsexual crime like trespass makes it extremely difficult to get an accurate sense of the prevalence of voyeurism as a clinical and legal issue.

Voyeurism as a criminal matter has become even more complex with the advances in technology. Videotaping others, or using some form of recording device to observe others in situations where there is a reasonable expectation of privacy, has necessitated statutory changes to address such behaviors. In 2004, the federal government created the Video Voyeurism Prevention Act making it illegal to use any device to record, broadcast, or distribute the image of another person's private areas in any situation where the individual has a reasonable expectation of privacy (National Center for Prosecution of Child Abuse/National District Attorneys Association [NCPCA/NDAA], 2009). This is an international issue and other countries, such as England and Wales, have also established criminal codes (Mann, Ainsworth, Al-Attar, & Davies, 2008). Canada successfully prosecuted an individual in 2006 for the first time using that country's new video voyeurism law (Canadian Privacy Law Blog, 2006). In reviewing state statutes, state legislatures have responded in a variety of ways in an attempt to make it unlawful to invade another's privacy in such a fashion. Some jurisdictions include the notion that the intent is for a prurient interest, others do not (NCPCA/NDAA, 2009). As an example, the Nevada Revised Statute 200.603 makes peeping a misdemeanor offense, but if the offender possesses any recording device, the offense is a gross misdemeanor. There is a separate statute, NRS 200.604, which addresses "Capturing image of private area of another person; distributing, disclosing, displaying, transmitting or publishing image of private area of another person" (NCPCA/NDAA, 2009, pp. 47–48). A case that became nationally prominent was that of Michael David Barrett who secretly made videos of an ESPN reporter, Erin Andrews, by cutting a hole in the wall of adjoining hotel rooms and filming her. He then posted the videos. In the course of that investigation, it was discovered that he had also videotaped over a dozen other women. He ultimately faced federal charges of interstate stalking (Canning, Netter, & Goldwert, 2009).

Crucial research questions which need to be addressed regarding the voyeur come easily to mind. Capturing recidivism rates, developing tools in hopes of predicting future risk, and identifying the most effective treatment techniques for voyeurs, are arduous research tasks at best, and definitely a work in progress. Perhaps because voyeurism is considered a noncontact offense, and therefore a "less serious" offense, there is a dearth of information in all of these research areas (Mann, Ainsworth, et al., 2008). In the criminal arena, given the cultural normalization of voyeuristic behaviors and the ease with which one person may now violate another's personal space through technological devices, the statutory changes which were summarized specify where such behaviors cross legal boundaries.

To bring clarity to this clinical discussion of voyeurism, we are distinguishing between those individuals engaged exclusively in acts of voyeurism versus those whose acts of voyeurism are precipitants to, or co-occurring with, other types of deviant or illegal sexual behaviors. The emphasis here is on the individual engaged exclusively in acts of voyeurism, or the "classic/contemporary voyeur." This is the individual who engages in the classic "Peeping Tom" types of offenses and who may or may not utilize recording devices to allow or accentuate access to his or her victims (the use of sophisticated recording devices being a more contemporary approach). Masturbation may have occurred during the commission of voyeuristic behaviors, and is generally directly associated with the act of voyeurism or the recall of the acts of voyeurism. These individuals do not have a substantiated history at clinical presentation of hands-on sexual offenses. They may have expressed the fantasy or intent to engage in hands-on offenses, but have not acted on the fantasy. Voyeurism can and does occur in conjunction with other types of sexual offense behaviors. That said, we are considering that there may be those engaged in voyeurism that do not commit other types of sexual offenses, and warrant a sound clinical response specific to voyeurism. This distinction may be akin to current challenges associated with formulating assessment and treatment responses to those engaged in viewing child pornography but who have no history of hands-on sexual offenses against a child.

The case study of Mr. V was chosen for this discussion because it exemplifies the behavior of a voyeur who is typical of the classic/contemporary voyeur. At the time he entered treatment, he had never been arrested or convicted for any other type of sexual offense. Although this case study may raise more questions than it provides answers, we hope that it can offer a framework to further our understanding of the issues relevant to the assessment and treatment of the "classic/contemporary" voyeur.

The Case of Mr. V

Introduction

The following information is provided in advance of the case formulation itself, so that the factors impacting the clinician's decisions throughout that process are evident. The information provided here is specific to the case of Mr. V and was attained through clinical interviews and the review of records. This information will be incorporated in the ensuing case formulation that includes: results of clinical interviews; assessment of risk/needs; and treatment response.

Presenting Information

Mr. V, a 32-year-old Caucasian male, was referred for evaluation after being charged with "peeping," and with using technology to capture the images of the private areas of another person. Mr. V was caught "peeping" into the bedroom window of an adult female neighbor. The woman was in the process of disrobing when she observed him outside her residence. The woman notified law enforcement immediately and Mr. V was apprehended within a few hours of the offense. The second charge involved Mr. V using a cellular telephone with a built-in camera device to capture the images of females utilizing the employee restroom at his place of work. The hidden recording device was discovered by a female coworker after Mr. V had been detained on the peeping charge. He was charged with both offenses within the same week. Mr. V pled guilty to the charges and was sentenced to a 5-year term of probation.

Approximately 10 years prior to the index offenses, Mr. V was charged with voyeurism while attending college in another state. He drilled a hole in a wall to spy on an adult female neighbor. He had been attending college for almost 2 years when he was caught and charged with that offense. At the time, Mr. V. admitted to numerous instances of "peeping" on female coeds in various off-campus apartments. On these occasions Mr. V would stake out apartments where he could easily observe women through their windows with minimal chance of being noticed. The charge was reduced to a trespassing charge and was ultimately dismissed, but Mr. V was asked to leave the college. Upon returning to his community, at the insistence of his family he participated in limited outpatient treatment (12 sessions) to address the voyeurism. Mr. V then resided with his family for several years and was employed sporadically in various food service and retail related jobs. Mr. V never continued his college education. At the time of the index offenses he was working at a restaurant and living alone.

Mr. V reported being able to keep himself from acting out during the 12-session therapy by considering consequences, participating in the treatment, and on one occasion going to a brothel for "release." However, he resumed the acts of voyeurism within 2 months of the 12-session treatment ending. The behaviors continued for 10 years until his arrest for the index offenses. The use of a recording device to view adult females using the restroom at his workplace began about 3 years prior to his arrest for the index offenses.

This introduction to Mr. V provides evidence of potential problems associated with legal responses that tend to minimize or dismiss the potential seriousness of voyeuristic offenses (Mann et al., 2008). There are voyeurs who will discontinue the offending behaviors after being caught; however, the challenge lies in developing assessment procedures to separate the low risk from moderate and high risk offenders. Examining risk and needs becomes a critical part of assessment.

Background Information

Mr. V was born and raised in a metropolitan community. His family was intact through his childhood and his parents remain married. His family resides in the same community as Mr. V. He has an older sister and brother. Family life was stable in regard to care and circumstances. He lived in the same residence throughout his youth. His father's employment was consistent. His mother did not work outside the home. His family is close and there was consistent involvement with extended family members. He exhibited no problems associated with alcohol or substance abuse and did not report incidents of physical or sexual abuse. No family members were reported to have criminal records. Mr. V denied the presence of pornographic or sexually explicit materials within the residence when he was younger. Mr. V graduated from high school with average to above average grades. Within one year of graduating from high school Mr. V had moved to another state to attend college from which, as noted above, he was expelled 2 years later.

Social Status

Mr. V has not had close friends. He views himself as a "loner." He has no negative peer associations, and historically did not gravitate to negative associates. Most of the activities that he pursued, such as video games and watching television, did not require the involvement of others. He had not dated, ever lived with a partner, or been married. Mr. V has never had children.

Mental Health History

During the 12-session treatment noted above, he did not openly report his extensive history of voyeurism, and claimed the offense at age 21 was his first. As noted previously, the acts of voyeurism had subsided while he was in treatment, but resumed within 2 months of treatment termination, and had been ongoing up until his recent arrest for the index offenses. He had no history of mental health treatment or any mental health diagnosis prior to the treatment for voyeurism at age 21.

Mr. V had no juvenile arrest record, although he reported the onset of voyeurism at age 14 and that it occurred on a persistent and consistent basis throughout his juvenile years.

Nonoffending Sexual Experiences and History

Mr. V had no history of sexual victimization or sexual experiences with others prior to age 18. He did not date in high school. His first experience with intercourse was at age 18 with a prostitute. He began masturbating at age 13, and did not have access to pornography at that time. In the ensuing years, up until the age of 18, he would masturbate, sometimes two to three times a day. His masturbatory fantasies from age 14 were primarily linked to acts of voyeurism. He denied homosexual behaviors or having engaged in acts of intentional indecent exposure.

Sexual Offense History

Mr. V's first offense was at the residence of a female neighbor whom he believed was in junior high school and who was about 13 or 14 years old. He described the act as opportunistic and began "peeping" in her window. He claimed that he had seen her disrobe on a few occasions, after which he became fixated. He estimated having "peeped" on her over 30 times during a 7- to 8-month time frame. He would often engage in masturbation to ejaculation while looking through the window. Typically these acts occurred at night. He denied rape fantasies associated with this behavior, but he reported recurring fantasies of consensual sexual encounters with her while surreptitiously observing her undress. He reported that these voyeuristic behaviors stopped after the family living in the residence moved away. He then began looking for other opportunities to spy on others, and would routinely search the neighborhood, targeting adolescent and adult females. He estimated peeping through windows and spying on over 20 women, engaging in hundreds of such acts until he moved away to attend college at about age 19. The offending pattern was always the same, occurring at night, and accompanied by masturbation to ejaculation. There were times when he came close to getting caught, as he reported being chased away from a few different residences. Mr. V claimed that he would discontinue the peeping behavior for a few weeks after each "close encounter," but then the pattern would soon resume.

Over the following years from 21 to 31, he estimated he peeped at over 30 victims. He would have primary targets, and would frequently return, as he thought he had less chance of being discovered due to the secluded surroundings and safe hiding places. The victims were always older adolescent females and adult females. He did not observe couples engaged in sexual behaviors, and focused on opportunities to observe females disrobing.

Mr. V described a period of becoming bored with voyeurism and around age 28 began accessing adult pornography via the Internet. He would spend a few nights per week, up to 3 hours an evening, viewing older adolescent and adult female nudity. He denied arousal to watching pornography depicting others engaged in sexual behaviors. His arousal would come from masturbatory fantasies of sexual encounters with the women depicted in the pornographic videos and still pictures. All told, Mr. V estimated having engaged in hundreds of incidents of voyeurism since the age of 14, with the majority of the incidents paired with masturbation to ejaculation. He also reported three separate occasions, beginning around age 31, of hiding a video recording device in the employee bathroom used by female coworkers in places where he was employed. He would retrieve the recording device, and if he had captured images of females nude, or partially nude, he would download the material to his computer, and masturbate while viewing the images. Mr. V reported primary arousal to adult females and older adolescent females. He denied rape fantasies. He reported having sexual encounters with prostitutes at a brothel about five times. His experiences with prostitutes were the only sexual experiences in which he had actual physical contact with another person.

Case Formulation: Results of Clinical Interview with Mr. V

Based on Mr. V's extensive history of voyeurism, the starting point was to conduct a comprehensive evaluation, with the goal to assess Mr. V's risk for sexual re-offense and needs that go to mitigating risk. "Sex offender specific assessments are of great value in developing supervision and treatment strategies to put in place necessary external controls and to effectively aid offenders in developing their ability to self-regulate" (California Sex Offender Management Board [CASOMB], 2012, p. 6). This request for evaluation typically comes from a supervising agency (parole/probation), at the request of an attorney, or at times directly from the offender. Evaluations can occur pre- or postdisposition depending on the jurisdiction. Mr. V was referred for evaluation after entering a guilty plea to the charges, and prior to disposition.

A standardized sex offense specific risk assessment process was utilized in response to Mr. V's offenses. This approach is consistent with the assessment of various paraphilia, or sexually related crimes. The fact that Mr. V had no history of hands-on offenses does not alter the risk assessment process. Prior to conducting the evaluation, it is critical to obtain all the collateral information related to the charges, including police reports, court documents, any prior psychological/treatment reports, and the history of legal charges. Once sufficient information has been obtained, the evaluator needs to review all of this information prior to beginning the evaluation. Informed consent is reviewed with the offender prior to the evaluation process, and the appropriate releases of information are obtained so that the evaluation can be provided to the necessary parties. Briefly stated, the sex offense specific evaluation includes a review of records and an extensive clinical interview focusing on the offender's psychosocial history (Freund & Dougher, 2011). This clinical interview process will address information relevant to family of origin and childhood to assess for early exposures/experiences and trauma. The body of work associated with the clinical interview would encompass the following:

- Current functioning/status and family constellation
- Medical, mental health, legal, substance use, educational, employment, military, and relationship history
- Comprehensive examination of sexual history
- Account of the index offenses, and sexual offending history

Upon completion of the clinical interview, the evaluator is in a better position to decide which tests, instruments, and scales would be best suited to further assess for risk and needs. The Center for Sex Offender Management advises that, "Treatment is more effective when research-supported assessment tools are used to determine the appropriate level of service (i.e., dosage and intensity), to identify the specific risk factors that should be targeted in treatment, to assess progress that offenders are making in treatment, and to make ongoing adjustments to treatment plans" (2008, p. 16).

The information resulting from clinical interviews and record review tells us that Mr. V came from a relatively stable childhood, with no significant negative exposures or experiences that would increase risk or be indicative of trauma. His history was devoid of sexual, physical, or emotional abuse, and there was no evidence of substance abuse or early exposures to sexually explicit or pornographic materials. Mr. V did not report having relationships with females through adolescence or in his adult life. His only hands-on sexual experiences were with prostitutes. He was disconnected socially in his adult life and turning to prostitutes to get sexual needs met helped exacerbate the sexual objectification process. He also began viewing adult pornography on a persistent and repetitive basis around age 28.

During the examination of his offending history, in the clinical interview Mr. V revealed that the early onset of his voyeuristic behavior at age 14 was impulsive, and opportunistic. The most obvious dynamic factors associated with the onset of voyeurism for Mr. V were puberty which increased, albeit naturally, a heightened interest in sexual behaviors and in females, and that he had no significant peer centered connections. The initial occurrence, or ground zero, in regard to the onset of voyeurism, was rewarding in that he had an opportunity to observe an adolescent female disrobing without facing fear of rejection. He was not caught, and arousal was enhanced as he engaged in masturbation to ejaculation during the offense. These dynamics served to reinforce interest in the voyeuristic behaviors. He never dated and was likely challenged in regard to his sense of confidence and esteem, especially with female peers. These circumstances helped motivate Mr. V's interest in voyeurism, to satisfy his sexual interest, enhance arousal, and in a very distorted sense, make connections with others. This conditioning process was reinforced over time in that he engaged in hundreds of incidents without being caught or interrupted. In fact, Mr. V reported almost being caught or interrupted on only a few occasions, aside from the instances leading to his arrest. This is one factor that makes sexual offenses such as voyeurism and indecent exposure a high risk for recurrence, in that the perpetrators don't get caught. In the assessment, Mr. V identified specific beliefs and attitudes associated with his voyeuristic behaviors. Early on, it was, "I'll just look this once and see what I see." Other beliefs that allowed the behaviors to continue included, "I won't get caught. I am not really hurting anyone if they don't know I am there. I just can't stop. If I could just get a girlfriend I would stop. It's not like I am raping her." These justifications continued when he began video recording female coworkers using the employee restroom at his place of work. Mr. V reported masturbating while watching the clips, though he found "peeping" to be more arousing. He viewed "peeping" as an act that moved him closer to having a hands-on sexual experience with another person. Mr. V did admit to having fantasies of consensual sexual acts with the victims of his acts of voyeurism. Given the behaviors spanned almost two decades, with no evidence of escalation to hands-on sexual offenses, it is less probable he would progress to hands-on offending. One recent study indicated that 4% of hands-off sexual offenders went on to commit a hands-on offense (Swinburne Romine, Miner, Poulin, Dwyer, & Berg, 2012). His experiences with prostitutes were limited to less than five occurrences, yet served to reinforce sexual objectification of women.

Assessment of Mr. V's Static and Dynamic Risk Factors

The risk assessment process is a preliminary estimation for re-offense risk that is strengthened when factors related to sexual re-offense risk for adults are considered. According to Hanson "Evaluators are most likely to provide valid assessments when they consider factors actually related to risk.... The strongest predictors of sexual offense recidivism are variables related to sexual deviancy, such as deviant sexual preferences, prior sexual offenses, early onset of sexual offending and the diversity of sexual crimes" (2000, pp. 1–2). In addition, Hanson suggests additional factors to consider, including: measures of criminal lifestyle, response to treatment, and well-established static risk factors such as prior sexual offenses and dynamic risk factors (acute and stable). Acute factors are those which are immediately associated with the offense, such as being intoxicated and experiencing arousal in the presence of a child. Stable dynamic factors are those that occur over a longer period of time, such as mood disorder, deviant sexual interest, and alcoholism (Hanson, 2000). In general, "sex offenders have been found to have significantly higher rates of sexual recidivism when they have a sexual interest in children, particularly male children, or have general paraphilias such as exhibitionism or voyeurism (Dempster & Hart, 2002; McGrath, Cumming, Livingston, and Hoke, 2003; Miner, 2002)" (Minnesota Department of Corrections, 2007, p. 7).

The Risk/Needs/Responsivity Model (RNR) provides a framework for directing the assessment and treatment process.

> Developed in the 1980s and first formalized in 1990, the risk-need-responsivity model has been used with increasing success to assess and rehabilitate criminals in Canada and around the world. As suggested by its name, it is based on three principles: 1) the *risk principle* asserts that criminal behavior can be reliably predicted and that treatment should focus on the higher risk offenders; 2) the *need principle* highlights the importance of criminogenic needs in the design and delivery of treatment; and 3) the *responsivity principle* describes how the treatment should be provided. (Bonta & Andrews, 2007)

The seven dynamic risk–needs factors identified in this model are: antisocial personality pattern; procriminal attitudes; social supports for crimes; substance abuse; family–marital relationships; schoolwork; pro-social recreational activities. These seven factors along with criminal history assist in the overall assessment of "criminogenic needs" (Bonta & Andrews, 2007).

The clinical interview creates an opportunity for the evaluator to rule in/out certain tests, measures, and instruments that go to further assessment of static and dynamic factors. *A caveat: In determining which instruments/scales to utilize, each clinician has the responsibility to select those instruments his or her respective training and licensure allows. Some of the proposed tools are not available for use by all and require specialized training/education. Some clinicians may not have access to certain assessment tools, namely, the Penile Plethysmograph (PPG), or the Abel Assessment for Sexual Interest* (AASI; Abel, 2011).

To assess static factors, some actuarial scales are available for use with adult sexual offenders. Some of those scales include the Rapid Risk Assessment for Sexual Offense Recidivism (Hanson, 1997), the Vermont Assessment for Sexual Offense Recidivism (McGrath & Hoke, 2002), and the Static-99R (Hanson, 2000), to name a few. Some jurisdictions are moving toward standardizing certain scales. In California it is standard to utilize the Static-99R. The Static-99R is a 10-item actuarial assessment instrument created by Hanson and Thornton (1999) for use with adult male sex offenders. This does not preclude evaluators from administering additional scales/instruments. Standardization may lead to more consistent research regarding more accurate prediction of risk.

In the case of Mr. V, the Static-99R was utilized based on the nature of his offenses because this instrument is widely accepted across jurisdictions. The strength of the Static-99R is that it targets risk factors that research has shown to be associated with sexual recidivism (Harris, Phenix, Hanson, & Thornton, 2003). The 10 items on the Static-99R address the following: the offender's age; if the offender has ever lived with a lover/partner for at least 2 years; index of nonsexual violence convictions; prior nonsexual violence convictions; prior sexual offenses; prior sentencing dates excluding the index offense; any convictions for noncontact sex offenses; any unrelated victims; any stranger victims; and any male victims. The developers of the Static-99 and Static-99R provide explicit rules for combining these factors into a total risk score. The Static-99R coding rules specifically indicate the scale can be applied in the risk assessment of voyeurs. Mr. V's static risk assessment based on the Static-99R suggested high risk. Of the 10 factors Mr. V had a total score of six points, placing him in the high risk category based on coding rules. Those factors included: his current age; history of prior sexual offense charge (no conviction); victims were unrelated and strangers; no evidence of having lived with a lover/partner, conviction for non-contact sex offense.

Typical areas of focus in regard to assessment of dynamic factors include the following areas: criminogenic needs, personality/regulation of moods, sexual interests/deviance, attitudes supportive of sexual deviance, intelligence, social and interpersonal competence, and substance use.

In turning to the assessment specific to the case of Mr. V, criminogenic needs were assessed by addressing the eight core factors identified under the RNR Model. In Mr. V's case, he did not have a nonsexual criminal history (static factor addressed in the Static-99R scoring). There was some evidence of antisocial traits (to be distinguished from antisocial personality disorder) given the impulsive and repetitive nature of his offending behaviors leading to the violation of others' rights. He engaged in a persistent level of distorted thinking to maintain the behaviors over an extended period of time, therefore it can be assumed that "criminal (distorted) thinking" became a norm for him, but limited to acts of voyeurism. He did not associate with a criminal element. There was no evidence of substance abuse, but Mr. V had no history of established peer centered relationships and was socially isolated; he had a sporadic and inconsistent employment history and was dismissed from college in response to his criminal behaviors, and there was no evidence of prosocial recreational interests or activities. Further assessment of needs was accomplished by using the Structured Risk Assessment-Forensic Version Light (SRA-FVL) (Thornton & D'Orazio, 2012). The SRA-FVL considers three domains: sexual interests, relational style, and self-management. In Mr. V's case, he was assessed in the typical needs/high risk category when the results of the SRA-FVL were combined with his Static-99R score. In addition, the Minnesota Multiphasic Personality Inventory-II (MMPI-II) (Butcher, 1989) was administered, but the profile was invalid as he was a "fake good" responder. This means Mr. V was overly representing himself in a positive light. His response to the MMPI-II was consistent with his response to the Social Desirability Scale in the AASI questionnaire. For those who present with antisocial traits or criminal histories the Psychopathy Checklist-R (Hare, 2012) and the Level of Service-Case Management Inventory (Multi Health System, 2004) can be utilized.

To strengthen the assessment of "risk/needs," additional measures were applied to further examine some of the factors associated with the RNR Model. Based on Mr. V's history of social isolation, further examination of personality/regulation of moods and perception of self was warranted. The Burns Depression Checklist (Burns, 1990), a brief examination of symptoms associated with depressed mood, was administered in conjunction with the Burns Anxiety Inventory. Mr. V's responses to these scales gave evidence of slightly depressed mood and prevailing anxiety, especially in response to social situations and challenges. Other measures to consider would include the Beck Depression Scale (Pearson Education, 1996), Center for Epidemiologic Studies Depression Scale (CES-D), available through the National Institute of Mental Health (Radloff, 1977). There are more elaborate testing measures, such as the MMPI-II (Butcher, 1989) and the Millon Clinical Multiaxial Inventory-III (MCMI-III; Pearson Education, 1994), that provide more in-depth analysis regarding personality traits.

To assess Mr. V's sexual interests, the Abel Assessment for Sexual Interest computer generated questionnaire was utilized. Further assessment of sexual interests and arousal via physiological measures were not taken in that Mr. V had no substantiated history of sexual behaviors with prepubescent children or any history of sexual violence. An argument could be made for administering the PPG based on limited evidence that some voyeurs escalate to sexual aggression/assault. This presents an ethical debate in that if Mr. V were to show a response to violence, yet has no history of such behavior, would this place Mr. V in a negative light with the court? Is this issue best reserved for the treatment setting? The AASI questionnaire was selected in Mr. V's case due to the comprehensive nature of the questionnaire. In addition to a summary of deviant sexual behaviors and experiences, the Abel questionnaire includes scales that screen for sexual fantasies/arousal, cognitive distortions, social desirability, a danger registry, and self-reported history of accusations, arrests, and convictions for sexual offense behaviors. Mr. V's responses to the AASI questionnaire were consistent with information provided in the clinical interview. He reported acts of voyeurism occurring since age 14, accessing adult Internet pornography from age 28 to the present, and sexual behaviors with prostitutes. On this test he did not reveal sexual interest in children or sexual violence. He did not report a history of sexual victimization. Mr.

V reported sometimes having fantasies about sex with prostitutes, adult sex partners who are strangers, masturbating in public without being seen, and using adult Internet sexual materials excessively. He indicated he often had fantasies and sexual arousal associated with window peeping or secretly watching others undress. The social desirability scale indicated Mr. V was having difficulty reporting honestly regarding topics unrelated to sexual deviance. This means he was likely attempting to "fake good," which is not uncommon in the evaluation process. On the one hand, in the clinical interview Mr. V was forthcoming in discussing the known sexual offenses, and provided new information regarding his sexual offending behavior, and nonoffending sexual behaviors; that is, sex with prostitutes. On the other hand, the fake good results on the social desirability scale and the MMPI-II suggested that he was attempting to make a good impression. This could be attributed to his need to impress the court and the evaluator in light of the serious potential negative outcomes in regard to the charges against him. The deception cannot be ignored, but should become a treatment issue. Other instruments to consider for further assessment of sexual interests/deviance include: the Clarke Sexual History Questionnaire (Patich et al., 1977); the Multiphasic Sexuality Inventory (Nichols & Molinder Assessments. Inc., 1984).

Based on information attained during the clinical interview, Mr. V. engaged in thinking that allowed for the sexually deviant behaviors to occur and progress (i.e., "I'll just look this once and see what I see"; "I am not really hurting anyone if they don't know I am there"). Further assessment of his attitudes/beliefs that suggest tolerance for sexual deviance was warranted. The Abel Questionnaire includes a cognitive distortion scale, and was utilized in Mr. V's case. His cognitive distortion score did not reveal attitudes tolerant of sexual aggression or sexual acts with children. The Empathy for Women Test (Hanson & Scott, 1995) was utilized to assess his ability to distinguish between sexually abusive and nonabusive interactions between men and women. His responses fell within the normal range based on scoring criteria and demonstrated that Mr. V could distinguish between abusive and nonabusive situations. Other scales to consider include: the Hanson Sex Attitudes Questionnaire (Hanson, Gizzarelli, & Scott, 1994); Wilson Sex Fantasy Questionnaire (Wilson, 1978); and Bumby Cognitive Distortion/Rape Scale (Bumby, 1995).

Mr. V completed high school and attended some college, suggesting adequate intellectual functioning. Therefore, no intelligence or educational assessment was conducted. Instruments to consider that go to assessment of intelligence include the Kaufman Brief Intelligence Test (Kbit-2; Pearson Education, 2012.), and the Wechsler Adult Intelligence Scale-III (WAIS-III; Pearson Education, 1997).

Further assessment beyond the clinical interview of Mr. V's social and interpersonal competence was deemed necessary based on his history of

social isolation, avoidance, and lack of positive social and emotional connections. These factors were considered significant dynamics in his offense
history. The Social Avoidance and Distress Scale (Watson, 1969) and Fear
of Negative Evaluation Scale (SADS; Watson, 1969) were utilized with
Mr. V. The SADS is a 28-item, self-rated scale used to measure various
aspects of social anxiety including distress, discomfort, fear, anxiety, and
the avoidance of social situations. His responses were consistent with
information obtained in his social history, and suggested significant difficulty in social situations. The Fear of Negative Evaluation Scale (Watson,
1969) is another assessment of social anxiety. Mr. V had a high score,
indicating significant apprehension about what other people think of him.
Other scales to consider include: The Buss-Durkee Hostility Inventory
(1957), and the Interpersonal Reactivity Index (Davis, 1980).

Mr. V did not present with a history of substance abuse, and therefore no further assessment occurred. Instruments available to assess for
substance abuse include the Substance Abuse Subtle Screening Inven-
tory-3 (SASSI-3; Miller, 1988), the Michigan Alcoholism Screening Test
(MAST; Selzer, 1971), the Drug Abuse Screening Test (DAST; Skinner,
1982), and urine/blood testing.

With information available from the clinical interview, responses to
tests/inventories, application of risk scales, and factual accounts of the
referral offense, the clinician is better prepared to provide an estimation of
sexual re-offense risk, address the offender's needs and response to those
specific needs in treatment planning.

In considering dynamic factors consistent with the RNR Model, Mr.
V was estimated to be in the high risk range for continued acts of voyeurism. The primary factors associated with this risk estimation included:
significant history of offending behavior; impulsivity; criminal thinking that maintained offending behaviors and re-offense after treatment
despite prior legal and social consequences; social isolation and relationship challenges; a lack of employment stability; and no positive leisure
activities. The mitigating factors included: no evidence of substance abuse;
no nonsexual criminal history; no evidence of severe psychopathology;
adequate level of intellectual functioning; and a willingness to report on
the progression of offense behaviors thus allowing for closer examination
of motivational and dynamic factors which allow for early relapse prevention planning. These conclusions were consistent with his Static-99R
score, and the SRA-FVL score, which placed him in the high re-offense
risk range. Mr. V was diagnosed with Voyeurism *DSM-IV-TR* 302.82 as
a result of his evaluation. The following recommendations were offered to
the court regardless of the legal outcome:

*Mr. V should be directed to participate in an outpatient treatment program
designed to specifically address voyeurism, in conjunction with a treatment*

plan that incorporates the acute and prevailing dynamic factors associated with the offense behaviors. An individualized treatment plan is important, and Mr. V should be encouraged to include his primary support system in the treatment planning process. Treatment can occur individually or in conjunction with group therapy. Group treatment, however, should be specific to those engaged in acts of voyeurism, and not hands-on offenses against children or adults. Given no evidence of hands-on offenses, it would be important not to align Mr. V with that type of offender. This treatment approach would incorporate standard, sex offense specific treatment goals: acceptance of responsibility for behavior without minimization or externalization of blame; develop accountability for behaviors and relationships; develop motivation for change; identify and address risks to healthy living and build skills for getting needs met in prosocial ways; learn about the impact of sexual abuse on others; formulate a basic understanding of the fundamental principles of relapse prevention planning while moving toward healthy life promotion; learn to identify and confront cognitive distortions in general and specific to sexual offending behaviors; develop skills for positive self-regulation of emotions and impulses; develop and maintain healthy relationships and relationship skills, while demonstrating responsible day to day behaviors; decrease deviant sexual interests and build skills to effectively manage deviant arousal. If released to the community, probation or parole supervision should assist with compliance of treatment mandates. It is further recommended that treatment and progress reports are made available on a regular basis to supervising law enforcement agencies (parole/probation). Failure to comply with terms of parole/probation should be considered an immediate risk factor, and responded to expeditiously by the court. Having continued access to pornographic material, via the Internet or otherwise, is a significant risk factor for Mr. V. Restricting access to such material is recommended, as he works to break through the obsessive-compulsive elements of his behavior, while building skills necessary to create and maintain healthy peer centered relationships and interests. Further assessment of Mr. V's mental health (psychiatric/psychological) is recommended, for consideration of psychotropic medications to assist in the management of anxiety, depression, and compulsive traits.

In Mr. V's case, the evaluation was submitted to the court and he was placed on probation for 5 years and mandated to participate in treatment specific to his sexual offense history.

Treatment

There is very little in regard to "best practice" models identified in the literature specific to the "classic/contemporary" voyeur (Lavin, 2008). There are references to the application of cognitive-behavioral interventions with voyeurs, and various combinations of interventions including psychotropic response (Mann et al., 2008). Mr. V was assessed as high risk for sexual re-offense. An individualized treatment plan was developed to address his specific needs in response to his risk for sexual re-offense. This approach is consistent with the RNR model, accepted as a "best practice" response for managing various types of sexual offenders in the community (CASOMB, 2012). In the absence of compelling research specific to the treatment of voyeurs, we would argue that the RNR model offers a practical response in the treatment of sexual offenders.

In meeting with Mr. V to establish the treatment plan, the concept of the "Containment Team" approach was reviewed and he gave consent to that approach being incorporated into his treatment plan. Essentially, this approach maintains consistency with California sex offense treatment provider requirements. "Although there is no specified theoretical upper limit to the number and roles of Containment Team members, the model views the minimum essential membership as consisting of three specialists: (a) the supervising probation officer or parole agent or similar representative of judicial authority; (b) provider of specialized sex offender treatment services; (c) polygraph examiner" (CASOMB, 2012).

Mr. V was provided with an informed consent document that addressed some of the risks and benefits associated with this treatment approach. He was also provided with a summary regarding the clinician's background, office practices, and additional consent for psychotherapy.

Mr. V agreed to a waiver of confidentiality consistent with the recommendations outlined in the Containment Model of sex offender management. His agreement to the confidentiality waiver allowed for open communication between the provider and identified professionals/agencies in the Containment Model (i.e., probation officer, polygraph examiner). He was required to review and sign a document delineating information about his privacy and confidentiality prior to the onset of treatment.

Mr. V entered into a treatment contract that estimated the length of treatment, and the rules/responsibilities associated with his level of treatment. This contract specified that since Mr. V was on probation, upon completion of core treatment phases, he would participate in a structured follow-up process that would coincide with his 5-year term of probation. This contract specified the following terms, rules, and agreements:

1. I agree to be honest and assume full responsibility for my offenses and my behavior.
2. I agree to notify my therapist in advance (24 hr) if I must miss a session. There must be a strong rationale for missing any scheduled appointments. All missed appointments will be reported to my probation/parole officer.
3. I agree to pay my assigned fee at the time of each session, or in advance.

4. I agree not to come to any session under the influence of alcohol/drugs.
5. I agree not to engage in verbally or physically assaultive behaviors, in treatment or in the community.
6. I agree to make my best efforts to cooperate in the treatment process.
7. I agree to complete all treatment related tasks, homework, and assignments.
8. I agree not to commit any crimes.
9. I agree not to involve myself in any activity/situation in which I may be creating greater risk for re-offense or where I have access to the person(s) I have sexually victimized (unless approved by those in a position to do so).
10. I agree not to disclose the identity of other participants in treatment (for participation in sex offense specific group therapy).
11. I agree to abide by all treatment rules.
12. I agree to share with my treatment provider any contact I may have with a treatment participant outside of therapy.
13. I will not have in my possession at any time, sexually explicit or pornographic materials, in the event my terms of probation prohibit such use, and comply with court mandates regarding Internet access.
14. I consent to information being released to my parole/probation officer on a consistent basis regarding my participation in treatment and to address specific concerns about my status with parole/probation.
15. I consent to release information about my treatment to a certified sex offense specific polygraph examiner.
16. I will develop a treatment plan specific to my risks and needs.
17. I will sign waivers of confidentiality/release of information to allow for open communication with other professionals responsible for my treatment and supervision.
18. I have the right to refuse treatment and not sign confidentiality waivers while acknowledging certain consequences may be imposed; for example, arrest for violation of parole/probation.

Mr. V participated in the formulation of a treatment plan specific to his risk and needs. The treatment plan specified problem areas (criminogenic needs), with specific goals, treatment methods, and measures for progress. The treatment plan incorporated evidence based interventions supported by the professional literature in the field of sex offender treatment and as well as other psychotherapeutic interventions.

The following treatment plan specific to Mr. V was based on the RNR Model, a diagnosis of Voyeurism 302.82. The following table identified his criminogenic and noncriminogenic risk–need factors on the left and the corresponding treatment responses/goals on the right.

1) Antisocial personality pattern: Mr. V engaged in a persistent and repetitive pattern of voyeuristic behaviors violating the rights of others for almost 20 years.

Decrease deviant sexual interests and build skills to effectively manage deviant arousal.
Acceptance of responsibility for voyeuristic behaviors without minimization or externalization of blame.
Formulate a basic understanding of the fundamental principles of relapse prevention planning while moving toward healthy life promotion.
Identify and address risks to healthy living and build skills for getting needs met in prosocial ways.
Develop skills for positive self-regulation of emotions and impulses.

2) Procriminal attitudes: Mr. V presented evidence of distorted beliefs that maintained acts of voyeurism including denial associated with the intrusive nature of the behavior.

Develop accountability for behaviors and relationships.
Develop motivation for change.
Learn about the impact of sexual abuse for others.
Learn to identify and confront cognitive distortions, in particular those attitudes that maintained the offense behaviors.

3) Social supports for crime: Mr. V did not have antisocial or negative peer associations; however, he lacked significant positive peer associations and connections and was socially isolated. His social isolation was a contributing factor to the offense behaviors.

Develop and maintain healthy relationships and relationship skills, while demonstrating responsible day-to-day behaviors.

4) Family/marital relationships: Mr. V lacked significant long- term, intimate, and healthy relationships outside of his immediate family.

Develop and maintain healthy relationships and relationship skills, while demonstrating responsible day-to-day behaviors. Identify and address risks to healthy living and build skills for getting needs met in prosocial ways.

5) School/work: Mr. V frequently changed jobs, with low levels of satisfaction associated with work experience.

Create motivation and develop skills for pursuit and maintenance of gainful employment on a consistent basis, while addressing educational options in regard to future employment/vocational goals.

6) Prosocial recreational activities: Mr. V had no history of involvement in organized prosocial activities and interests.

Improve time-management skills, incorporate hobbies and positive/social and leisure activities.

7) Social anxiety/Depressed mood: Mr. V presented with a moderate range of symptoms associated with depressed mood and moderate to high levels of anxiety when faced with social situations.

Refer for psychiatric assessment to consider use of psychotropic medication.
Enhance skills for responding to and managing factors that precipitate negative moods, including anxiety and depression.

| 8) Problems related to self-esteem: Mr. V presented with negative attitudes and poor perception of self. | Learn to identify and confront cognitive distortions that diminish self-esteem, and replace with attitudes that promote optimism and motivation for change. |

Progression through treatment was based on multiple factors, including: attendance; participation; completion of treatment assignments and materials; completion of treatment phases; satisfactory scores on quizzes/evaluations; reports from family and probation officers; compliance with terms of probation; evidence of day-to-day responsible behaviors; and no recurrence of sexual deviance or nonsexual offense behaviors. Prior to treatment completion Mr. V had to demonstrate an ability to clearly recognize behavioral and thought patterns that contributed to offense behaviors and develop adaptive coping responses to effectively manage social and sexual functioning. To remain in the treatment program, he needed to demonstrate a willingness and ability to apply newly learned behaviors. Throughout the process the Sex Offender Treatment Needs and Progress Scale (McGrath, Cumming, Livingston, & Hoke, 2003) was utilized to assist in evaluation of progress. This scale contains 22 risk factors linked to sexual offending. The factors identified are dynamic and targets for intervention. There is an updated version newly named the Sex Offender Treatment Intervention and Progress Scale (SOTIPS) (McGrath, Cummings, & Lasher, 2012).

In response to identified needs utilizing the RNR model, strategies and interventions consistent with sex offense specific treatment were applied. Mr. V was referred for psychiatric assessment at the onset of treatment and it was determined that the use of psychotropic medication was not warranted. The consulting physician ascertained that although Mr. V presented with a significant history of compulsive sexual behaviors, there was no evidence of compulsive features in other areas of his life. It was further assessed that his depressed mood was primarily situational in response to his legal consequences, and his anxiety in response to social challenges could be managed effectively via cognitive-behavioral interventions. It was agreed that Mr. V would remain open to further psychiatric assessment.

The primary method of treatment with Mr. V was individual based cognitive-behavioral therapy (CBT). There is evidence for CBT as being an effective response to sexual offending behaviors in general (Grossman, Martis, & Fichtner, 1999). Frequently with CBT in response to sexual deviance, interventions are enhanced by using various workbooks, such as *The Sex Addiction Workbook* (Sbraga & O'Donohue, 2003); *The Adult Relapse Prevention Workbook* (Steen, 2001); and *Cybersex Unhooked* (Delmonico, Griffin, & Moriarity, 2001). Group therapy is often the treatment of choice and preferred in larger sex offense specific treatment programs which respond to various types of offending behaviors. That format was available to Mr. V., although the treating clinician opted not to involve Mr. V in that treatment method as the type of offenders were primarily hands-on, and Mr. V had no history of hands-on offending. The clinician referred Mr. V to a community based non-sex-offense specific treatment program that provided a range of skill building groups for adults. He began weekly participation in group therapy after completing his first 3 months of individual therapy. The social skills group addressed basic conversational skills, and progressed to management of anxiety in social situations. He provided consent for the individual and group therapists to exchange information, and for the group therapists to report directly to his probation officer regarding attendance and participation. Mr. V consented to having his parents and siblings participate in family therapy periodically to assist in relapse prevention planning and monitoring. To address treatment goals, specific phases were developed in response to Mr. V's needs. Below is a brief description of each phase and what Mr. V addressed:

Phase I Psychoeducational: Create motivation for change; introduction to strength and promotion based strategies; introduction to relapse prevention: develop early safety and RP plan; factors for true consent in sexual situations; identification of laws associated with sexual behaviors; consequences for offenders; deviant sexual interests vs. healthy sexual interests; factors to consider in pursuit of healthy relationships; introduction to lapse reporting and the abstinence violation effect (AVE); test on Phase I.

Phase II Accountability/Responsibility: Introduction to the CBT as core program philosophy and technique for promoting personal responsibility; thinking errors/cognitive distortions general and specific to offense history; the problem of immediate gratification (PIG); examination of motivational factors associated with problems in life management and how they were linked to offending behaviors; introduction to emotional regulation; revisit offense history and full disclosure; introduction to accountability to others via clarification process (to be initiated after demonstrating competence with empathy); continue theme of healthy life promotion; revisit safety/RP plan; continue to monitor lapses; continued reporting on efforts to promote healthy living; test on Phase II.

Phase III Empathy Training: Introduction to empathy as critical life skill; strategies for building empathy; empathy as a barrier to the problem of immediate gratification (PIG) and the manager of thinking errors; empathy in general and specific to offense behaviors; empathy-remorse-shame; examination of impact of sexual abuse: general and specific; empathy for self in regard to any history of negative life exposures/experiences; continue clarification process; continue healthy life promotion; revisit safety/RP plan; monitor lapses; test on Phase III.

Phase IV Healthy Living/Positive Self-Regulation: Mission statement for healthy living; simple reminders for assumption of responsibility; internal compass for the path to healthy living; revisit the problem of immediate gratification and thinking errors; primary risks to healthy living; examination and use of CBT interventions to confront history of negative exposures/experiences; introduction to assertiveness, problem solving, and review of emotional regulation; additional skills to promote healthy living concepts and relationships; revisit safety and RP plan; monitor lapses; test on Phase IV.

Phase V Relapse Prevention: Revisit core RP concepts as offender prepares for treatment follow-up phase; test on RP concepts and review of written RP plan. Relapse prevention is based on the notion that certain factors, if not managed, create greater risk for re-offense. Therefore, the core strategies are associated with identification of those factors, while developing skills, techniques, and strategies for responding that prevent recurrence of the targeted behavior. Relapse prevention planning is attained by incorporating the components addressed throughout the course of treatment: accountability/responsibility; confrontation of thinking errors; lapse reporting; empathy training; social skills training.

Phase VI After Care-Follow-Up: Review structure for follow-up sessions; assign summary report form to prepare for each follow-up session that addresses strengths, challenges, interventions, and personal goals for that time period.

Mr. V was able to complete the core treatment steps within 18 months, while attending on a weekly basis. Upon completion of the comprehensive program, a follow-up period was provided. Mr. V participated in 6 months of twice per month therapy sessions (individual or family). Follow-up sessions continued at a reduced frequency with a minimum of one per month until his release from probation, with the understanding he could increase the frequency of sessions as needed.

Through the course of treatment, reports were provided to supervising agencies within the containment team that addressed his progress and participation. Monthly summaries continued during follow-up and a final report was sent upon completion of the follow-up phase.

Treatment Issues

Therapists often encounter the constraints of the real world versus the ideal when attempting to implement "best practice" treatment. Constraints can include therapist licensure limitations or scope of practice limitations for available treatment providers, agency protocols, legal/jurisdictional issues, availability of certain types of interventions (testing, polygraph, arousal assessment, group therapy), and financial resources available to the offender. Although these are often issues for any treatment provider, the impact of such constraints is more problematic as a therapist attempts to respond to the needs of the sex offender. Not only does the therapist have an obligation to provide best practice response to the client, the therapist also has an obligation to consider community safety. This double edged sword necessitates the therapist finding the delicate balance between his or her responsibility to the community and yet establishing a therapeutic alliance with the client. Many states are experiencing extensive legislative responses in regard to the management of sexual offenders who reside in the community. These mandates often require application of interventions that are not readily available in a given community, or interventions where no funding is attached. Often providers are put in a position to do the best they can with what they have available.

In treating Mr. V, an ethical dilemma presented itself at the onset of treatment regarding his placement in group therapy, which has often been cited as "best practice" and standard in sex offender treatment programs (Sawyer, 2011). In Mr. V's community, although a sex offense specific group based treatment response was available, that program did not distinguish between hands-off and hands-on offenders for participants. The model was "one size fits all." Mr. V's provider opined it was not in the best interest of Mr. V to align him therapeutically with hands-on sexual offenders ("careful what you wish for" philosophy), given no evidence of progression toward such behaviors. As pointed out by Ball,

> For several reasons, whenever possible we recommend that sexually compulsive clients not be placed in the same group as sexual abusers of children. First, there are few real similarities between the offenses of each and between the personality organizations of the offenders themselves. In most cases there are few similarities between the compulsive urges that exhibitionists struggle with and the chronic emotional and physical attraction of pedophiles to children. (Ball & Seghorn, 2011, pp. 35–12)

There is a lack of scientific data regarding the best practice response to voyeurs who have not escalated to hands-on sexual offending behaviors. With the lack of such data, the therapist is left only with clinical judgment in response to the client's needs. Mr. V presented with significant skills deficits and personality inadequacies. The need was to focus on promoting prosocial skills and development, and he received group therapy specific to those needs. A treatment group specific to hands-off offenders would have been considered if available.

Apart from the constraints to successful therapy that the therapist and the community bring, are the complications/limitations that the offender brings to the treatment process. Mr. V did not have challenges intellectually that would have required finding a sex offense treatment provider with expertise in responding to the needs of the intellectually challenged offender. Availability of such providers can be an issue. Although Mr. V presented with some degree of depression and anxiety, other than a consultation with a psychiatrist, these issues were successfully treated within the context of his treatment program. In situations where the issues of comorbidity present more of a challenge it often becomes necessary to expand the treatment team and to coordinate treatment with these additional providers. Establishing a coordinated treatment approach and ongoing consistent interactions among the providers and the probation/parole officer are critical components for successful treatment, and would maintain consistency with the Containment Model. The offender's cultural background could also influence the treatment process. The therapist needs to be aware of cultural differences and how they impact the treatment process. Given the complex nature of sex offender treatment, some degree of cross-cultural competence is necessary (Carrasco & Garza-Louis, 2011).

The offender's level of motivation and cooperation in treatment are evidenced by attendance, active participation, completion of tasks, and additional prepost test measures. Treatment can be more challenging when the offender's personality style negatively impacts the process. Mr. V had excellent attendance, and was compliant with treatment tasks, contracts, and probation terms. For those individuals who are noncompliant with treatment, closer communication within the containment team is often required and makes a strong case in support of the Containment Model. A more intensive response might include more frequent probation/parole visits, electronic monitoring, surveillance, more frequent therapy sessions, and consultation with other providers. Noncompliance in treatment, or treatment failure could lead to probation/parole violations. An offender may require residential treatment or periods of incarceration due to increased risk to the community.

Most offenders initially present with levels of denial that extend through phases of treatment (Freeman-Longo, & Blanchard, 1998). With Mr. V, the primary level of denial was "denial of impact." This occurs when the offender minimizes harm to a victim. For the voyeur this is a typical level of denial, as they often perceive no harm to a victim if they have not been caught looking and the offense was hands-off (Hanson & Harris, 1997). The treatment task was to help Mr. V understand the potential harm for others that resulted from his acts of voyeurism. This was initially achieved by discussing vignettes about other life circumstances depicting an individual's rights being violated unbeknownst to the victim, and the offender escaping without detection. This level of denial was further challenged with Mr. V by addressing the notion of harm to self, in that repeated acts of "peeping" supported by his belief of no harm to others had maintained the behaviors, ultimately leading to his legal situation and other negative consequences. The latter was initially more useful in promoting his assumption of responsibility for the offending behaviors because in doing so it appealed to his self-interest. His awareness of "harm to self" helped generate motivation to prevent recurrence and opened the door for enhancement of empathy. He was able to grasp the distorted thinking associated with the offense pattern and began to understand how empathy could create a barrier to continued offenses. Essentially the goal was to get Mr. V creatively engaged in establishing as many roadblocks as possible so as to enable him to avoid re-offending, and that included awareness of harm to others. This aspect of treatment was strengthened as he completed the treatment phase associated with empathy training. Categorical denial is more challenging because the offender maintains the behavior did not occur yet pleaded or was found guilty to a sexual offense related charge. This level of denial creates ethical challenges for the treatment provider. "Denial might also be considered as a responsivity factor that can interfere with treatment progress. Offering a reasonable time period for therapeutic engagement might provide a better alternative than automatically refusing treatment to categorical deniers" (Levenson, 2011, p. 346). Some programs develop specialized responses to these types of situations (Marshall, Thornton, Marshall, Fernandez, & Mann, 2001).

In responding to the needs of any offender, motivating the client to "buy into" the relapse prevention concept can be difficult. Adhering to this approach requires self-monitoring and willingness to report on thoughts, feelings, and behaviors that could go to identifying increased risk. For the client, reporting on these matters can create concern about not being seen in a favorable light by the provider, and interpreted as not progressing in treatment. The other challenge for the offender is "giving up" the pleasure based behavior and turning toward other means for getting core needs met. Mr. V had some challenges in this regard, especially given his ongoing need to be viewed in a favorable light. There were times in which he lapsed in regard to accessing adult pornography via the Internet. These unreported lapses were uncovered during prepolygraph interviews, then confirmed in polygraph examinations. Essentially Mr. V would "come clean" with the lapses when it was time to undergo a maintenance polygraph examination. It was important for the clinician to be empathetic in responding to Mr. V's lapses to prevent polarization in the therapeutic relationship. Helping Mr. V see lapse reporting as part of a "team" approach for promoting a healthy life was critical. There is emerging evidence that supports the promotion versus avoidance concept in relapse prevention programming because it serves to enhance an offender's motivation in treatment (Mann, Webster, Schofield, & Marshall, 2004). An empathetic response, while also working to enhance motivation toward treatment compliance was necessary with Mr. V given his pervasive challenges with self-esteem. A central task with Mr. V was helping him develop trust in the therapeutic process as he worked to acquire "new skills" to replace old negative styles for coping and responding to life challenges. Anechiarico (2011) wrote, "To say that offenders have low self-esteem is incomplete. It is more accurate to say that their self-esteem is fragile and unstable—a sense of self that is vulnerable to assault and feelings of shame without adequate resources to make repairs when damaged" (pp. 6–3).

The consistency of the Containment Model with Mr. V eventually motivated him to report lapses as they occurred rather than waiting until he was scheduled for a polygraph. His lapse reporting was also verified via polygraph examinations and toward the end of treatment he was no longer disclosing new lapses during the polygraph. There was never evidence of continued acts of voyeurism in his lapse reporting or polygraph examinations. An ethical dilemma is presented when an offender fails relevant polygraph questions specific to offense behaviors, yet fails to admit to the behaviors, or admits, yet victims are not identified. Should the offender be charged again? Can the offender be legally charged? Does the failed polygraph examination constitute a parole/probation violation? Should a failed polygraph examination result in dismissal from treatment, or be a condition to warrant further or more intensive treatment? Many sex offense specific treatment programs consider the polygraph to be a tool to assist with treatment compliance, "the polygraph should be used as an investigative, risk assessment, and treatment tool, not as a final arbitrator of guilt or innocence" (Green, Franklin, & Lanzafama, 2011, pp. 67–69). Other programs resist use of this tool due to the ethical challenges, and at times, lack of availability in a specific community. As Vess points out, "Despite its increasing use, polygraph testing is considered controversial, with little consensus regarding its accuracy or appropriate applications. On the basis of the current state of the professional literature regarding the polygraph, its use with sex offenders raises unresolved ethical concerns" (Vess, 2011, p. 381).

Mr. V's lapses involved continued use of Internet pornography. The issue of pornography as it relates to sex offender treatment is also creating considerable debate in the therapeutic community. Specifically, is it harmful and significantly linked to re-offense rates? Are there some benefits to be derived for the offender from continued viewing of pornography? Are the assumptions about the harm essentially just that—assumptions? What is the empirical evidence that indicates harm? With Mr. V, it was not a stretch to link repeated and persistent viewing of others via pornography to his offending behaviors. Eliminating the use of pornography during his term of probation was a court sanction and violating that sanction could have led to significant consequences. Prohibiting the use of pornography is typical and consistent with most jurisdictions subscribing to the Containment Model. According to the Center for Sex Offender Management, jurisdictions have imposed additional special conditions of supervision that address: Computer/Internet Restrictions: Offenders must not use the Internet without permission of their supervising officer and offenders must submit to an examination and search of their computer to verify that it is not utilized in violation of their supervision and/or treatment conditions. Other Technology Restrictions: Offenders will not possess a camera, camcorder, or videocassette recorder/player without the approval of their supervising officer. (2000, p. 8)

The treatment task was to help Mr. V understand the potential costs associated with continued use of pornography, while working to develop healthy connections with others that were not based primarily in sexual gratification.

Treatment Outcome/Termination

The possibility of a positive treatment outcome is enhanced when the therapist is willing to stay informed and knowledgeable about best practice standards in the field of sex offender treatment, and also has the ability to be innovative and creative if the ideal components for successful treatment prove to be elusive. Perhaps that combination is really the art of any effective therapy: clinical judgment as to how to implement best practice standards within the confines of one's own therapeutic context. The sex offender treatment field is ever evolving, but fortunately for the interested provider, ongoing training and resources are available. Additionally, effective treatment is more likely when the therapist can maintain an empathetic stance while still holding the offender accountable. The level of motivation an offender brings to the treatment process varies by individual, but can definitely be diminished if the therapist turns the accountability process into an adversarial process. As previously mentioned, this would be even more detrimental when treating an individual like Mr. V where he entered therapy lacking the skills to cope effectively with negative social emotion and with social anxiety. The therapy process can be experienced as overwhelming for the offender, simply in terms of the financial and time commitment required, never mind the amount of information and skill sets an individual must learn to incorporate in his or her daily life. Creating a structured treatment plan with clear-cut and concrete expectations addressed in a stepwise fashion, allows the individual to experience successes throughout the treatment process. The focus is not just on the end result, but also on the process of getting there.

Termination of treatment can be abrupt, as in situations where the offender is incarcerated for a probation/parole violation, treatment failure, or for a re-offense. Treatment can end prematurely if the legal mandate requiring treatment ends prior to the completion of treatment, and the offender does not choose to voluntarily continue. Ideally, the decision to terminate treatment results from the offender having completed all the elements of a detailed treatment plan. Having such a specific treatment plan clarifies for both the therapist and the offender when it is appropriate to terminate treatment.

Mr. V was on probation for 5 years. He participated in weekly outpatient therapy for the first 18 months of his probation, complemented by weekly non-sex-offense specific group therapy emphasizing social skills and management of anxiety and depression. He participated in follow-up therapy for the remainder of his probation. Strengths associated with his treatment and supervision experiences were reviewed with Mr. V prior to termination to encourage continued compliance and promote the healthy living concept. His relapse prevention plan was thoroughly reviewed, with an emphasis on strategies for responding to primary risks associated with lack of connections, social isolation, and reliance on Internet pornography to get social and sexual needs met. Mr. V maintained a treatment binder which was available for him to keep post-treatment. That binder included various treatment "reminder cards" to encourage application of core treatment concepts beyond therapy. The reminder cards were designed not to reveal his sexual offense history. These reminder cards were provided due to the unlikelihood that any offender actually maintains treatment materials that reveal their sexual offense history and could possibly be found by others.

At time of release, Mr. V had been employed for 3 years at a local restaurant. He completed his skills training group therapy, and established some healthy peer centered connections and interests. Mr. V joined a local gym, and began to actively pursue recreational and educational interests. Mr. V was taking two college level courses and was interested in pursuing a degree in business. He also began volunteering at a local senior center in an attempt to "give back" to his community. The final polygraph examinations did not indicate deception in regard to treatment contracts, and terms of probation.

During Mr. V's 5-year imposed hiatus from viewing Internet pornography, the world of Internet pornography continued to expand, offering more options and variations for the viewer. Even with restrictions in place, and knowing that he would undergo polygraph examinations, Mr. V struggled with lapses regarding the viewing of Internet pornography. Despite all the therapeutic interventions that were put in place prior to his release from probation and treatment, his most significant challenge might be how he manages his choices regarding the use of pornography now that he is living with unrestricted access to the Internet. Obviously, many outcomes are possible.

Conclusions/Future Directions

"Looking at others" is a popular modern pastime. Although many enjoy the intrusiveness of technology and social media into the lives of others, evidenced by the upswing in TV reality shows, when an individual's privacy is invaded without their permission, the resulting feelings are those of violation, fear, and outrage. The legal system has specified the limits of that unsolicited "looking," and when a person violates those limits and is arrested for voyeurism, stalking, capturing the image of another or a related crime, clinical intervention is often mandated. In the absence of compelling research support for a particular assessment or treatment approach specific to the voyeur, we would advocate the use of the Risk Need Responsivity Model. It is an encompassing model that is currently considered a "best practice" for the treatment of many types of sexual offenders. The vast use of the RNR makes it possible to gather data specific to the application of that model, which might increase the possibility of developing a body of research specific to working with the voyeur. Relevant to that research direction we would encourage research addressing the impact of sex offender group work specific to the voyeur. As noted earlier, Mr. V was referred to a non-sex-offending social skills group rather than a mixed sex offender group. Research looking at the impact of the voyeur participating in a group that mixes hands-off sexual offenders with hands-on sexual offenders, and groups that are exclusive to hands-off sexual offenders, or no sex offender group treatment are relevant research topics.

The RNR Model in conjunction with the Containment Model promotes the use of the polygraph as an adjunct to treatment. Use of the polygraph in sex offender treatment programs is still considered controversial by some, so research clarifying the application of the polygraph in treating the "classic/contemporary" voyeur merits further exploration. In the case of Mr. V the polygraph examinations influenced honest lapse reporting, especially regarding use of pornography. Relying solely on the therapeutic connection to encourage honest reporting by the client that could lead to negative outcomes for the client may not be realistic. That said, we are not implying it doesn't happen. Hence the controversy and need for more research.

Another issue is the need for a legal response to those who engage in acts of voyeurism that would hold them accountable and allow for early interventions to occur rather than downplaying or minimizing the behaviors as nuisance offenses. The possibility of escalating to a compulsive pattern and creating more victims is great with this type of offense given the low behavior-to-getting-caught ratio. Had Mr. V's case been responded to more seriously early on the escalation may have been prevented.

A lively debate is occurring in the sex offender treatment field regarding the harm associated with sexual offenders continuing to view pornography while in treatment. One prevailing question is, "Should viewing pornography for sexual offenders always be prohibited?" Some sex offender treatment providers are wondering, "Are there instances in which allowing a sexual offender to access pornographic materials during treatment warranted and even therapeutic?" In the case of the voyeur, they are already associating with the world through looking. It would seem that Internet or other types of pornography are methods that continue to promote looking at others for sexual pleasure and arousal versus promoting healthy, prosocial relationships. It would seem that continued viewing of pornography by the voyeur would perpetuate avoidance of relationships, and keep the voyeur invested in viewing others as a primary means for getting a range of needs met. An argument could be made that in the case of most voyeurs, consistently restricting use of such material during their period of supervision makes greater sense given the obvious association with the offending behaviors.

As promised, we likely have raised more questions than provided answers. Maybe the best way to raise self-esteem is to lower expectations?

References

Abel, G. G. (2011). Abel assessment for sexual interest. Retrieved from http://www.abel-screening.com

American Psychiatric Association. (2000). *Diagnostic and statistical manual of mental disorders* (4th ed., text rev.). Washington, DC: Author.

Anechiarico, B. (2011). A closer look at sex offender character pathology and relapse prevention—An integrative approach. In B. K. Schwartz (Ed.), *Handbook of sex offender treatment* (pp. 6-1–6-7). Kingston, NJ: Civic Research Institute.

Ball, J., & Seghorn, T. K. (2011). Diagnosis and treatment of exhibitionism and other sexual compulsive disorders. In B. K. Schwartz (Ed.), *Handbook of sex offender treatment* (pp. 35-1–35-17). Kingston, NJ: Civic Research Institute.

Bonta, J., & Andrews, D. A. (2007). Risk-need-responsivity model for offender assessment in rehabilitation. Retrieved from http://www.publicsafety.gc.ca/res/cor/rep/risk_need_200706-eng.aspx

Bumby, K. (1995). Bumby Cogitive Distortion Scale In R. P. Edmunds (Ed.), *Assessing sexual abuse: A resource guide for practitioners* (pp. 81–84). Brandon, VT: Safer Society Press.

Burns, D. D. (1990). *The feeling good handbook*. New York, NY: Penguin.

Buss, A., & Durkee, A. (1957). An inventory for assessing different kinds of hostility. *Journal of Consulting Psychology, 21,* 343–349.

Butcher, J. N. (1989). *Minnesota Multiphasic Personality Inventory-2.* Retrieved from http://psychcorp.pearsonassessments.com/HAIWEB/Cultures/en-us/Productdetail.htm?Pid=MMPI-2&Mode=summary

California Sex Offender Management Board (CASOMB). (2012). Sex offender treatment program certification requirements. Retrieved from http://casomb.org/

Canadian Privacy Law Blog. (2006.). First conviction under Canada's new voyeurism law. Retrieved from http://blog.privacylawyer.ca/2006/08/first-conviction-under-canadas-new.html

Canning, A., Netter, S., & Goldwert, L. (2009). Erin Andrews' lawyer: Stalker secretly taped 17 other women. Retrieved from http://abcnews.go.com/GMA/espns-erin-andrews-attorney-hotel-security-lax-guests/story.

Carrasco, N., & Garza-Louis, D. (2011). Hispanic sex offenders—Cultural characteristics and implications for treatment. In B. K. Schwartz (Ed.), *Handbook of sex offender treatment* (pp. 45-1–45-10). Kingston, NJ: Civic Research Institute.

Center for Sex Offender Management. (2008). *Twenty strategies for advancing sex offender management in your jurisdiction.* Silver Spring, MD: U.S. Department of Justice.

Davis, M. H. (1980). A multidimensional approach to individual differences in empathy. *The Journal Supplement Abstract Service Catalog of Selected Documents in Psychology, 10,* 85.

Delmonico, D. L., Griffin, E., & Moriarity, J. (2001). *Cybersex unhooked: A workbook for breaking free of compulsive online sexual behavior.* Wickenberg, AZ: Gentle Path Press.

Dempster, R. J., & Hart, S. D. (2002). The relative utility of fixed and variable risk factors in discriminating sexual recidivists and nonrecidivists. *Sexual Abuse: A Journal of Research and Treatment, 14,* 121–138.

Department of Justice Canada. (2012, August). *Voyeurism as a criminal offence: A consultation paper.* Ottawa, ON, Canada: Author. Retrieved from www.justice.gc.ca/eng/cons/voy/toc-tdm.html

Freeman-Longo, R. E., & Blanchard, G. T. (1998). *Sexual abuse in America: Epidemic of the twenty-first century.* Brandon, VT: Safer Society Press.

Freund, R. A., & Dougher, M. J. (2011). Clinical assessment of sex offenders. In B. K. Schwartz (Ed.), *Handbook of sex offender treatment* (pp. 19-1–19-12). Kingston, NJ: Civic Research Institute.

Green, P., Franklin, B., & Lanzafama, R. S. (2011). The sex offender, the polygraph, and community corrections. In B. K. Schwartz (Ed.), *Handbook of sex offender treatment* (pp. 67-1–67-11). Kingston, NJ: Civic Research Institute.

Grossman, L. S., Martis, B., & Fichtner, C. G. (1999). Are sex offender's treatable? A research overview. Retrieved from http://www.ps.psychiatryonline.org/article

Hanson, R. K. (1997). *The development of a brief actuarial risk scale for sexual offense recidivism: User report 1997–04.* Ottawa, ON, Canada: Solicitor General of Canada.

Hanson, R. K. (2000). *Risk assessment* (ATSA Informational Packages, No. 1). Beaverton, OR: Association for the Treatment of Sexual Abusers.

Hanson, R. K., Gizzarelli, R., & Scott, H. (1994). Hanson Sex Attitude Questionaire. In R. P. Edmunds (Ed.), *Assessing sexual abuse: A resource guide for practitioners* (pp. 94–95). Brandon, VT: Safer Society Press.

Hanson, R. K., & Harris, A. J. R. (1997). Voyeurism: Assessment and treatment. In D. R. Laws & W. T. O'Donahue (Eds.), *Sexual deviance: Theory, assessment and treatment* (pp. 297–310). New York, NY: Guilford.

Hanson, R. K., & Scott, H. (1995). Assessing perspective taking among sexual offenders, non-sexual criminals and non-offenders. *Sexual Abuse: A Journal of Research and Treatment, 7,* 259–277.

Hanson, R. K,. & Thornton, D. (1999). *Static-99 Improving actuarial risk assessments for sex offenders.* Ottawa, ON, Canada: Department of the Solicitor General.

Hare, R. (2012). *Psychopathy Checklist Revised*. Retrieved from http://www.hare.org/scales/

Harris, A., Phenix, A., Hanson, K. R., & Thornton, D. (2003). Static 99 coding rules revised. Retrieved from http://www.publicsafety.gc.ca/res/cor/rep/_fl/2003-03-stc-cde-eng.pdf

Kaplan, M. S., & Krueger, R. B. (1997). Voyeurism: Psychopathology and theory. In D. R. Laws & W. T. O'Donahue (Eds.), *Sexual deviance: Theory, assessment and treatment* (pp. 297–310). New York, NY: Guilford.

Lavin, M. (2008). Voyeurism: Psychopathology and theory. In D. R. Laws & W. T. O'Donahue (Eds.), *Sexual deviance: Theory, assessment and treatment* (pp. 305–319). New York, NY: Guilford.

Levenson, J. S. (2011). "But I didn't do it": Ethical treatment of sex offenders in denial. *Sexual Abuse: A Journal of Research and Treatment, 23*(3), 346–364.

McGrath, R. J., Cumming, G. F., Livingston, J. A., & Hoke, S. E. (2003). Outcome of a treatment program for adult sex offenders: From prison to community. *Journal of Interpersonal Violence, 18*, 3–17.

McGrath, R. J., & Hoke, S. E. (2002). *Vermont assessment of sex offender risk manual*. Retrieved from http://www.csom.org/pubs/vasor.pdf

Mann, R. E., Ainsworth, F., Al-Attar, Z., & Davies, M. (2008). Voyeurism: Assessment and treatment. In D. R. Laws & W. T. O'Donahue (Eds.), *Sexual deviance: Theory, assessment and treatment* (pp. 320–335). New York, NY: Guilford.

Mann, R. E., Webster, S. P., Schofield, C., & Marshall, W. L. (2004). Approach versus avoidance goals in relapse prevention with sexual offenders. *Sexual Abuse: A Journal of Research and Treatment, 16*(1), 65–71.

Marshall, W. L., Thornton, D., Marshall, L. E., Fernandez, Y. M., & Mann, R. (2001). Treatment of sexual offenders who are in categorical denial: A pilot project. *Sexual Abuse: A Journal of Research and Treatment, 13*(3), 205–215.

McGrath, R. J., Cumming, G. F., & Lasher, M. P. (2012). *SOTIPS: Sex Offender Treatment Intervention and Progress Scale*. Retrieved from http://www.nij.gov/funding/2012/sotips-manual.pdf

Miller, G. A. (1988). SASSI Institute. Retrieved from http://www.sassi.com

Miner, M. H. (2002). Factors associated with recidivism in juveniles: An analysis of serious juvenile sex offenders. *Journal of Research in Crime and Delinquency, 39*, 421–436.

Minnesota Department of Corrections. (2007). Sex offender recidivism in Minnesota. Retrieved from http://www.doc.state.mn.us/documents/04-07SexOffenderReport-Recidivism.pdf

Multi Health System Inc. (2004). *LS/CMI Level of Service/Case Management Inventory*. Retrieved from http://www/mhs.com/product.aspx?gr=saf&prod=ls-cmi%id=resources

National Center for Prosecution of Child Abuse/National District Attorneys Association. (2009, March). *Voyeurism statutes*. Retrieved from http://www.ndaa.org/pdf/voyeurism_statutes_mar_09.pdf

Nichols & Molinder Assessments, Inc. (1984). *The original Multiphasic Sex Inventory (MSI)*. Retrieved from http://www.nicholsandmolinder.com

Paitich, D., Langevin, R., Freemen, R., Mann, K., & Handy, L. (1977). The Clarke SHQ: A clinical sex history questionnaire for males. *Archives of Sexual Behavior , 6*(5) 421–436.

Pearson Education. (1994). Million Clinical Multiaxial Inventory-3. Retrieved from http://psychcorp.pearsonassessments.com/HAIWEB/Cultures/enus/Productdetail. htm?Pid=PAg505

Pearson Education. (1996). Beck Depression Inventory. Retrieved from http://www. pearsonassessments.com/HAIWEB/Cultures/en-us/Productdetail. htm?Pid=015-8018-370

Pearson Education. (1997). Wechsler Adult Intelligence Scale-Third edition. Retrieved from http://pearsonassessments.com/HAIWEB/Cultures/en-us/Productdetail.htm?Pid= 015-8980-727

Pearson Education. (2012). Kaufman Brief Intelligence Test, Second Edition. Retrieved from http://www.pearsonassessments.com/HAIWEB/Cultures/en-s/Productdetail. htm?Pid=PAa32300

Radloff, L. (1977). The Center for Epidemiologic Studies Depression Scale. Retrieved from http://cesd-r.com

Sawyer, S. P. (2011). Group therapy with adult sex offenders. In B. K. Schwartz (Ed.), *Handbook of sex offender treatment* (pp. 37-1–37-16). Kingston, NJ: Civic Research Institute.

Sbgraga, T. P., & O'Donohue, W. T. (2003). *The sex addiction workbook.* Oakland, CA: New Harbinger.

Selzer, M. L. (1971, June). The Michigan Alcoholism Screening Test: The quest for a new diagnostic instrument. *American Journal of Psychiatry, 127,* 1653–1658.

Skinner, H. A. (1982). European Monitoring Centre for Drugs and Drug Addiction. Retrieved from Drug Abuse Screening Test (DAST). Retrieved from http://www. emcdda.europa.eu/html.cfm/index3618EN.html

Steen, C. (2001). *The adult relapse prevention workbook.* Brandon, VT: Safer Society Press.

Swinburne Romine, R. E., Miner, M. H., Poulin, D., Dwyer, S. M., & Berg, D. (2012). Predicting reoffense for community-based sexual offenders: An analysis of 30 years of data. *Sexual Abuse: A Journal of Research and Treatment, 24*(5), 501–514.

Thornton, D., & D'Orazio, D. (2012, May). Assessing criminogenic needs using SRA-FLV to assess. Paper presented at the California Coalition on Sexual Offending 15th Annual Training Conference.

Vess, J. (2011). Ethical practice in sex offender assessment: Consideration of actuarial and polygraph methods. *Sexual Abuse: A Journal of Research and Treatment, 23*(3) 381–396.

Watson, D., & Friend, R. (1969a). Measurement of social-evaluative anxiety. *Journal of Consulting and Clinical Psychology, 33,* 448–457.

Watson, D., & Friend, R. (1969b). Social Avoidance and Distress Scale (SADS). Retrieved from http://www.statisticssolutions.com/resources/directory-of-survey-instruments/ social-avoidance-and-distress-scale-sads

Wilson, G. (1978). Wilson Sexual Fantasy Questionnaire (SFQ). Retrieved from www. cymeon.com/fsq.asp

7

EXHIBITIONISM

A Case Study

Jill S. Levenson

Introduction

Exhibitionism is defined in the *Diagnostic and Statistical Manual of Mental Disorders* (4th ed., Text Rev., *DSM-IV-TR*; American Psychiatric Association, 2000) as a paraphilia characterized by "recurrent, intense sexually arousing fantasies, sexual urges, or behaviors involving the exposure of one's genitals to an unsuspecting stranger" (p. 569), which occurs over a period of at least 6 months and causes distress or impairment for the person engaging in the behavior. In an effort to better establish a pattern of deviant behavior, *DSM-V* proposals (which at this writing have not yet been finalized) add that the person "has sought sexual stimulation from exposing the genitals to three or more unsuspecting strangers on separate occasions" and also propose a specifier related to preferred age of the victim (American Psychiatric Association, 2010). A review of the literature from 1980 through 2008 found limited support for any further substantial changes in the criteria for this disorder (Langstrom, 2010).

The best known and most well-developed conceptual model of exhibitionism is that of the *courtship disorder* (Freund, 1990; Freund & Blanchard, 1986). Freund and his colleagues construed exhibitionism as a disturbance in the affiliation phase of courtship, which typically involves engaging potential partners through smiling, posturing, and conversation. The exhibitionist's exposure of his genitals was seen as an anomalous and misguided attempt to initiate an intimate interaction prior to appropriately establishing a relationship. In clinical settings, it is not uncommon for exhibitionists to describe their behavior not as a prelude to an interaction, but rather as a complete sexual act in and of itself (Morin & Levenson, 2008). The behavior is often described by clients as compulsive and habitual, and many exhibitionists have engaged in the act hundreds or thousands of times. It is unclear how a pathway to this deviation occurs within normal courtship development, and other researchers have questioned the concept of courtship disorder in favor of narcissism, suggesting that a more general and pathological need and desire for admiration and validation may contribute to the development of exhibitionistic behavior (Lang, Langevin, Checkley, & Pugh, 1987).

The *DSM-IV-TR* (American Psychiatric Association, 2000) does not offer a category in which we might classify a client with various sexually compulsive behaviors. In fact, excessive or habitual sexual behaviors do not conform to the *DSM* definition of compulsions, which are "repetitive behaviors that the person feels driven to perform in response to an obsession, or according to rules that must be applied rigidly" and which are aimed at "reducing distress..." (p. 462). Excessive sexual behaviors may be more analogous (but not quite identical) to the criteria described for substance abuse disorders, in which "a maladaptive pattern" (p. 199) of use leads to impairment or distress as manifested by a failure to fulfill roles or obligations, engaging in the behavior in situations involving risk, legal problems, or recurrent negative consequences. Kafka (2001a) suggested altogether avoiding the confusing use of the terms *sexual addiction* and *sexual compulsivity* and instead proposed a classification for *hypersexual disorders*.

Kafka and his associates (Kafka, 2001a, 2001b; Kafka & Hennen, 2002) argued that there are hypersexual individuals who engage excessively in a wide range of unconventional sexual behaviors. Kafka wrote: "Paraphilic disorders may be the proverbial tip of the iceberg of a broader range of sexual disorders characterized by excessive sexual appetite, sexual preoccupation, and repetitive impulsive enactment of sexual behavior despite adverse consequences" (Kafka, 2001a, p. 236). Kafka suggested that Paraphilia-Related Disorders can include engaging excessively in masturbation, promiscuity, pornography use, cybersex, or telephone sex—behaviors that when practiced with privacy and in moderation, are generally socially acceptable and not unlawful. Morin and Levenson (2008) noted that an important component of assessing exhibitionism is to distinguish between true exhibitionists (whose fantasies, urges, and behaviors involve exposing their genitals expressly for the sexual excitement they derive from being seen); public masturbators (who masturbate in public places with the possibility of being seen but without a clear desire to be observed); and compulsive masturbators (those whose hypersexual behavior—no matter how excessive or disruptive to their lives—is kept within the bounds of law and social acceptability).

This chapter will discuss a case study of a man diagnosed with Exhibitionism. The client acknowledged a pattern of exhibitionistic behavior almost daily from his college years until the age of 40 when he was sanctioned for the behavior by his medical licensing board. First, his psychosocial history will be described, followed by a case conceptualization. Next, the assessment process will be discussed, including assessment tools, differential diagnosis, and prioritization of treatment needs. Finally, the client's initial and maintenance treatment plans and progress will be described, along with some discussion about therapeutic process with this client specifically and when treating exhibitionism more generally.

Description of the Presenting Problem

The client, a 43-year-old white male who is a practicing medical doctor, was self-referred after a series of exhibitionistic incidents that ultimately resulted in loss of his employment. He reported that he engaged in public masturbation in front of hospital staff at his workplace. After local news coverage, he was asked to resign from his medical practice. He then reported himself to his state's impaired practitioner program, requesting therapeutic intervention. He initially entered into therapy voluntarily and is currently under a corrective action contract with the impaired practitioner program which reports to the state medical licensure board. No other disciplinary action was taken, nor was he arrested.

Client Background and History

The client reported that he was born in the Midwestern United States but was raised after age 7 in a Southern state. He has one older sister. He stated that he was raised by both parents; his father traveled frequently as a salesman and his mother ran a family owned store. He reported that his parents fought loudly and even violently at times and were often verbally abusive to each other and to the children. He said that his mother physically disciplined the children with a flyswatter and that he perceived her as "pretty scary at times." His father was not physically abusive, but regularly became enraged and verbally aggressive. However, the client also related many positive feelings toward his parents, whom he described as offering a strong sense of values and exposure to a variety of enriching activities and experiences. He described his parents as supportive and involved in his childhood extra-curricular activities. Education was highly emphasized.

The client described himself as growing up in an affluent home and community with parents who were strict disciplinarians. His parents, he said, took great pride in decorating the house, making certain it was immaculate and impressive, and were always the first on the block to have the newest technology, the best cars, and the nicest clothes. His parents were depicted as measuring value by what could be seen by others. He described a home in which love was expressed through material gifts, and where hard work and goal achievement were highly respected. The client, a sickly child with asthma, was unable to play sports and viewed himself as somewhat of a misfit among his peers. Because his parents greatly valued education, the client excelled in school, creating an identity for himself by which his worth to others (initially his parents) was measured by his intelligence and knowledge. Though he knew his parents loved him and that he could count on them for support, they had a keen ability to make the client feel small and inadequate through scalding verbal altercations. In fact, he reports feeling as though he constantly had to "prove himself" to gain his father's admiration and he did so through educational and occupational achievement.

He viewed his mother as critical and demanding, though he perceived her intentions as good. Both parents were emotionally distant, and nurturing was offered through gifts and rewards. His father, who traveled frequently, would spend time with the client doing household or garden chores, where the purpose of the activity was to accomplish a goal rather than to enjoy their time together. Efforts to express his feelings were often met with disapproval or disregard, and when he misbehaved or disappointed his mother he would "incur her wrath," leaving him with a perpetual feeling of being emotionally dismissed and perceiving that it was only his achievements that made him lovable. There were no indications that his father suffered from any sexual deviations; however, this is difficult to ascertain in a history.

The client reported that he was sexually abused at the age of 7 over a period of several months by a 13-year-old who was a friend of the family. The older boy introduced the client to a "game" in which he took the younger child outside in the woods, sexually fondled and fellated him, then took his clothes and ran away. The abuse occurred exclusively outdoors. The client found the "game" disturbing and humiliating but recalls that his body responded to the touch and he became aroused. This arousal produced a feeling of guilty confusion and led him to later question whether he was bisexual. Though the client never specifically disclosed the abuse to his parents, he did eventually express to his mother that he did not want to "play" with this boy anymore, and subsequently was not left alone with him.

At around age 12 or 13, the client discovered masturbation by accident while swimming in the family's pool. He was surprised by the outcome, and began to experiment to try to reproduce the orgasm. Eventually, he found copies of Playboy *magazine belonging to his father, and would masturbate to the pictures while fantasizing about the women. When anxious, he would masturbate to alleviate anxiety, and he reports he became "hooked." His first sexual relationship occurred at age 14 with a female schoolmate; they would "make out" and masturbate each other to orgasm while lying on her living room couch. He recalled that his arousal was heightened by the risk of being caught. While in high school, he and his girlfriend would engage in heavy petting, kissing, and on occasion even intercourse under the cover of a blanket while on a school bus transporting the students to band trips. According to the client, this behavior was common among students and it therefore appeared to him to be normal and acceptable.*

While in college, he would masturbate daily, sometimes multiple times per day, as a way to relieve tension and anxiety. Eventually, he began to masturbate in department store bathrooms, in the car when alone, or at work after hours. He would make certain that his genitals were obscured from view, but would watch women through the windows while he masturbated, using them as objects of stimulation. He sought out pornography depicting individuals engaged in outdoor sexual acts or acts that were performed in a car. He describes using masturbation like a drug, by which the orgasmic "high" could combat feelings of loneliness, worthlessness, and anxiety.

While the client was attending medical school, he would often watch young-adult to middle-aged women from inside his apartment, and would masturbate as they walked past the window. Typically the blinds were open just enough so that he could see out the window without being clearly visible from the outside. The behavior progressed to masturbating in the car while driving or in parking lots, using the visual stimulus of women for his arousal. While driving, he began to masturbate as another car was passing, and raise his hips so that they could get a glimpse as they passed. At other times, he would masturbate while placing an order at a drive through restaurant. He played a "game" to see if he could reach orgasm before arriving at the window to pick up his food. He claims that in these scenarios, he never showed his genitals to the individual at the pick-up window, due to fear of being arrested. Similarly, he masturbated in empty department store bathrooms trying to reach orgasm before someone would enter.

The client stated that he is exclusively heterosexual. He has been married for over 20 years and has two children from this marriage. He reported having "hundreds" of sexual partners in his life, all female. Currently, he and his wife are sexually active infrequently, and he has had no other partners in the past 2 years. He previously had numerous sexual encounters during his marriage, including with coworkers and escorts. In the past he viewed Internet pornography and masturbated daily but denies ever chatting with or arranging to meet someone he met online. He said that the pornography he viewed was consensual adult erotica only. He had engaged in soliciting prostitutes and had visited lingerie shops and Asian massage houses. He engaged in sexual behavior in the workplace in the form of pornography use, masturbation, exhibitionism, and extramarital affairs.

The client stated that aside from his current problems he had no prior psychiatric or psychological treatment with the exception of some brief marital counseling which was reportedly not very helpful. Following the incident of exposure at his workplace, he sought an evaluation facilitated by the state's impaired practitioner program and was referred to a treatment provider where he attended group and individual therapy. He reported currently taking Zoloft (150 mg daily) and believed that this medication helped minimize his sexual tendencies. He reported occasional alcohol use but denied excessive drinking or use of any other illicit drugs. He had never been arrested for a sexual or nonsexual offense.

Case Conceptualization

The client's description of his early childhood painted a picture of family life in which poor affect regulation was modeled by both parents, who yelled and screamed at each other and at the children as an expression of emotion and needs. His nurturing but demanding and critical mother was overly involved in her children's activities, and this enmeshment was viewed by the client as an expression of her interest in him but probably also represented her desire to monitor and control her children's behavior. His emotionally distant father emphasized performance and success as a way to accomplish personal well-being, and both parents may have used their children's achievements as a reflection of their own worth and successful parenting. As a result of the rejecting nature of these early relationships, the client appears to have suffered a narcissistic injury manifesting in a profound need for attention and external validation. His parents' focus primarily on his accomplishments—while at times devaluing the client's thoughts and feelings or implying that he was inferior or inadequate—appeared to have created a lasting pattern of attention-seeking and a need for approval. Most of his childhood validation was derived from performing and excelling in intellectual endeavors, whereby being noticed and praised was the vehicle for meeting emotional needs for acceptance, attention, and affection. Validation of his worth and value based on attributes other than his intellect was absent or limited in his interactions with both family and peers. Morin and Levenson (2008) noted that enmeshed, intrusive, or rejecting parents may "deprive a child of an appropriate sense of personal integrity or identity. Such a child may grow into adulthood with an intense need for attention and acknowledgement that manifests itself in a behavior which metaphorically cries 'look at me!' and 'notice me!'" (pp. 93–94).

Moreover, the family system appears to have modeled poor interpersonal boundaries in terms of frequent bouts of verbal abuse and name calling, violating both generational and emotional boundaries. The home environment lacked modeling of appropriate affect regulation, and masturbation quickly revealed itself to the client as an antidote to anxiety or internal distress. At the same time, his parents may have unwittingly reinforced, as a part of their affluent lifestyle, entitlement notions of being "deserving" and needing instant gratification. The poor boundaries and limited strategies for affect management, along with entitlement notions, seem to have paved the way for sex to be used to meet emotional needs, with his own immediate gratification taking priority over concern for the ways in which his behavior might violate the rights of others.

It appears that many of the client's earliest sexual experiences occurred out of doors, in public places, or with a risk of being caught. His first sexual experience was one of being sexually abused by a teen male; this abuse took place in the woods and involved leaving the abused boy naked, humiliated, and powerless. His early consensual sex with female age-mates also took place in semipublic settings (the living room, the bus) with a risk of being seen by others. He described his discovery of masturbation while in the swimming pool. His sexual arousal which occurred in outdoor or public settings, coupled with knowledge that the sexual behavior might be viewed as wrong and "getting away with it," appears to have produced a classical conditioning association that remained part of the client's sexual template for years to come. In other words, his sexual arousal appears to have been paired with an outdoor setting and risk of discovery. This classical conditioning response appears to have been incorporated into his romantic relationships early on, becoming part of his arousal patterns.

Furthermore, the client reports that he felt confused about his sexual orientation because he found the sexually abusive acts perpetrated upon him to be physically pleasurable. Consequently, though he knew he was attracted to women, he wondered if he was bisexual. This concern led to a pattern of excessive masturbation to pornography in an effort to "prove" to himself that he was heterosexual. He masturbated to female erotica and eventually escalated to masturbation while watching real women outside of his apartment or car windows. While the early manifestation of this behavior involved masturbation with a desire to remain unseen, he ultimately began increasing the risk of being seen through "games" (e.g., masturbating in a drive-through line hoping to finish before he reached the window). The apparent excitement of the risk of discovery finally led to a pattern of intentional exposure of his genitals while masturbating in public places.

The client described escalation in his behavior over the years as he and his wife grew distant in their marriage. Emotionally estranged from her, he longed for intimacy but felt rebuked by his wife, reinforcing his feelings of inadequacy and helplessness. He described his exhibitionism as a way to indulge his need for sexual gratification while controlling the situation, taking on little risk of rejection, and using the long-distance sexual encounter to manage his ambivalence about intimacy. Morin and Levenson (2008) noted that "an exhibitionist may feel extremely vulnerable and may avoid truly intimate relationships in an effort to protect himself from emotional harm. Thus, exposing may be a way to have sexual encounters and be validated in a type of distorted and protected long-distance illusion of intimacy. By establishing and maintaining control over the sexual encounter, the exposer is able to avoid the inherent risks of true emotional intimacy" (p. 94).

The case conceptualization above was driven primarily by self-report. Since reported history may not always be reliable, objective assessment strategies were utilized to further evaluate the client's strengths and needs.

Assessment Protocol and Differential Diagnosis

Assessment protocols or testing instruments specifically for exhibitionists have not been developed, and physiological measures of sexual interest have not been adequately studied to draw conclusions about their utility with exhibitionist populations. No significant research in the use of penile plethysmography (PPG) with exhibitionists over the past decade appears to have been conducted (Morin & Levenson, 2008), and Marshall (2006) concluded that there was "little support for the idea that these assessment procedures produce meaningful evidence on these offenders" (p. 18). The Abel Assessment for Sexual Interest (AASI; also referred to as the Abel Screen) has been used as a nonintrusive alternative to PPG for the assessment of sexual interest (Fischer, 2000; Hanson, 2002). Using viewing time as a measure of sexual interest, the AASI is easier to use in outpatient settings than the PPG, but has displayed shortcomings that have precluded its wide application, including concerns about its scoring format, reliability, and validity (Fischer, 2000). Although the test purports to include a scale that assesses exhibitionism (www.abelscreen.com) no information about the psychometric properties of the scale appears to be available for nonsubscribers. Published research papers on the psychometric properties of the instrument (Abel, Huffman, Warberg, & Holland, 1998; Letourneau, 2002) make no mention of the exhibitionism scale.

A recent survey asked mental health practitioners who treat exhibitionists about the primary areas they assess when evaluating such clients (Morin & Levenson, 2008). The most common areas identified were offense patterns and victim preferences (98%), frequency of behavior (98%), compulsivity (93%), duration of behavior (92%), motivation and amenability for treatment (85%), and variety of offending behaviors (85%). The clinicians also described other areas of focus, including attachment styles, early childhood victimization, symptoms of sexual addiction, and substance abuse. Most of this information can come only from the offender, and therefore it is the client's self-report that leads to the primary diagnosis and treatment plan for an exhibitionist (Maletzky, 1997; Morin & Levenson, 2008).

Morin and Levenson (2008) highlighted the importance of effective interviewing skills and creating a therapeutic alliance when assessing exhibitionism. Given the shame and stigma attached to sex offenses, clients may be reluctant to fully disclose behaviors in the initial stages of treatment. For these reasons, review of all available official documents can assist the clinician in obtaining as much objective information as possible. Police reports, victim statements, presentence investigation reports, criminal records of prior sexual and nonsexual offenses, prior mental health evaluations, and treatment progress updates can be used to better understand the offender's patterns, to challenge contradictions between his report and official versions, and to uncover important information that might be otherwise unrevealed by the client (Morin & Levenson, 2008).

A full history polygraph can also be useful in assessing the breadth and depth of a client's sexually abusive patterns. Many have criticized the clinical polygraph exam, citing poor validity and reliability and questioning whether the technique might be coercive and therefore unethical (Cross & Saxe, 1992, 2001). While not perfect, polygraph exams are more valid and reliable than commonly believed, and their utility lies not in the deceptive or truthful finding, but in their ability to facilitate disclosure of behavioral patterns and risk factors that might otherwise remain unknown (Levenson, 2009). It is well-established that polygraph examination elicits increased numbers of disclosures from offenders and that these disclosures are useful in assessment of offense patterns, case management, safety planning, and treatment planning (Ahlmeyer, Heil, McKee, & English, 2000; Emerick & Dutton, 1993; English, Jones, Pasini-Hill, Patrick, & Cooley-Towell, 2000; Heil, Ahlmeyer, & Simons, 2003; Hindman, 1988; Hindman & Peters, 2001; Humbert, 1990; O'Connell, 1998). A survey of sex offenders about the accuracy and utility of polygraph examination revealed a remarkable degree of similarity between offender reports and examiner reports; sex offenders reported that they agreed with examiners' opinions 90% of the time, reported increased honesty in therapy and with others in their lives, and reported that polygraph helped them comply with supervision and treatment requirements (Kokish, Levenson, & Blasingame, 2005).

In the case of Exhibitionism, Morin and Levenson suggested that the most crucial components in the assessment of exhibitionists appear to be the differential diagnoses of psychiatric comorbidity; the most prevalent disorders among sex offenders are mood disorders, anxiety disorders (especially social phobia), ADHD, and substance abuse (especially alcohol) (Kafka & Hennen, 2002). As well, diverse paraphilias and paraphilia-related disorders are often common among this population (Abel, Becker, Cunningham-Rathner, Mittelman, & Rouleau, 1988; Kafka, 2001b), and only by obtaining the most thorough psychosocial and offense history possible can the evaluator accurately assess the treatment needs of the exhibitionist (Morin & Levenson, 2008).

In the current case, some objective assessments were utilized in addition to self-report. MMPI-2 results indicated slight elevations on scales measuring depression, hypochondriasis, conversion hysteria, and psychopathic deviate. These scales suggest that the client may experience depressive, pessimistic, or guilt feelings. He may tend to exaggerate or complain about physical symptoms, and may have a tendency to convert internal conflicts related to dependency, sexuality, or aggression to physical symptoms; these characteristics may also suggest a tendency to manipulate. His slightly elevated score on the psychopathic deviate scale may reflect his tendency toward poor impulse control, poor judgment, entitlement, and breach of societal norms related to the problematic sexual behaviors.

An Abel Assessment of sexual interest was administered when the client received treatment at an intensive partial hospitalization program. The screening confirmed the client's report of sexual interest in exhibitionism, public masturbation, and voyeurism. Results indicated primary sexual interest in adult and adolescent females, with no elevated scores related to young children.

The client ultimately was found truthful on a full disclosure polygraph exam, further clarifying his sexual history. There were no indications that the client had any hands-on contact with victims of any age. The *DSM-IV* diagnosis was,

Axis I: 302.4 Exhibitionism, currently in remission
Axis II: No diagnosis, narcissistic personality traits

The client met criteria for Exhibitionism, as he had engaged in recurrent exposure of his genitals to unsuspecting strangers for over 20 years. The client appeared to suffer from an additional paraphilia-related hypersexual disorder involving excessive pornography use and scores of extramarital sexual encounters involving escorts, massage parlors, coworkers, and patients. He repeatedly engaged in these behaviors despite significant risks to his health, safety, marriage, and career.

According to the *DSM-IV-TR*, personality disorders represent an enduring pattern of experience and behavior that deviates from cultural expectations. This pattern is manifested in two or more domains of cognition, affect, interpersonal functioning, or impulse control. The pattern is inflexible and pervasive across a range of social situations, and leads to social or occupational distress or impairment. The client displayed several markers of narcissism, including grandiosity, a need for excessive admiration, and entitlement, but he did not meet full criteria for Narcissistic Personality Disorder. Though he had behaved in an interpersonally exploitive fashion in the context of his victimizing behaviors, and displayed arrogance at times, his behaviors appeared to be ego-dystonic and he demonstrated insight and empathy regarding the impact of his behavior on others.

In terms of prioritizing his treatment needs, the main concern was to help the client gain control of his exhibitionistic behavior. As the client entered a period of remission from his excessive sexual urges, treatment needs centered around affect regulation, interpersonal functioning in relationships, and cognitive reframing.

Treatment Plan

As noted above, exposing oneself can be a highly repetitive behavior and relapse is not unexpected. Notably, in the Static-99 (Hanson & Thornton,

1999), "any conviction for a non-contact offense" is a risk factor which increases the likelihood of any future sexual offending. A treatment outcome study which followed 61 exhibitionists for periods of up to 8 years found that treated exhibitionists recidivated at rates of 24 to 39%, depending on the treatment administered (Marshall, Eccles, & Barbaree, 1991). Of the untreated control subjects, 57% were charged with new sex offenses. However, the authors reported that when they gained access to subjects' police files containing reports of exposures that had not led to official charges, the recidivism rates were 2.3 times higher.

Initial Plan

Following his job loss and sanctioning by the medical ethics board, the client initially received an 8-week intensive day treatment program at a well-known sexual behavior institute designed to help him establish a period of remission in a safe, supportive, restricted environment. An intensive combination of group and individual therapy provided cognitive-behavioral treatment focused on building skills that would facilitate rapid improvement in self-regulation and problem solving.

Kafka's (2001a, 2001b) hypersexuality model links compulsive masturbation with poor impulse control, which in combination are likely to increase the risk for repetitive sexually deviant behavior. Similarly, Hanson and Harris (1998) described poor sexual self-regulation and sexual preoccupation as important dynamic risk factors for reoffense. Therefore, the client was immediately placed on Zoloft to help decrease sexual preoccupation and compulsive masturbation. In a series of studies (summarized in Greenberg & Bradford, 1997) it was found that three different SSRIs, fluoxetine (Prozac), fluvoxamine (Luvox), and sertaline (Zoloft) were equally effective in reducing deviant sexual fantasies and decreasing sexual impulsivity. Other studies have found statistically significant improvement in hypersexual symptoms associated with a variety of paraphilic and paraphilia-related behaviors (including compulsive masturbation and exhibitionism) when treated with SSRIs (Kafka, 1991, 1994; Kafka & Prentky, 1992).

The counseling curriculum included 15 hours of ammonia olfactory aversion therapy and covert sensitization training. These strategies were designed to reduce inappropriate sexual interests. In a survey of mental health providers working with exhibitionists, 48% reported using covert sensitization (Morin & Levenson, 2008). In this procedure, the offender visualizes an offense scenario and then pairs that image with a vividly detailed scenario of severe adverse consequences that would potentially follow from the offense (e.g., being arrested or sitting in court). A variant of this procedure, called *assisted covert sensitization*, is designed to boost the power of the method by adding a foul odor during the rehearsal of the aversive scene. Maletzky reported a relapse rate of only 13.3% with this technique in a sample of 155 patients (cited in Marshall et al., 1991). In Morin and Levenson's 2008 survey of clinicians, 20% reported using covert sensitization with ammonia as the noxious odor.

Although the client did not report any traditional issues with anger management (i.e., violent tendencies), his sexual acting out was hypothesized to be partly related to resentments and feelings of deprivation in his intimate relationships. He was therefore also exposed to 16 hours of anger management training to focus on identifying and responding to areas of resentment and anger. The client tended to avoid conflict and confrontation in an effort to maintain the approval and affection of those he deemed as being important to him. By focusing on better understanding the origins and triggers of his anger, he was helped to learn to manage situations that tended to elicit feelings of resentment as well as to express anger appropriately without fears of rejection. Along these same lines, the client also engaged in 8 hours of assertiveness training using role play, modeling, and social reinforcement. These techniques were designed to teach him to express his feelings appropriately and assertively in order to set limits with others and get his needs met in healthier ways. These strategies were also aimed at helping him with affect regulation and practicing more suitable interpersonal coping mechanisms. Intimacy education sought to increase awareness of what is required to achieve more balanced relationships, improve conflict resolution, and enhance communication with his wife and others in his life.

Cognitive restructuring training assisted the client to examine core beliefs and distorted schema about himself and others. As well, he was helped to identify the rationalizations, minimizations, and justifications he commonly used to excuse his own sexually deviant behavior. For instance, the client repeatedly told himself that he was entitled to satisfy his sexual needs and that his behavior was not harmful to others. By closely examining these thoughts, and observing the true and untrue components, he learned to recognize and correct distorted belief systems and to substitute more appropriate and healthy thoughts to guide his behavior and decision making.

The client also received 16 hours of relapse prevention training in which he examined his motivation for change, learned to identify risk situations, and developed a detailed plan to decrease the probability of reoffending (Laws, Hudson, & Ward, 2000; Marques & Nelson, 1989; Morin & Levenson, 2002). The plan and how it was implemented is discussed in more detail below in the maintenance section.

Sixteen hours of victim impact education assisted the client to become more aware of the various ways his inappropriate sexual behaviors impacted others, including his victims and his family (Fernandez, 2002; Marshall, Hamilton, & Fernandez, 2001). Because the client is a physician, 16 hours of sexual boundary training was added, designed to help him better understand the special obligations that clinical professionals have toward the patients they serve. Sexual harassment ethics, laws, and policies were reviewed, as were the harmful nature of dual relationships and the potential for coercion or exploitation. Furthermore, he participated in a professional misconduct group made up of other practitioners who had sexually violated others in the workplace.

Individual and group therapy were concurrently provided to focus on understanding personality issues, exploring the development of the sexual behavior problems, and increasing awareness of interpersonal patterns. Group therapy included both sex offender groups and sex addiction groups. The sex addiction groups used a 12-step model for maintaining recovery from problematic behaviors.

The client successfully completed the treatment plan described above. Success was determined by his compliance and attendance, his written work demonstrating intellectual understanding and application of treatment concepts, his verbal communication with staff and other clients, his observed and reported behavior demonstrating change in interpersonal interactions with others, and truthful polygraph examinations. A history polygraph exam was used to clarify the client's reported history of sexually problematic behavior and to rule out the existence of other paraphilias. Subsequent monitoring polygraph exams were utilized to determine whether he was currently abstaining from sexually inappropriate behavior in the community (for a more thorough discussion of the use of clinical polygraph exams in the assessment and treatment of sex offenders, see Levenson, 2009; Morin & Levenson, 2008). After successfully completing the treatment plan described above in an 8-week intensive day treatment setting, it was recommended that the client could return to the practice of medicine under conditions of a maintenance plan and the continuation of therapy on an outpatient basis. The client continued to be monitored by his state's impaired practitioner program, which made recommendations about practice to the medical licensing board.

Maintenance Treatment Plan

At the current time, the client remains in outpatient treatment. He is monitored by the state's impaired practitioner program, and participates in polygraph exams twice yearly to verify that he is not engaging in sexually inappropriate behavior in the workplace or community. He attends weekly group therapy in a sex offender group made up mostly of non-contact offenders, the focus of which included boundary issues, intimacy deficits, and cognitive distortions supporting inappropriate sexual behavior (Morin & Levenson, 2002, 2008; Murphy & Page, 2008). He attends individual therapy on a monthly basis to continue to explore the origins and development of his sexually problematic behavior, and to be purpose-fully cognizant of consequences to self and others resulting from these behaviors. He continues to monitor his thoughts, feelings, precursors, and behaviors associated with hypersexual patterns and to intervene accord-ingly. These interventions include a wide range of methods designed to avoid or escape from potentially risky situations, and to employ appropri-ate coping strategies to manage negative thoughts and feelings in difficult circumstances. He uses a daily log to chart his relapse prevention strate-gies and these specifically include: reading and listening to talk radio to deal with boredom and idle time; using cognitive strategies and self-talk to combat self-deprecating thoughts and depression; daily affirmations; exer-cising 30 minutes several times per week; 12-step meetings and readings several times per week; avoiding staying up at night watching television while family members sleep, as this behavior was a frequent precursor in the past to watching and masturbating to sexually explicit movies on TV; keeping his computer in a public area of the house; avoiding looking at pornography; and taking certain routes while driving that facilitate avoid-ance of temptations to masturbate while in the car.

The client also continually works on identifying and correcting dis-torted cognitions related to sexually problematic behavior and profes-sional boundaries in the workplace. For instance, in an effort to maintain more firm professional boundaries in the workplace, he avoids socializ-ing or personal talk with patients, coworkers, and subordinates; refrains from making sexual jokes or innuendos in the office; avoids lunching with female employees or hospital personnel; and no longer shares personal stories and information about himself at work.

Another area of treatment focus involves enhancing appropriate com-munication and intimacy skills, which is designed to achieve healthy, hon-est, and fulfilling sexual and emotional relationships. Particularly with his wife, the client works on assertiveness in expressing his needs, using "I" statements to focus on how he feels without blaming others, making more of an effort to understand and meet his wife's emotional needs on a daily basis, and to utilize conflict resolution strategies such as negotiation, compromise, and validation. The client has incorporated many important changes in his attitude toward and behavior with his wife. Despite these changes, however, he and his wife remain somewhat emotionally distant and unable to meaningfully discuss their marital problems. Their sexual relationship is infrequent and sporadic. The client is plagued with inner conflict about his marriage; on one hand, he is grateful to his wife for sticking with him throughout his professional crisis and relocating the family with him to another city, but on the other hand he is resentful that he still "walks on eggshells," feeling unable to express his needs to her in a way that allows him to feel heard and validated. This scenario, of course, is an ominous formula for re-creating the very circumstances contributing to his exhibitionism in the past in an effort to meet his emotional needs through sexual gratification.

The client attends Sex Addicts Anonymous meetings at least once per week in order to share and receive support from peers who are also attempting to manage sexually problematic behaviors. He completed his 12-step work with a sponsor, and is now considering becoming a sponsor for a fellow SAA groupmate. Empirical and theoretical literature suggests that self-help support groups can be instrumental in assisting individuals to combat compulsive behaviors, including sexual compulsivity (Wright, 2010).

In terms of sexual behavior management and monitoring, he participates in polygraph examinations twice per year to encourage honesty regarding his sexual behavior. The polygraph reports, along with monthly treatment progress summaries, are shared with the state's impaired practitioner program to demonstrate compliance with his licensure board corrective action plan and to ensure the safety of patients and coworkers. The client has also installed Internet filtering software to prevent use of pornography and other sexual material online.

The primary therapeutic modality currently used with the client is an interpersonal process approach, which combines elements of developmental, family systems, and cognitive models of understanding client behavior (Teyber & McClure, 2011). Exhibitionist clients often present for therapy with a range of interpersonal problems that stem from longstanding relational deficits and distorted thinking about themselves and others (Morin & Levenson, 2008). The interaction between client and therapist allows opportunities for immediacy interventions by responding to relational patterns as they present themselves in the therapeutic relationship (Teyber & McClure, 2011). Similar opportunities exist in the group process (Jennings & Sawyer, 2003). Relationship skills can be experienced and practiced, rather than simply taught, in a therapeutic environment that offers an opportunity for true intimacy, trust, and emotional safety. This is accomplished by exploring relational themes and maladaptive patterns that developed through rehearsal in response to significant events and relationships throughout the client's life (Teyber & McClure, 2011). Clients ultimately generalize new relational skills to others in their lives, enhancing both interpersonal experiences and general well-being. This type of personal growth would be expected to mitigate future urges to offend as the client adapts more healthy and successful strategies for meeting emotional needs.

For example, in an individual session the client related that he had recently masturbated, in private, in his home, while looking at an arousing photo of a partially dressed celebrity in a mainstream entertainment magazine. He asked the therapist if she thought that it was necessary for him to remain totally abstinent from masturbation. Instead of answering the question directly, the therapist empowered the client to examine this question for himself by talking through the important aspects of the behavior. The therapist facilitated exploration of the client's definitions of "healthy sexuality," the behavioral boundaries and parameters he'd set for himself, an appraisal of his sexual self-regulation, and definitions of "addictive" or "compulsive" that he might utilize to assess his own behavior. By encouraging self-reflection and self-determination, the therapist allowed the client to rehearse the problem-solving skills he needs to be able to draw upon in his daily life. Perhaps equally important, the therapist then wondered out loud why the client felt the need to ask the therapist her opinion in the first place. The client speculated that he was engaging in a long-term pattern of relating by which he seeks the approval of those he views as "authority" figures. By first asking the therapist her opinion, he was attempting to seek approval and avoid being chastised if he proffered the "wrong" answer. As well, he anticipated that his own ideas would not be valued (as was often his experience with his parents) and realized that he does not expect others to trust his judgment. In processing these core beliefs, the therapist was then able to assist the client to reaffirm his own worth, to take ownership of his recovery by trusting his own instincts, and to use new skills to critically reason out decisions. The process of using what was going on immediately within the session helped the client recognize relational themes, correct distorted cognitive schemas, rehearse healthy interpersonal encounters, and undergo a corrective emotional experience. He is beginning to recognize the myriad ways that his interactions with others are shaped by the filter of his own expectations.

Individual therapy also aims to help the client examine his behaviors in other contexts. For instance, in his professional life, he has had confrontations with other doctors after imposing himself in situations not truly requiring his intervention. He readily acknowledges his need to be a "hero" and to be seen as the smartest doctor in the practice. He recognizes that the "white coat" has allowed him to nurture his need to be valued and respected by others and to be viewed as special and important. As noted above, he has expressed a desire to become a sponsor to a groupmate in his 12-step program, and he and his therapist have processed the importance of being careful not to use sponsorship as a vehicle for indulging his own needs. In other words, he has to be vigilant in remembering that as a sponsor his role is to guide and support another person in his own recovery, not to act as an all-knowing teacher whom others must admire.

In the group therapy setting, the client sometimes responds to others by giving advice, offering information, or sharing his own experiences in a way that redirects the focus from other group members onto himself. Through gentle verbal observations of this dynamic, the therapist is able to help the client become aware of his tendency to be self-aggrandizing or self-absorbed, which is fueled by his need for admiration and validation from the therapist and other group members. Again, through the use of immediacy in the therapeutic setting, the therapist helps the client to process his interpersonal dynamics and recognize maladaptive behavior patterns.

Conclusion

Exhibitionism can be a highly compulsive and repetitive behavior and is therefore in some cases very difficult to treat. Because exposing is so easily and unobtrusively performed, many clients have engaged in hundreds or even thousands of offenses and have eluded sanctions in the vast majority of those events. In the current case, the client had engaged in this behavior thousands of times, and the behavior had become habitual. For this reason, the initial treatment plan involved psychiatric assessment and SSRI treatment, behavioral conditioning interventions, and cognitive-behavioral therapy modules in a restricted setting. The initial intensive 8-week day treatment program allowed the client an opportunity to attain remission in a safe and supportive setting where he would not encounter his usual triggers and opportunities. Over time, outpatient group and individual therapy were utilized to assist the client to address his relationship and intimacy issues and learn to meet his needs for attention, affirmation, affection, control, and approval in socially acceptable ways. A process approach to psychotherapy within a cognitive framework allowed the client to explore and recognize relational themes and repetitive interpersonal patterns while experiencing and practicing more healthy patterns in both the individual and group therapy settings.

References

Abel, G. G., Becker, J. V., Cunningham-Rathner, J., Mittelman, M. S., & Rouleau, J. L. (1988). Multiple paraphilic diagnoses among sex offenders. *Bulletin of the American Academy of Psychiatry and the Law, 16*(2), 153–168.

Abel, G. G., Huffman, J., Warberg, B., & Holland, C. L. (1998). Visual reaction time and plethysmography as measures of sexual interest in child molesters. *Sexual Abuse: A Journal of Research and Treatment, 10*(2), 81–94.

Ahlmeyer, S., Heil, P., McKee, B., & English, K. (2000). The impact of polygraphy on admissions of victims and offenses in adult sexual offenders. *Sexual Abuse: Journal of Research & Treatment, 12*(2), 123–138.

American Psychiatric Association. (2000). *Diagnostic and statistical manual of mental disorders* (4th ed., text rev.). Washington, DC: Author.

American Psychiatric Association. (2010). *DSM-5 development.* Retrieved from www.dsm5.org

Cross, T. P., & Saxe, L. (1992). A critique of the validity of polygraph testing in child sexual abuse cases. *Journal of Child Sexual Abuse, 1*(4), 19–33.

Cross, T. P., & Saxe, L. (2001). Polygraph testing and sexual abuse: The lure of the magic lasso. *Child Maltreatment, 6*(3), 195–206.

Emerick, R. L., & Dutton, W. A. (1993). The effect of polygraphy on the self-report of adolescent sex offenders: Implications for risk assessment. *Annals of Sex Research, 6*(2), 83–103.

English, K., Jones, L., Pasini-Hill, D., Patrick, D., & Cooley-Towell, S. (2000). *The value of polygraph testing in sex offender management* (National Institute of Justice No. D971.BVX0034). Denver: Colorado Department of Public Safety, Division of Criminal Justice, Office of Research and Statistics.

Fernandez, Y. L. (2002). *In their shoes: Examining the issue of empathy and its place in the treatment of offenders*. Oklahoma City, OK: Wood'N'Barnes.

Fischer, J. (2000). The Abel Screen. In D. R. Laws, S. M. Hudson, & T. Ward (Eds.), *Remaking relapse prevention with sex offenders: A sourcebook* (pp. 303–318). Thousand Oaks, CA: Sage.

Freund, K. (1990). Courtship disorder. In W. L. Marshall, D. R. Laws, & H. E. Barbaree (Eds.), *Handbook of sexual assault: Issues, theories, and treatment of the offender* (pp. 331–342). New York: Plenum.

Freund, K., & Blanchard, R. (1986). The concept of courtship disorder. *Journal of Sex and Marital Therapy, 12*(2), 80–92.

Greenberg, D. M., & Bradford, J. M. W. (1997). Treatment of the paraphilic disorders: A review of the role of the selective serotonin reuptake inhibitors. *Sexual Abuse: A Journal of Research & Treatment, 9*(4), 349–360.

Hanson, R. K. (2002). Associate editor's introduction to Dr. Letourneau's paper. *Sexual Abuse: A Journal of Research and Treatment, 14*(3), 205.

Hanson, R. K., & Harris, A. J. R. (1998). *Dynamic predictors of sexual recidivism* (No. 1998–01). Ottawa, ON, Canada: Department of the Solicitor General of Canada.

Hanson, R. K., & Thornton, D. (1999). *Static-99: Improving actuarial risk assessments for sex offenders* (No. 1999–02). Ottawa, ON, Canada: Department of the Solicitor General of Canada.

Heil, P., Ahlmeyer, S., & Simons, D. (2003). Crossover sexual offenses. *Sexual Abuse: A Journal of Research and Treatment, 15*(4), 221–236.

Hindman, J. (1988, July–August). Research disputes assumptions about child molesters. *National District Attorneys Association Bulletin, 7*(4), 1, 3.

Hindman, J., & Peters, J. M. (2001). Polygraph testing leads to better understanding adult and juvenile sex offenders. *Federal Probation, 65*(3), 8–15.

Humbert, P. (1990). The impact of polygraph use on offense history reporting. *ATSA Professional Forum, 4,* 20–21.

Jennings, J. L., & Sawyer, S. (2003). Principles and techniques for maximizing the effectiveness of group therapy with sex offenders. *Sexual Abuse: A Journal of Research and Treatment, 15*(4), 251–268.

Kafka, M. P. (1991). Successful antidepressant treatment of nonparaphilic sexual addictions and paraphilias in men. *Journal of Clinical Psychiatry, 52*(2), 60–65.

Kafka, M. P. (1994). Sertraline pharmacotherapy for paraphilias and paraphilia-related disorders: An open trial. *Annals of Clinical Psychiatry, 6,* 189–195.

Kafka, M. P. (2001a). The paraphilia-related disorders: A proposal for a unified classification of nonparaphilic hypersexuality disorders. *Sexual Addiction and Compulsivity, 8*(3), 227–239.

Kafka, M. P. (2001b). Paraphilias and paraphilia-related disorders. In G. O. Gabbard (Ed.), *Treatments of psychiatric disorders* (3rd ed., pp. 1952–1979). Washington, DC: American Psychiatric Press.

Kafka, M. P., & Hennen, J. (2002). A *DSM-IV* Axis I comorbidity study of males (n

= 120) with paraphilias and paraphilia-related disorders. *Sexual Abuse: A Journal of Research and Treatment, 14*(4), 349–366.

Kafka, M. P., & Prentky, R. (1992). Fluoxetine treament of of nonparaphilic sexual addictions and paraphilias in men. *Journal of Clinical Psychiatry, 53*(10), 351–358.

Kokish, R., Levenson, J. S., & Blasingame, G. D. (2005). Post conviction sex offender polygraph examination: Client-reported perceptions of utility and accuracy. *Sexual Abuse: A Journal of Research and Treatment, 17*(2), 211–221.

Lang, R. A., Langevin, R., Checkley, K., & Pugh, G. (1987). Genital exhibitionism: Courtship disorder or narcissism? *Canadian Journal of Behavioural Science, 19*(2), 216–232.

Langstrom, N. (2010). The *DSM* diagnostic criteria for exhibitionism, voyeurism, and frotteurism. *Archives of Sexual Behavior, 39*(6), 1235–1237.

Laws, D. R., Hudson, S. M., & Ward, T. (2000). *Remaking relapse prevention with sex offenders: A sourcebook.* Thousand Oaks, CA: Sage.

Letourneau, E. (2002). A comparison of objective measures of sexual arousal and interest: Visual reaction time and penile plethysmography. *Sexual Abuse: A Journal of Research and Treatment, 14*(3), 207–223.

Levenson, J. S. (2009). Sex offender polygraph examination: An evidence-based case management tool for social workers. *Journal of Evidence Based Social Work, 6*, 361–375.

Maletzky, B. M. (1997). Exhibitionism: Assessment and treatment. In D. R. Laws & W. T. O'Donohue (Eds.), *Sexual deviance* (pp. 40–74). New York, NY: Guilford.

Marques, J. K., & Nelson, C. (1989). Elements of high–risk situations for sex offenders. In D. R. Laws (Ed.), *Relapse prevention with sex offenders* (pp. 35–46). New York, NY: Guilford.

Marshall, W. L. (2006). Clinical and research limitations in the use of phallometric testing with sexual offenders. *Sex Offender Treatment, 1*(1), 1–32.

Marshall, W. L., Eccles, A., & Barbaree, H. (1991). The treatment of exhibitionists: A focus on sexual deviance versus cognitive and relationship features. *Behavior Research and Therapy, 29*(2), 129–135.

Marshall, W. L., Hamilton, K., & Fernandez, Y. (2001). Empathy deficits and cognitive distortions in child molesters. *Sexual Abuse: A Journal of Research & Treatment, 13*(2), 123–130.

Morin, J. W., & Levenson, J. S. (2002). *The road to freedom.* Brandon, VT: Safer Society Press.

Morin, J. W., & Levenson, J. S. (2008). Exhibitionism: Assessment and treatment. In D. R. Laws & W. O'Donohue (Eds.), *Sexual deviance* (2nd ed., pp. 76–107). New York, NY: Guilford.

Murphy, W., & Page, J. (2008). Exhibitionism: Psychopathology and theory. In D. R. Laws & W. O'Donohue (Eds.), *Sexual deviance* (2nd ed., pp. 61–75). New York, NY: Guilford.

O'Connell, M. A. (1998). Using polygraph testing to assess deviant sexual history of sex offenders. *Dissertation Abstracts International Section A: Humanities & Social Sciences, 58*(8-A), 3023.

Teyber, E., & McClure, F. (2011). *Interpersonal process in therapy: An integrative model* (6th ed.). Florence, KY: Brooks Cole.

Wright, P. J. (2010). Sexual compulsivity and 12-step peer and sponsor supportive communication: A cross-lagged panel analysis. *Sexual Addiction & Compulsivity, 17*(2), 154–169.

8

TELEPHONE SCATOLOGIA

Kirk A. B. Newring

Penix (2008) provided a cogent summary of state of the field surrounding telephone scatologia. She noted:

> Casual, obscene telephone calling is often mistaken for telephone scatalogia.[1] Whereas prank phone calls are a relatively common phenomenon in modern society (Price, Kafka, Commons, Gutheil, & Simpson, 2002), scatalogia, in which the caller becomes sexually aroused by exposing an unsuspecting victim to sexual material and may masturbate during or while remembering the call, is far less widespread. A review of the characteristics of telephone scatalogists by Pakhomou (2006) indicates that they are typically heterosexual, discovered in young adulthood, possess an average or elevated sexual drive, do not evidence significant cognitive deficits, have no significant psychopathology, and have typically attempted but failed to maintain a long-term committed relationship (often with children). They also tend to have limited social interactions, criminal histories involving theft, a high school or some college education, and menial jobs. (Alford, Webster & Sanders, 1980; Almansi, 1979; Dalby, 1988; Kentsmith & Dastani, 1974; Price et al., 2002)

> Three major types of scatological telephone calls were identified by Masters, Johnson, and Kolodny (1982). Most prevalent is the type in which the perpetrator boasts about himself and his sexual organs, and describes his masturbation. Another sort is characterized by sexual and other threats towards the listener, and the final variety attempts to manipulate the respondent into revealing intimate sexual or otherwise intimate information about herself. Characteristic ruses for obtaining private information include posing as another female (Almansi, 1979; Dalby, 1988; Pakhomou, 2006), and acting as a sexual survey researcher. (Schewe, 1997; Skinner & Becker, 1985, p. 420)

The present case involves a man fitting some, but not all, aspects of the telephone scatalogist described above.

Case Background

Mr. Bradley Graham[2] is a 61-year-old man of Mexican and Irish descent. He was recently charged with three counts of Intimidation by Phone, and agreed to enter a plea of guilty to two of these counts, and he anticipated being placed on probation. Mr. Graham's probation officer requested that a psychosexual evaluation and risk assessment be completed prior to sentencing.

Mr. Graham reported that he was arrested in April 2010 for telephone calls he had made to young women in 2008, 2009, and perhaps 2010. He acknowledged making inappropriate calls to young women that were living in dorms at the university in the county where he was arrested, though he lived more than one hundred miles away from the university. Mr. Graham said that he was tracked through his use of a credit card to purchase disposable cell phones that were used in making these calls.

Bradley Graham reported that he was born in Papillion, Nebraska and grew up in Omaha. He was the oldest of four children born into an intact nuclear family. He reported an unremarkable childhood, save for one traumatic event. Bradley reported that he watched from his yard as his best friend was hit by a semi-truck while crossing a road and died as a result of the injuries he sustained. Bradley stated that he enjoyed school and got along well with his teachers. He noted that several teachers were physically abusive (e.g., metal edge of rulers rapped on knuckles). He also reported some difficulties in growing up due to his mother's alcoholism. Mr. Graham denied having been placed out of the home as a child or adolescent.

Bradley has married and divorced twice, has four adult children, and two grandchildren. He stated that he is on good terms with his three sons, but has an estranged relationship with his daughter following one of his previous arrests. Bradley's marriages lasted 8 and 10 years. He stated that he is not on good terms with either of his ex-wives.

Bradley stated that he is not currently dating, and indicated that he did not view himself as a desirable mate. He reported having several friends. When challenged, he acknowledged that while he had friends that support him, he has not disclosed his history of sexual misbehavior to them, and did not seek their solace and support when contemplating sexually motivated misbehavior. When challenged about this, Bradley noted that he is more of a resource to his friends than vice-versa, and that he has difficulty soliciting social support.

Bradley reported that he has had several jobs of several years duration. He is currently self-employed as a truck driver, and has contracted with the same company for the past 15 years, despite his arrests and incarcerations.

Bradley denied any abnormalities in his sexual health and development. He reported having had approximately 12 different sexual partners in his lifetime, with some of those being dating/married relationships, and others being casual or one-night encounters. When asked about his sexual practices, Bradley acknowledged an interest or past history of exhibitionism, voyeurism, and telephoning strangers to engage them in sexual discussions while he masturbated. He also reported having frequented massage parlors and prostitutes in past decades. He denied other sexual variances such as nonconsent, hebephilia, pedophilia, transvestic fetishism, fetishism, and zoophilia. He stated that he is currently abstinent from all forms of sexual activity, including intercourse and masturbation.

Mr. Graham reported that he was in fair health. He acknowledged being slightly overweight, and stated that he is on medication for high cholesterol and high blood pressure. He stated that he had a recent physical, and maintained good dental hygiene. Mr. Graham denied having had any formal law enforcement contacts as a juvenile.

According to police records, Mr. Graham had two prior charges for DUI. He also noted that his mother was an alcoholic. Mr. Graham denied recalling one of his DUIs, stating that he has no recollection of having his license suspended. Mr. Graham also reported that while he may have consumed alcohol concurrent with his inappropriate telephone calls, alcohol did not play a disinhibitory role in these offenses. Mr. Graham denied being addicted to any drugs or alcohol.

Mr. Graham's criminal history includes:

1980: Indecent Exposure, dismissed
1981: DUI, dismissed
1985: DUI, license suspended; 3 days in jail
1987: Attempted Sexual Assault: 2 years in prison; 3 years on probation
*1996: Harassing, six counts: 18 months in prison; 18 months on
    probation*
*2003: Public Indecency, two counts: 30 days in jail; 12 months on
    probation*
2006: Disturbing the Peace: Fine and court costs

The 1987 charge related to Mr. Graham attempting to sexually assault his babysitter's sister. The 1996 charges were similar to the index charges of obscene telephone calls, as were the 2003 charges. The 2006 charge resulted from Mr. Graham drinking to the point of intoxication and being expelled from a drinking establishment, and "causing a scene" outside, which resulted in law enforcement officers being called to intervene. Mr. Graham stated that there have been other incidents of making inappropriate phone calls for which he was not sanctioned.

Mr. Graham reported that he was arrested in December 2010 for telephone calls he had made to young women in 2007, 2008, and perhaps 2009. He acknowledged making inappropriate calls to young women that were students at the local university in the county of his arrest. Mr. Graham made these calls from his home, to a university several hundred miles away. He reported that he would research the telephone numbers for the dormitories, and chart which dorms' prefixes led to females, and then he would later use this list when making calls. He noted that the calls would not become sexualized until the second or third time he called the same person. Bradley reported that he would begin the calls by intimating that he was in emotional distress, had no one to talk to, and was calling numbers at random to try to find someone "just to talk to." After conversing with the person for 5 to 30 minutes, he would thank them, and ask if he could call again later, if he needed to. He reported that on the follow-up call he would seek reassurance and emotional intimacy, and then proceed to masturbate and at times, he would ask the person he called to masturbate as well.

Behavioral Health Treatment History

Bradley had attended individual and group counseling for at least two intervals during his life. He is currently participating in counseling with his previous therapist. He had previously been in counseling with her, and discontinued on his own volition. Bradley reported that treatment was consistent with a Relapse Prevention (Newring, Loverich, Harris, & Wheeler, 2009) approach toward an identified problem of sexual addiction. He read several works by Patrick Carnes and completed the workbook, *Out of the Shadows: Understanding Sexual Addiction* (2001), on two separate occasions. Bradley reported that he does well in treatment, and understands his sexual addiction, and describes his offense and reoffense in terms of preoccupation, ritualization, compulsivity, and despair. However, despite this level of insight, he dropped out of treatment on two prior occasions because things appeared to be going well in his life. He failed to return to treatment on his own volition, and returned to his sexual offending behavior of telephone scatologia.

In reviewing his treatment knowledge and treatment experiences, Bradley reported that he was able to identify the Relapse Prevention components of his sexual offense behaviors. He described his high-risk situations, seemingly unimportant decisions, thinking errors and cognitive distortions, red flags and warning signs, and lapses and relapses. However, Bradley also noted that just going to treatment and having someone to talk to helped keep him out of trouble. That is, in hindsight Bradley reported that the active treatment ingredient in his previous therapy experiences was the combination of having a place to seek and enlist support, coupled with supervision, monitoring, and accountability. Bradley stated that when he had been in treatment before, after 6 to 18 months, he would feel confident, having his support needs addressed, and not perceive any risk factors for lapses or relapses in his daily life. Once he discontinued treatment, he later found himself without the support and accountability that treatment provided, and Bradley did not enlist the support of his friends, previous treatment providers, or other forms of intervention. Bradley did not list overconfidence as a high-risk situation, nor did he describe lack of support and accountability as a risk factor. In sum, while Bradley had the knowledge of Relapse Prevention, he was unsuccessful in applying it in his daily life without the additional supports of ongoing treatment.

Likewise, Bradley reported that he has maintained sobriety as a function of his attendance and participation in Alcoholics Anonymous. Bradley noted that substance abuse was addressed in his counseling sessions, but that he found the support and accountability in AA as the main contributing factors in his maintenance of sobriety. Bradley has included ongoing attendance and participation in AA as one of the features of his ongoing safety plan.

Prior Diagnoses

Bradley Graham has past diagnoses of

302.9 Paraphilia Not Otherwise Specified
309.29 Adjustment Disorder with Mixed Anxiety and Depressed Mood

Clinical Assessment

For adult men with sexual behavior problems or sexual offense behaviors, there are three approaches to risk assessment: unstructured clinical judgment, actuarial risk assessment, and structured professional judgments.

Unstructured Clinical Judgment. This approach relies on the clinician or evaluator to provide an assessment of risk based upon their clinical judgment. While this may include empirically identified risk factors, there is no specific algorithm for the assessment of risk. This approach is generally unsupported by research due its relatively low intrarater reliability, low inter-rater reliability, and low predictive accuracy.

Actuarial Risk Assessment. This approach relies on the clinician or evaluator to provide an assessment of risk based on the application of specified coding rules on a specific set of risk factors. The coding rules often specify a weight or value for each item, with a specific algorithm for deriving a total score. The total score is then compared to known-outcome data sets for developmental and follow-up studies for offenders with a certain score or within a certain score range, thus the name actuarial (e.g., for men with a score of X, in the developmental population on which the measure was developed, Y% of men with that score were categorized as having sexually recidivated within a 10-year follow-up period). Authors of different actuarials have included or eschewed including nominal categories with derived scores (e.g., Low, Moderate, High). Notably, within the actuarial approach, there is a requirement for clinical assessment on some measures. For example, the Sex Offender Risk Appraisal Guide (SORAG) includes variables that require current *DSM* diagnosis (i.e., personality disorder), as well as a current score on the Psychopathy Checklist-Revised (PCL-R), as well as an assessment of deviant sexual interest (e.g., phallometry, *DSM* Axis I diagnosis of Pedophilia). Some examples of Actuarial Risk Assessments include the SORAG, the Static-99R (which was previously known as the Static-99, which includes the previously developed RRA-SOR), as well as some state-developed tools such as the Minnesota Sex Offender Screening Tool-Revised (Mn-SOST-R), the Iowa Sex Offender Risk Assessment (I-SORA), and the Vermont Assessment of Sex Offender Risk (VASOR). In addition to these sexual offender specific risk assessments, there are actuarial risk assessments for general violence prediction, for use when there is a prior charge of violence, but no charges for sexual misbehavior (e.g., Violence Risk Appraisal Guide; Level of Service-Case Management Inventory).

The strengths of actuarial approaches are in the relatively high intra-rater reliability, inter-rater reliability, and positive predicative accuracy (typically measured through Receiver Operator Characteristics or ROC analysis). The Static-99/99R and SORAG have been thoroughly reviewed, replicated, and cross-validated in several studies.

In their meta-analysis of predictive factors in sexual offense recidivism studies, Hanson and Morton-Bourgon (2007) concluded,

> The sex offender risk scale that was most strongly related to general recidivism was the SORAG (d. =.79), which was a significantly better predictor than the Static-99 (d. = .52) or SVR-20 (d. = .52). The RRASOR significantly predicted general recidivism (d. = .26), although it was a poorer predictor than the other scales (their confidence intervals did not overlap). (p. 14)

However, there are several limitations to the use of actuarial risk assessment instruments. Foremost, as an approach, is that they provide data about large groups, but as some have argued little meaningful data about what to do at an individual level. For example, if we know that 60% of men with a certain score on an actuarial reoffended within 15 years, at the level of the individual it does not tell the decision maker if the specific man is more likely to be one of the 60% or one of the 40%. Within the larger body of psychological assessment, scores are sometimes reported as a score, with a "confidence interval" to include the range of scores that likely represents the true score, a process that includes the margin of error.

In some social science survey, this is sometimes seen in opinion polls reported as +/– X%, or in IQ scores it is often reported, obtained score 100, 95% Confidence Interval 94-106. While the authors of the actuarial risk assessments have often included confidence intervals for the group/bin scores, individual scores had not been subject to the level of analysis. Hart, Michie, and Cooke (2007) concluded that "the 95% Confidence Intervals were large for risk estimates at the group level; at the individual level they were so high as to render risk estimates virtually meaningless" (p. s63). For example, Hart et al. (2007) reported that for the Static-99 score of 6, 95% of CI at the level of the individual was reported as .06–.95.

Actuarials also require initial training in the approach and the specific instrument, as well as ongoing education and recalibration to reduce rater-drift (the deviation from rating rules after the rater has become familiar with the instrument). Actuarials often have specific inclusion and exclusion criteria for the populations on whom the instrument can defensibly be used (e.g., the Static-99R lists prerequisites charges and should not be used on women, or on men with only noncontact pornography charges, such as Possession of Child Pornography).

Other actuarials are limited in the normative samples on which they were developed and later replicated. Another limitation of some of the state-developed actuarials (e.g., Mn-SOST-R, VASOR) is the requirement that the rater make a determination about the quality of the previous treatment received by the ratee. While the manuals accompanying the instruments provide some guidance, it may prove difficult for a rater to defend making an estimation of a person's risk for reoffense based upon the analysis of a treatment program, about which the rater has little or no familiarity or knowledge.

Another limitation of the actuarial approaches is the implicit assumption that treatment does not matter. For most of the actuarial approaches, the score on the actuarial assessment will be the same for the individual on the day he leaves treatment as it was on the day he began treatment. This may be an artifact to the lack of controlled studies demonstrating the benefit of treatment in the inclusion of the development of the actuarial.

Lastly, some professionals using actuarial risk assessment report data from more than one actuarial instrument (e.g., using both the Static-99 and VASOR) as part of a risk assessment, perhaps under the notion of "more is better." Seto (2005) evaluated the impact of combining multiple actuarial assessments in predicting recidivism in adult male sexual offenders. Seto concluded, "No combination method provided a statistically significant or consistent advantage over the predictive accuracy of the single best actuarial scale" (2005, p. 156).

Structured Professional Judgment (SPJs). This approach relies on the clinician or evaluator to provide an assessment of risk based on clinical assessment using empirically derived risk factors. However, while there may be weighting or other algorithms included, SPJs do not include actuarial estimates of risk (e.g., men with a score of X had reoffense rates of Y), rather, they rely on the evaluator to make a clinical statement about the assessment of risk and recommendations about the management of risk, based on those specific factors in the instrument. Examples of SPJs include the Sexual Violence Risk-20 (SVR-20) and the Risk for Sexual Violence Protocol (RSVP).

The authors of the Static-99R have developed an SPJ-like assessment, designed to assess so-called dynamic risk factors related to reoffense risk. While not having the actuarial numbers like the Static-99R, the current iteration of this model, the Stable-2007, has research supporting its use as a dynamic risk assessment measure, to be used in conjunction with the Static-99R, in informing decisions about the amount of supervision recommended for a specific offender, in comparison with other offenders under community supervision.

The strength of an SPJ approach is that it is informed by research, and typically limited only to those risk factors. However, the utility of the SPJ often rests on the clinical skills and abilities of the person using the approach. Further, while some are fond of numbers and statistics like those offered by actuarial measures, SPJs typically do not include numbers or values in recommendations of risk in the same manner. For example, on the SVR-20, the evaluator may include the number of factors identified, or the values for each factor, but this would not be linked to a known-outcome reoffense risk vis-à-vis a developmental sample.

A quick point about the use of nominal categories to convey risk assessment; the authors of some instruments, most notably the Static-99R and its companion instrument, the Stable-2007, include nominal categories to convey assessment of risk. To the lay reader, these labels can be pejorative, confusing, and misleading. The nominal categories provided in the Static-99R include: Low, Low-Moderate, Moderate-High, and High. The nominal categories provided in the Stable-2007 are not referred to as "risk" categories; rather, they are referred to as "Need Category" and include: Low, Moderate, and High. In point of fact, when combining the Static-99R and Stable-2007, the instrument authors do not refer to the nominal categories as risk; rather, they refer to them as "Overall Supervision Priority" and list them as: Low, Moderate-Low, Moderate-High, High, and Very High. Thus, it could be construed as a misrepresentation to describe the combination of Static-99R and Stable-2007 as "risk" estimates, when the authors of the instruments eschew that language in favor of supervision priority. Furthermore, without context, the nominal categories of risk themselves are meaningless. A more useful description is qualifying the risk category vis-à-vis the average offender, and including reoffense rates. Lay people typically overestimate the average rates of reoffending in men previously convicted of sexual offenses. Thus, with a Static-99R score of 2 (the median score) about 1/3 of these men have a new violent offense (including sexually violent) within 10 years. Static-99R scores lower than those convey a relatively lower risk of reoffense, and scores higher than that convey a relatively higher risk of reoffense. However, even at scores of 5 and 6, reoffense rates are nearly 50% (48.2 and 53.2) over a 10-year interval. By using a label such as high risk, to apply to all men in a certain bin, where about half reoffend in 10 years may not accurately convey the relevant data. Risk is a relative and probabilistic statement about unknown future occurrences, and without a context, statements such as "low" or "high" are not appropriate.

In the meta-analysis noted above, Hanson and Morton-Bourgon (2004) concluded:

> Risk assessments were most likely to be accurate when they were constrained by empirical evidence. Unstructured clinical assessments were significantly related to recidivism, but their accuracy was consistently less than that of actuarial measures. The predictive accuracy of clinical assessments was slightly higher in the current review (d. = .40; k = 9) than in Hanson and Bussière's earlier review (r = .10; d ~ .20, k = 10), although the difference was not statistically significant (their confidence intervals overlap). Part of the improvement involved inclusion of a recent study in which clinical assessment did quite well (Hood, Shute, Feilzer, & Wilcox, 2002), and removing to a separate category post-treatment assessments of "benefit from treatment." The extent to which recent advances in research knowledge have improved routine clinical assessments remains unknown. Empirically-guided professional judgments showed predictive accuracies that were intermediate between the values observed for clinical assessments and pure actuarial approaches. The same pattern of results applied to the prediction of sexual recidivism, violent non-sexual recidivism, and general (any) recidivism. There were no sex offender recidivism studies that examined the accuracy of risk assessments in which judges were presented with actuarial results and then allowed to adjust their overall predictions based on external risk factors (Webster et al., 1994). Future research should consider such adjusted actuarial risk assessments because this approach has proven the most accurate in other domains (e.g., weather forecasting; Swets, Dawes, & Monahan, 2000).

> For the prediction of general recidivism, the general criminal risk scales were superior (d. = 1.03) to measures designed to predict sexual recidivism (d. = .52). The general criminal risk scales were

also as good at predicting any violent recidivism (d. = 79) as the scales specifically designed to assess violent recidivism among sexual offenders (SORAG, d. = .75/.81). Further research is required to determine whether the specific sexual offender risk scales provide useful information that is not already captured in the general criminal risk scales. (pp. 17–18)

As noted in the Hanson and Morton-Bourgon meta-analysis above, the SORAG and Static-99R appear to be the best measures available at this time. The Static-99R is designed for use by probation officers. The SORAG is perhaps more cumbersome for the probation officer to use, though with proper training and adequate file information (e.g., recent diagnostic information and psychopathy assessment), a probation officer could use the SORAG.

Ultimately, the decision to use an assessment approach is often specific to the referral question being asked. Referral questions in cases such this can include one or more of the following: is this person a suitable candidate for probation (or parole), what is this person's risk to reoffend, what are the treatment needs for this individual, how should we best manage this person in the community? The Static-99R and Stable-2007, when used in conjunction, appear to be a satisfactory combination of instruments for probation suitability assessments. As noted above, these instruments in combination have been used to inform resource deployment prioritization and management prioritization for men in community placement. For more dichotomous determinations (e.g., risk-informed treatment program), lower scores on actuarial assessment (e.g., SORAG, Static-99R) may lead to a recommendation for a lower intensity treatment recommendation, and conversely, high static risk may lead to a more intensive treatment recommendation. Treatment planning is often beyond the scope of actuarial instruments, as there is little a person can do through treatment to change his scores on actuarial. On the Static-99R, a person can achieve a lower score through the process of aging, as well as developing a romantic relationship once they are in the community. For treatment planning purposes, the Stable-2007 can be useful (Newring & Wheeler, 2010). Structured Professional Judgments (SPJs) have strength in all areas. They can be useful in risk assessment, risk management, treatment activities, and dichotomous decision-making referrals (e.g., civil commitment).

The referral question, casually phrased by the probation officer was, "should we be worried about Bradley Graham, and if so, what do we need to focus on?" Based on this referral, several assessment methods were used, including, clinical interview, collateral contacts, functional analysis/behavior chain analysis, Static-99R, Stable-2007, Acute-2007, Garos Sexual Behavior Inventory (GSBI), Minnesota Multiphasic Personality Inventory-II (MMPI-II), and the Psychopathy Checklist-Revised (PCL-R).

Assessment Results

Mr. Graham cooperated with the interview process and exhibited little resistance to answering general interview questions. On a self-report symptom inventory, Bradley endorsed current problems such as feelings of guilt and regret, as well as chronic pain. During the interview, Bradley reported anxiousness, some dissatisfaction with sleep, and feelings of guilt and shame. Bradley described his strengths as being caring. He reported hobbies of spending time with his sons and grandchildren, fishing, stamp collecting, NASCAR, and watching University of Texas Longhorn football games. Bradley reported sporadic church attendance over his lifetime, and has not attended any church events for the last 5 years. He is not currently active in any social or philanthropic clubs or organizations.

When asked about the events that led to his arrest, Bradley admitted engaging in the acts of calling strangers in hopes of maintaining a discussion that would fulfill prurient interests. He stated that he would masturbate during some of these phone calls, but not all. He stated that he had successfully been in treatment before, and did not make use of his treatment and supports. He stated that the phone calls for which he is now charged were all impulsively made.

When asked about risk and protective factors related to reoffense, Bradley reported that remaining in individual and group counseling, as well as working his 12 steps in Sex Love Addicts Anonymous would assist him in maintaining a healthy life. He also reported that taking care of his physical and emotional health would help keep him safe. It appears that seeking acceptance from others was a motivating factor for his sexual misbehavior, and that were he able to address his personal problems related to this issue, his motivation for misbehavior may abate (e.g., increased distress tolerance for feeling unaccepted, increased interpersonal effectiveness in enlisting support, establishing caring and curative relationships, mood management skills for assisting him in managing negative affect).

The MMPI-2 was administered to identify any treatment responsivity issues that could potentially be of concern. Using the Revised Clinical Factors interpretation, Bradley presented himself as well adjusted. He did not endorse problems in the areas of somatic, cognitive, emotional, thought, or behavioral dysfunction. He disavowed cynical beliefs about others and may be overly trusting.

Mr. Graham's scores on the PCL-R are generally unremarkable, other than his total score being much lower than the average score for a male prison inmate.

Garos Sexual Behavior Inventory (GSBI)

The Garos Sexual Behavior Inventory (GSBI; Garos, 2008) is a self-report measure designed to assist forensic specialists and mental health professionals in making assessments and treatment decisions about individuals with problems related to sexuality and sexual behavior. The GSBI's seven scale scores can be used to evaluate the cognitive, affective, and behavioral dimensions of a client's overall sexual adjustment. The GSBI can help identify atypical or disordered sexual behavior, and paraphilic interests, such as exhibitionism, sexual masochism, and voyeurism.

Garos (2008) reported favorable psychometric properties, with subscale internal consistency coefficients ranging from .57 to .82, and test-retest reliabilities ranging from .62 to .84. Validity indices were established through correlations with existing measures, such as the Sexual Opinion Survey, Sexuality Scale, Zuckerman-Kuhlman Personality Questionnaires, Beck Depression Inventory, Sexual Addiction Screening Test, and Rosenberg Self-Esteem Scale. Discriminant validity was established through comparison of groups of known "Sex addicts" and "Nonaddicts" with significant differential responding by these groups on specific subscales of interest. Similar comparisons were made with incarcerated offenders; with one group sex offenders, and the other group nonsex offenders. In the offender samples, the groups showed significantly different responding using Wilks' Lambda, with p values ranging from .001 to .040.

GSBI

Scale Name	T Score[3]
Discordance	68
Sexual Obsessions	54
Permissiveness	39
Sexual Stimulation	41
Sexual Control Difficulties	57
Sexual Excitability	39
Sexual Insecurity	61

An analysis of Mr. Graham's responses on the GSBI indicates that his score profile was valid. Mr. Graham's score was elevated on the Discordance scale. Men with elevations on this scale are often described as being judgmental and self-punitive about their sexual conduct, and are often self-critical about their physical bodies and appearance.

Static-99R

Mr. Graham was scored on Static-99R, which is an actuarial measure of relative risk for sexual offense recidivism. Given that Static-99R was found to fully incorporate the relationship between age at release and sexual recidivism, whereas the original Static-99 scale did not (Helmus, 2009), the developers of Static-99 recommend that the revised version of the scale (Static-99R) replace Static-99 in all contexts where it is used. Static-99R has shown moderate accuracy in ranking offenders according to their relative risk for sexual recidivism. Furthermore, its accuracy in assessing relative risk has been consistent across a wide variety of samples, countries, and unique settings (Helmus, 2009). As the table below illustrates, Mr. Graham received a total score of (+4), which places him in the nominal Moderate-High Risk Category for being charged or convicted of another sexual offense, relative to other men charged with sexual offense behaviors.

Of the individuals in the reference group who had a score of +4 on the Static-99, 7.7 to 19.1% *sexually* reoffended within 5 years, and 8.2 to 27.3% *sexually* reoffended within 10 years. Of the individuals in the reference group who had a score of +4 on the Static-99, 21.1 to 33.7% *violently* reoffended within 5 years, and 25.3 to 43.2% *violently* reoffended within 10 years.

At this time, it is not possible to determine where within those ranges Mr. Graham's risk for reoffense is best described; though Mr. Graham appears to be more similar to the population comprising the lower-bound of the ranges provided the so-called routine correctional samples. However, Mr. Graham has sexually reoffended twice, which is consistent with aspects of the nonroutine samples.

Static-99 Score Summary (Helmus, Hanson, & Thornton, 2009)[4]

	Risk Factor Yes = 1, No = 0	Scores
1	Under age 25 at release? (Score range is -3 to 1)	-3
2	Single (no two year relationship)?	0
3	Index nonsexual violence, any conviction?	0
4	Prior nonsexual violence, any convictions?	0
5	Prior sex offenses? (Score range is 0–3)	3
6	Prior sentencing dates (excluding index)?	1
7	Convictions for noncontact sex offenses?	1
8	Any unrelated victims?	1
9	Any stranger victims?	1
10	Any male victims?	0
	Total Score =	4
	Risk Category	Mod-High

Stable-2007

The Stable-2007 is an empirically informed risk assessment instrument designed to assess dynamic variables that have been demonstrated to be related to sexual reoffense. Using the semistructured interview, Mr. Graham received a total score of 10 out of 24. Mr. Graham indicated elevated risk on 7 items.

His greatest areas of concern, as assessed by the Stable-2007 were

- General Social Rejection, Loneliness
- Sex Drive/Sex Preoccupation
- Sex as Coping
- Deviant Sexual Preference

To a lesser degree, but still of concern, Bradley indicated risk in the areas of

- Capacity for Relationship Stability
- Poor Problem Solving Skills

To his credit, he identified relative strengths in all remaining areas, such as

- Significant Social Influences
- Emotional Identification with Children (absent)
- Hostility toward Women (absent)
- Impulsive (absent)
- Lack of Concern for Others (absent)
- Negative Emotionality (absent)
- Cooperation with Supervision

Notably, when reviewing the Stable-2007 with Mr. Graham, he reported that several of the areas identified as relative strengths currently, were not present in his life during each instance when he was making the unwanted sexualized telephone calls.

Acute-2007

The Acute-2007 is an empirically informed risk assessment instrument designed to assess the relatively shorter-term dynamic variables (e.g., 0–90 days) that have been demonstrated to be related to sexual reoffense. Hanson, Harris, Scott, and Helmus (2007) reported favorable ROC data for the Acute, ranging from .65 to .74, though with only 17 of the 7050 Acute assessments during the developmental studies preceded a next sexual crime, the imminent predictive validity of the Acute warrants further research.

Using a semistructured interview, Mr. Graham did not indicate elevated or imminent risk in any of the areas assessed (e.g., hostility, sexual preoccupation, rejection of supervision, substance abuse). However, consistent with his statements about the Stable-2007 assessment, Mr. Graham noted that several of these risk factors were present in the weeks and days before the telephoning that led to his most recent arrest.

Functional Analysis/Behavior Chain Analysis (BCA)

Mr. Graham completed Behavior Chain Analysis on several of his acts of sexual offending behavior. Functional Analysis or a BCA involves identifying relevant precursors, co-occurring and antecedent events that appear to establish or maintain the target behavior.

Mr. Graham identified several precursors to his sexual offense behavior. He reported increasing amounts of stress within his romantic relationships, social isolation from peers, depressed mood, negative affect (i.e., rumination and blaming himself for past failures and the death of his childhood friend). He also reported that in making the obscene phone calls, he achieved a sense of intimacy, albeit contrived, distraction from negative emotions or avoidance of negative emotions, and for some, but for not all acts, orgasm. He also noted that he was often feeling lonely and ineffective in his interpersonal relationships at the time he was calling, and that he often sought and then received reassurance from the women he called. Bradley had noted that his use of alcohol did not appear to play a disinhibitory role in his phone calling, rather, he surmised that it was the depressant effects of the alcohol that made him more despondent, which may have increased his emotional distress, which then functioned to prompt the escape behavior of telephone scatologia.

Case Formulation

Diagnostic Impressions

Axis I   309.29 Adjustment Disorder with Anxiety and Depressed Mood
302.9 Paraphilia Not Otherwise Specified (telephone scatologia)
In history, 302.4 Exhibitionism
Axis II   V71.09 No Diagnosis on Axis II
Axis III   None reported that impact behavioral health
Axis IV   Problems related to the social environment;
Problems related to interaction with the legal system/crime
Axis V   GAF = 68

Mr. Bradley Graham had past and recent history of engaging in illegal sexual behavior. He had indicated that his misbehavior was best characterized as sexualized coping, in that his acts of misbehavior were preceded by periods of distress or isolation, and that the functional goals of his misbehavior were acceptance and reassurance from others.

Bradley attested that he had not engaged in problematic sexual behavior while under supervision. Bradley might also appreciate a benefit from occasional monitoring and supervision (e.g., checking LUDS/phone records, reviewing Internet usage) as well as monitoring for prosocial behavior (e.g., bowling leagues attended, philately events attended, church groups attended, etc.).

Treatment Plan and Implementation

Treatment was directed toward the dynamic treatment targets identified in the Stable-2007 assessment: General Social Rejection, Loneliness; Sex Drive/Sex Preoccupation; Sex as Coping; and Deviant Sexual Preference, as well as Capacity for Relationship Stability and Poor Problem Solving Skills. Treatment was directed toward the functional goals of distress tolerance, emotion regulation, and intimacy enhancement.

These treatment targets map on to what Wheeler (Wheeler, George, & Stephens, 2005; Wheeler, George, & Stoner, 2005) has termed Recidivism Risk Reduction Therapy (3RT). 3RT directs treatment for men with sexual offense behavior problem toward those empirically identified risk factors. Beggs and Grace (2011) provided preliminary empirically support, linking this manner of approach with reduced recidivism. In their sample of 218 men that had sexually offended against children, they found that treatment gain in areas of dynamic risk led to reduced recidivism, with an average follow-up of about 12 years. The study followed men in a prison-based treatment program from 1993 to 2000. The researchers noted that the program was based on cognitive-behavioral principles, and focused on relapse prevention, and was limited to men with sexual crimes against children. It was not a randomized control trial (RCT), though they made mention of how their approach was different, and perhaps more informative than an RCT.

In light of some of the recent criticisms of a Relapse Prevention-only approach program, treatment was tailored to include Mr. Graham's prior treatment experiences, in light of emerging research and practice. As noted in Newring and Wheeler (2010),[5] in the last several years, a movement has been undertaken to improve upon the noted limitations of Relapse Prevention (RP) as a primary treatment for sexual offending. In practice, RP for sexual offending typically involves a focus on avoidance-based interventions (e.g., do not go certain places, do not allow certain thoughts or feelings to persist), using a confrontational therapeutic approach. More recently, these typical confrontation-based and risk-centered treatment approaches have been challenged (Marshall, Ward, et al., 2005). While acknowledging the need to identify and manage risk for the individual offender, these new approaches offer a strength-based approach in which a therapeutic alliance provides the context in which good lives are fostered. For example, Marshall et al. (2005) assert that working collaboratively with the offenders toward these goals will enhance treatment compliance and maximize treatment effects. They also assert that offender self-esteem and hopefulness need to be early treatment targets, as deficits in those areas can impede treatment progress. The data supportive of these approaches are being collected, and are in the early stages of dissemination (Marshall, Marshall, Serran, & O'Brien, 2011).

In another example of this paradigm shift in sex offense treatment, a typical RP intervention for sexual offense behavior is modified to include an emphasis on approach goals (Mann, Webster, Schofield, & Marshall, 2004). This approach-based intervention was designed to be consistent with the Good Lives approach (Ward & Hudson 2000; Ward & Stewart, 2002). The Good Lives and Self-Regulation (c.f. Webster, 2005) models posit that sexual offending occurs for a reason and within a context. Furthermore, there is some empirical evidence to support that approach goals may be more salient factors in clients' risk to sexually reoffend (Hudson, Ward, & Marshall, 1992; Ward, Hudson, & Marshall, 1994; Wheeler, 2003). As noted above, the data supporting these newer approaches (vs. Relapse Prevention or treatment as usual) are emerging in the literature. At this time, there do not appear to be any RCT comparing Good Lives, Self-Regulation, Working Positively/Approach Goal-focused, and Relapse Prevention. As more men proceed through these treatment programs and protocols, and are followed in the community, the literature continues to grow. Inmates in working positively programs appear to show appreciation for those approaches (Newring, Raschke, Cacialli, & Rodriguez, 2012).

The motivation for sexual behavior often can be linked to a common human need, or needs, such as affiliation, mastery, competence, or efficaciousness. Many offenders may lack the agency to be interpersonally effective in sexual encounters with same-aged peers. In order to fulfill an otherwise normative human need to affiliate and feel competent, individuals who lack skills for engaging in prosocial sexual relationships may resort to sexual relationships that are characterized by coercion, exploitation, manipulation, or even force. Thus, the "goods" in the Good Lives model are those motivators, either establishing operations, antecedents, or consequences, common across clients (and people) which lead to maladaptive behaviors to obtain said goods (e.g., intimacy, agency, competence).

Synthesizing the Mann, Webster, Schofield, and Marshall (2004) and Marshall et al. (2005) works provides an example of an approach goal consistent with the Good Lives Model that can be addressed collaboratively—modification or suppression of deviant arousal versus enhancement of healthy sexual functioning. By focusing on what to increase, it is argued that the treatment participant will have a clear plan of what to do and how to do it, rather than a somewhat nebulous concept of what to avoid or not to do. The shift in "what to do" has also led to a shift in "how to do it."

As stated in the Marshall et al. (2005) article title, "working positively" calls for a shift in the therapeutic stance in which sex offense treatment is provided. Marshall (2005) calls for an inclusion of the research on therapeutic change to the field of sex offense treatment. Marshall recommends that sex offense treatment providers display "empathy and warmth in a context where they provide encouragement and some degree of directiveness" (p. 134). Marshall also recommends therapists demonstrate flexibility and adapt their style and focus to the needs of the patient over the needs of a treatment protocol or manual.

Dynamic Risk Factors. The last decade of research on sexual offense behavior has resulted in significant gains in our understanding of numerous personality and lifestyle variables associated with sexual recidivism risk. The term *dynamic risk factor* (DRF) refers to those aspects of an offender's behavior or environment that are associated with increased likelihood to reoffend, and that are potentially subject to change. Accordingly, if a stable dynamic factor can be reduced in treatment, this may affect longer-term change in an individual's reoffense risk. Although research on dynamic factors is an ongoing process, these preliminary findings provide a basic framework for integrating dynamic risk factors into extant approaches to sex offense treatment. Currently, available data indicate that dynamic risk factors for sexual offense recidivism appear to be associated with one of two broad categories: (a) a pathological orientation towards love and sex, or "erotopathic risk-needs" (Wheeler, George, & Stephens, 2005; Wheeler, George, & Stoner, 2005), or (b) a generally antisocial orientation (Hanson & Bussiere, 1998; Hanson & Harris, 2002; Hanson & Morton-Bourgon, 2004; Hudson, Wales, Bakker, & Ward, 2002; Quinsey, Lalumiere, Rice, & Harris, 1995; Roberts, Doren, & Thornton, 2002).

"Erotopathic risk-needs" refer to the dynamic risk factors that are associated with the development and maintenance of maladaptive sexual behaviors and romantic relationships. For example, a client's erotopathic risk-needs would include thoughts, emotions, relationships, or other behaviors that support the development and maintenance of emotionally detached, abusive relationships and avoidance of relationships and interactions that threaten his detachment; a preference for "relationships" with partners whom he can control (e.g. with minors, or through the use of force), and avoidance of partners who challenge his control. For clients with dynamic risk factors in this area, treatment should focus on building behavioral skills and activities to develop and maintain satisfying and pro-social intimate/sexual relationships that could serve to curtail future acts of sexual offending. Again, from an applied behavior analytic perspective, this approach is consistent with a differential reinforcement of alternative (or incompatible) behavior that achieves the same or similar acquisition of "good" at a more palatable social cost for the treatment participant and society.

The second broad category of dynamic risk factors, or "antisocial risk needs" (Wheeler, George, & Stephens, 2005; Wheeler, George, & Stoner, 2005), refers to the dynamic risk factors that are associated with the development and maintenance of a chaotic, irresponsible, defiant, or otherwise antisocial lifestyle. For example, antisocial risk-needs would include thoughts, emotions, relationships, or other behaviors that support a generally unstable lifestyle (e.g., unsteady employment, antisocial peers); facilitate and indulge the use of deception, manipulation, and secrecy (e.g., criminal activity, psychopathic personality traits); foster resentment of others and a sense of entitlement and self-indulgence (e.g. hostility, persecution); support noncompliance with rules and authority; and provide reinforcement for behavioral disinhibition (e.g. substance use, aggression, violence). For clients with dynamic risk factors in this area, treatment should focus on building behavioral skills and activities to develop and maintain a satisfying and prosocial lifestyle, which could serve to curtail future acts of sexual offending. From an applied behavior analytic perspective, this approach is consistent with a differential reinforcement of alternative (or incompatible) behavior that achieves the same or similar acquisition of good (à la Good Lives) at a more palatable social cost for the treatment participant and society.

Treatment for Bradley included individual as well as group therapy. While Bradley was the only member of his group with a diagnosis of telephone scatologia, group members were quick to identify the functional similarities of Bradley's sexual offense behaviors with their own.

Bradley's identified areas of dynamic risk included, General Social Rejection, Loneliness, Sex Drive/Sex Preoccupation, Sex as Coping, Deviant Sexual Preference, Capacity for Relationship Stability, and Poor Problem Solving Skills. Treatment initially focused on identifying his barriers in recognizing a need for social and emotional support, identifying his barriers in seeking and soliciting social and emotional support, and that practicing the skill set. Linehan's Dialectical Behavioral Therapy (Linehan, 1993a, 1993b) skills module of Interpersonal Effectiveness was the primary treatment component to address these areas of risk. Interpersonal Effectiveness skills were intended to address and ameliorate risk in the areas of General Social Rejection, Loneliness, Capacity for Relationship Stability, and Poor Problem Solving.

Dynamic risk assessment also indicated that Mr. Graham had risk-relevant deficits related to emotion regulation. Linehan's DBT skill set of Emotion Regulation was used specific to Bradley's identified sexual offense behavior risk, with emphasis on identification of emotions, non-sexual, prosocial, and behaviorally-active/social coping skills. Emotion Regulation skills were intended to address and ameliorate risk in the areas of General Social Rejection, Loneliness, Sex as Coping, and Poor Problem Solving Skills.

Linehan's DBT skill set of Distress Tolerance was used specific to Bradley's identified sexual offense behavior risk area of Sex Drive/Sex Pre-occupation, and Deviant Sexual Preference. Treatment in this area was expounded to include aspects of an Acceptance and Commitment Therapy (ACT; Hayes, Strosahl, & Wilson, 1999). ACT emphasizes the role of emotional avoidance as a precursor to maladaptive coping responses. Put simply, in an ACT approach, a client that lacks the ability to tolerate the distress of experiencing an unwanted, unpleasant, or distressing emotional or cognitive event is provided with therapeutic support to experience the unwanted, unpleasant, or distressing event without engaging in a maladaptive compensatory behavior to "make" the bad stuff go away. For men with sexual offense behavior problems, this involves helping the client identify the experience of unwanted or harmful sexual arousal—and then rather than suppress it, act on, or engage in something to make it go away (e.g., substance abuse), the client is taught to experience the sexual arousal as a point of data provided by their mind and body, and the client can then make a values-informed choice about how to act, not in response to that arousal, but in co-occurrence with that arousal.

Complications (Lapses, Nonattendance)

Mr. Graham's previous treatment experience proved to be both a blessing and a curse. His familiarity with treatment concepts and principles, as well as his motivation, led to quick establishment of rapport and treatment buy-in. However, Mr. Graham appeared to "know all the right words" and at times it was difficult to assess the sincerity of answers. He attended treatment as scheduled, and his probation officer made frequent contact with his treatment provider.

An emerging complication in treatment was Bradley's low self-esteem. After focusing treatment towards the Interpersonal Effectiveness skills, Bradley said with resignation in his voice, that even if he knows the skills to use, he does not deserve the support of his friends and family. We then changed the treatment approach to prioritize Bradley's Adjustment Disorder diagnosis and self-esteem concerns. Treatment including concurrent focus using Behavioral Activation (Martell, 2008) as well as self-esteem

exercises specific to sexual offense behavior treatment (Newring & Rodriguez, 2008; Newring et al., 2012).

Terminating Treatment and Relapse Plan

Mr. Graham has previously terminated treatment twice, at his discretion.
As with several behaviors, at times there are few reliable and valid ways to
measure the occurrence of unwanted behaviors, other than self-report or
report from others. While urinalysis and Breathalyzer tests can be used
with substance abuse problems, the field is lacking such tests for telephone
scatologia. While technology can help in monitoring the use of his land-
line and cell phone, disposable phones and long-distance calling cards are
just two of the ways to evade monitoring.

At the time he self-terminated therapy, he had made appropriate gains
and appeared to be doing well. He had a well-articulated safety plan, with
several immediate, intermediate, and long-term indicators of pending
relapse. However, he did not appear to make effective use of the plan, or
to share the plan, or to have his supports make effective use of his plan and
intervene effectively. As he has relapsed on multiple occasions following
treatment, Mr. Graham acknowledged that being alone or unsupervised
worked to his disadvantage. He noted that during each time he was on
probation, he reported positive self-esteem and compliance with all laws.
Given this, we included ongoing supervision as a requirement for continued treatment, and ongoing treatment as a requirement for ongoing
probation. Bradley acknowledged that being unsupervised was a necessary
precondition for his sexual offense behavior, and that if unsupervised, and
experiencing other dynamic risk (loneliness, social isolation, sexual coping) and acute risk (victim access, collapse of social supports, substance
abuse) he was at imminent risk of reoffense. At Bradley's request, his treatment team (including his probation officer, his therapist, and Bradley)
agreed that Bradley would never be terminated from treatment, though
the intensity of treatment could ebb and flow based on Bradley's needs.
Bradley was also encouraged to invite his care and support network to a
meeting with his probation officer and therapist, with Bradley discussing
frankly his sexual offense behaviors, lapse, and relapse indicators, prosocial and approach goals, support needs, and his ongoing health and safety
plan. While some of his support people expressed concerns (e.g., do they
have liability if Bradley reoffends), for the most part, and to Bradley's
surprise, his supports had some notion of Bradley's offense history and
needs. They reported appreciation of Bradley's asking for support, and
most noted that they felt uncomfortable bringing the topic up, and were
waiting for Bradley to do so.

Conclusions and General Advice/Nonspecific

At times, treatment was challenged by what appeared to be overattending to the technological aspects of the sexualized misbehavior. Treatment group members offered recommendations like, "don't ever have a cell phone," or "take the phone out of your house," in service of minimizing the temptations. Behavior prohibitions as part of probation were also concerning, again asking for no cell phones and monitored Internet. In Bradley's work as a truck driver, having access to his cell phone and e-mail was vital. It was his sexualized use of cell phones to enlist social support in service of distress tolerance that became problematic. Bradley had noted that he was aware of what not to do, and the warning signs of pending relapse, but he stated that he lacked the ability, or lacked confidence in his ability to engage in healthier alternatives to his maladaptive sexualized coping behaviors.

What Would You Have Done if Therapy Wasn't Working the Way You Thought it Would?

Bradley was knowledgeable about the treatment process, and pardon the pun, but at times it appeared that he was "phoning it in" and not taking treatment seriously. Bradley had not faced insurmountable consequences for his previous sexual offense behaviors, and at times he appeared cocksure about his chances for probation and community placement. Enlisting the support of his probation officer led to frank discussions amongst Bradley's attorney and the county prosecutor. Sadly, Bradley acknowledged needing a little bit more of the stick, and a little bit less of the carrot, to get motivated for treatment. If Bradley was not showing satisfactory treatment progress, treatment could have been modified to identify his barriers to progress. Motivational Interviewing (Levensky, Kersh, Cavasos, & Brooks, 2008) approaches could have been used, as well as "pep talks" from his probation officer.

What Ethical or Legal Considerations Came into Play?

During one session, Bradley reported that during one of his phone calls, the girl reported that she was only 16 and had gained early admission to college. He reported that she was living in a dormitory room with her older sister. Bradley stated that he was unsure if he was sexually inappropriate with the younger girl or the older sister during a follow-up call. He was also unsure whether that specific call had been reported to law enforcement. He stated that he assumed it had been, as he later learned that the dormitory administrative staff had asked all students to keep a log of incoming calls from strangers. After discussing this with Bradley and

Bradley's attorney, it appeared that law enforcement personnel had already investigated Bradley's interaction with this specific girl.

What Common Mistakes Did You Work to Avoid in Treatment?

A challenge during the group therapy sessions was to avoid spending too much time and resources on the unique topographical and technological aspects of the sexual offense behaviors, and redirecting Bradley and his cohort toward the functional elements of the behavior. Group members were often interested in the technical aspects and minutiae; such as asking about disposable cell phones, blocking caller identification, using cash to purchase disposable cell phones, and the like. This focus on the technical and technological aspects appeared to allow Bradley and his peers to avoid talking about the sexual offense specific and motivational aspects of his behavior. With Bradley's previous treatment experience, we also made a concerted effort to avoid his being placed in an elevated status vis-à-vis his peers; when this did happen, Bradley spent less time focusing on his treatment needs and more on his peers. Another challenge with Bradley was seeking evidence of application of the treatment concepts and principles. As noted earlier, his treatment experience left him quite knowledgeable and treatment savvy. When treatment focused more on what he did rather than what he said, we were able to refocus on the challenge of applying treatment terms and principles into his everyday life.

What Is the "Art" of this Case and How Was it Informed by Scientific Evidence?

There are no large-scale recidivism outcome studies assessing the impact of treatment on telephone scatologia. The art of this case was found in identifying the functional aspects of Bradley's sexual offense behaviors, and directing treatment approaches in light of the scientific evidence for problems of a similar function. Emerging research supports the use of using empirically supported problems towards dynamic risk factors for sexual offense recidivism.

What Cultural Factors Did You Consider and What Difference Did it Make?

Mr. Graham reported that he is of Hispanic/Irish descent. He reported that his mother's alcoholism and father's sense of machismo led to him having misogynistic views. Mr. Graham reported that through his earlier courses of therapy, he had been disabused of his sense of machismo and stereotypical gender roles; however, he reported that after having those ideals taken away, he did not develop healthier alternatives. His experience of this ethos was that as a man, he was to be self-sufficient and to suppress emotional needs. Part of the current course of therapy was to develop healthy gender role expectations.

Summary

Bradley Graham presented an interesting treatment challenge for his sexual offense behaviors of telephone scatologia. As the field lacks controlled outcome studies for the treatment of this specific sexual variance, assessment and treatment approaches were based on a functional understanding of his assessed risks and needs. Treatment was challenged by his previous treatment experiences, and his treatment group cohort's unfamiliarity with the behavior. Bradley made strong gains in treatment, and acknowledged that being unsupervised and not in treatment were likely lifelong risk factors for reoffense.

Notes

1. Different authors use the terms *telephone scatalogia* and *telephone scatologia*.
2. Name and identifying information has been changed, and aspects of the case have been further modified for pedagogic purposes.
3. T Scores are a statistical conversion of a raw score to a standard score. The T-score distribution has a mean (average) of 50 and a standard deviation of 10. Thus, scores above 65 are often considered unusual or noteworthy on the T-score metric.
4. Static-99 rates are based on the "new norms" as reported in Helmus et al. (2009).
5. Aspects of this portion of the present entry have been previously published in Newring and Wheeler (2010).

References

Beggs, S. M., & Grace, R. C. (2011). Treatment gain for sexual offenders against children predicts reduced recidivism: A comparative validity study. *Journal of Consulting and Clinical Psychology, 79*(2), 182–192.

Carnes, P. J. (2001). *Out of the shadows: Understanding sexual addiction* (3rd ed.). City Center, MN: Hazelden.

Garos, S. (2008). *Garos sexual behavior inventory (GSBI).* Los Angeles, CA: Western Psychological Services.

Hanson, R. K., & Bussiere, M. T. (1998). Predicting relapse: A meta-analysis of sexual offender recidivism studies. *Journal of Consulting and Clinical Psychology, 66*, 348–362.

Hanson, R. K., & Harris, A. (2002). *STABLE and ACUTE scoring guides: Developed for the Dynamic Supervision Project: A Collaborative Initiative on the Community Supervision of Sexual Offenders.* Ottawa, ON, Canada: Department of the Solicitor General of Canada. Retrieved from http://www.psepc.gc.ca

Hanson, R. K., Harris, J. R., Scott, T., & Helmus, L. (2007). *Assessing the risk of sexual offenders on community supervision: The dynamic supervision project.* (User Report

2007-05). Ottawa, ON, Canada: Public Safety and Emergency Preparedness Canada. Retrieved from http://www.psepc.gc.ca

Hanson, R. K., & Morton-Bourgon, K. (2004). *Predictors of sexual recidivism: An updated meta-analysis* (User Report 2004-02). Ottawa, ON, Canada: Public Safety and Emergency Preparedness Canada. Retrieved from http://www.psepc.gc.ca

Hanson, R. K., & Morton-Bourgon, K. E. (2007). *The accuracy of recidivism risk assessments for sexual offenders: A meta-analysis.* Ottawa, ON, Canada: Public Safety and Emergency Preparedness Canada. Retrieved from http://www.psepc.gc.ca

Hart, S. D., Michie, C., & Cooke, D. J., (2007). Precision of actuarial risk assessment instruments: Evaluating the "margins of error" of group v. individual predictions of violence. *British Journal of Psychiatry, 190*, s60–s65.

Hayes, S. C., Strosahl, K. D., & Wilson, K. G. (1999). *Acceptance and commitment therapy: An experiential approach to behavior change.* New York, NY: Guilford.

Helmus, L. (2009). *Re-norming Static-99 recidivism estimates: Exploring base rate variability across sex offender samples* (Unpublished master's thesis). Carleton University, Ottawa, ON, Canada.

Helmus, L., Hanson, R. K., & Thornton, D. (2009). Reporting Static-99 in light of new research on recidivism norms. *ATSA Forum, 21*(1), 38–45.

Hudson, S. M., Wales, D. S., Bakker, L., & Ward, T. (2002). Dynamic risk factors: The Kia Marama evaluation. *Sexual Abuse: A Journal of Research and Treatment, 14*, 103–119.

Hudson, S. M., Ward, T., & Marshall, W. L. (1992). The abstinence violation effect in sex offenders: A reformulation. *Behavior Research and Therapy, 30*, 435–441.

Levensky, E. R., Kersh, B. C., Cavasos, L. L., & Brooks, J. A. (2008). Motivational interviewing. In W. T. O'Donohue & J. E. Fisher (Eds.), *Cognitive behavioral therapy: Applying empirically supported techniques in your practice* (2nd ed., pp. 357–366). Hoboken, NJ: Wiley.

Linehan, M. M. (1993a). *Skills training manual for treating borderline personality disorder.* New York, NY: Guilford.

Linehan, M. M. (1993b). *Cognitive-behavioral treatment of borderline personality disorder.* New York, NY: Guilford.

Mann, R. E., Webster, S. D., Schofield, C., & Marshall, W. L. (2004). Approach versus avoidance goals in relapse prevention with sexual offenders. *Sexual Abuse: A Journal of Research and Treatment, 16*(1), 65–75.

Marshall, W. L. (2005). Therapist style in sexual offender treatment: Influence on indices of change. *Sexual Abuse: A Journal of Research and Treatment, 17*(2), 109–116.

Marshall, W. L., Marshall, L. E., Serran, G. A., & O'Brien, M. D. (2011). *Rehabilitating sexual offenders: A strength-based approach.* Washington, DC: American Psychological Association.

Marshall, W. L., Ward, T., Mann, R. E., Moulden, H., Fernandez, Y., Serran, G., & Marshall, L. E. (2005). Working positively with sexual offenders: Maximizing the effectiveness of treatment. *Journal of Interpersonal Violence, 20*(9), 1096–1114.

Martell, C. R. (2008). Behavioral activation for depression. In W. T. O'Donohue & J. E. Fisher (Eds.), *Cognitive behavioral therapy: Applying empirically supported techniques in your practice* (2nd ed., pp. 40–45). Hoboken, NJ: Wiley.

Newring, K. A. B., Loverich, T. M., Harris, C. D., & Wheeler, J. G. (2009). Relapse prevention. In W. T. O'Donohue & J. E. Fisher (Eds.), *Cognitive behavioral ther-*

apy: Applying empirically supported techniques in your practice (2nd ed., pp. 520–531). Hoboken, NJ: Wiley.

Newring, K. A. B., Raschke, V., Cacialli, D. O., & Rodriguez, P. J. (2012). The inmate-participant experience of a motivational/working positive treatment program for men convicted of sexual offenses. In B. Schwartz (Ed.), *The sex offender* (Vol. 7). Kingston, NJ: Civic Research Institute.

Newring, K. A. B., & Rodriguez, P. J. (2008, October). The inmate-participant experience of a positive/motivational sex offender treatment program: Qualitative data from the inpatient Healthy Lives Program. In L. E. Marshall (Chair), *The effect of a positive/motivational treatment program for sexual offenders on therapeutic process issues.* Symposium conducted at the 27th Annual Association for the Treatment of Sexual Abusers, Atlanta GA.

Newring, K. A. B., & Wheeler, J. G. (2009, May). Recidivism risk reduction therapy (3RT) and the juvenile sex offender. In K. A. B. Newring (Chair) & J. Apsche (Discussant), *Behavior therapies with juvenile offenders: Fire, sex, and violence.* Symposium conducted at the 35th Annual Association for Behavior Analysis, Phoenix, AZ.

Newring, K. A. B., & Wheeler, J. G. (2010). Functional analytic psychotherapy and sex offenders. In J. W. Kanter, M. Tsai, & R. J. Kohlenberg (Eds.), *The practice of functional analytic psychotherapy* (pp. 225–246). New York, NY: Springer.

Nicholaichuk, T., Gordon, A., Gu, D., & Wong, S. (2000). Outcome of an institutional sexual offender treatment program: A comparison between treated and matched untreated offenders. *Sexual Abuse: Journal of Research and Treatment, 12*(2), 139–153.

Penix, T. M. (2008). Paraphilia not otherwise specified: Assessment and treatment. In D. R. Laws & W. T. O'Donohue (Eds.), *Sexual deviance* (pp. 416–438). New York, NY: Guilford.

Penix Sbraga, T., & Brunswig, K. A. (2003, May). *The functions of sexual coping responses: Taxonomic, research and treatment implications.* Paper presented at the 29th Annual Association for Behavior Analysis, San Francisco, CA.

Price, M., Kafka, M., Commons, M. L., Gutheil, T. G., & Simpson, W. (2002). Telephone scatologia comorbidity with other paraphilias and paraphilia-related disorders. *International Journal of Law and Psychiatry, 25,* 37–49.

Quinsey, V. L., Lalumiere, M. L., Rice, M. E., & Harris, G. T. (1995). Predicting sexual offenses. In J. C. Campbell (Ed.), *Assessing dangerousness: Violence by sexual offenders, batterers, and child abusers* (pp. 114–137). Thousand Oaks, CA: Sage.

Roberts, C. F., Doren, D. M., & Thornton, D. (2002). Dimensions associated with assessments of sex offender recidivism risk. *Criminal Justice and Behavior, 29,* 569–589.

Seto, M. C. (2005). Is more better? Combining actuarial risk scales to predict recidivism among adult sexual offenders. *Psychological Assessment, 17*(2), 156–167.

Ward, T., & Hudson, S. M. (2000). A self-regulation model of the relapse prevention process. In D. R. Laws, S. M. Hudson, & T. Ward (Eds.), *Remaking relapse prevention with sex offenders: A source book* (pp. 79–101). Thousand Oaks, CA: Sage.

Ward, T., Hudson, S. M., & Marshall, W. L. (1994). The abstinence violation effect in child molesters. *Behavior Research and Therapy, 32,* 431–437.

Ward, T., & Stewart, C. A. (2002). Good lives and the rehabilitation of sexual offenders. In T. Ward, D. R. Laws, & S. M. Hudson (Eds.), *Sexual deviance: Issues and controversies* (pp. 21–44). Thousand Oaks, CA: Sage.

Webster, S. D. (2005). Pathways to sexual offense recidivism following treatment: An examination of the Ward and Hudson self-regulation model of relapse. *Journal of Interpersonal Violence, 20*(10), 1175–1196.

Wheller, J. G. (2003). The abstinence violation effect in a sample of incarcerated sexual offenders: A reconsideration of the terms Lapse and Relapse. *Dissertation Abstracts International: The Sciences & Engineering, 63,* 3946B.

Wheeler, J. G., George, W. H., & Stephens, K. (2005). Assessment of sexual offenders: A model for integrating dynamic risk assessment and relapse prevention approaches. In D. M. Donavan & G. A. Marlatt (Eds.), *Assessment of addictive behaviors* (2nd ed., pp. 392–424). New York, NY: Guilford.

Wheeler, J. G., George, W. H., & Stoner, S. A. (2005). Enhancing the relapse prevention model for sex offenders: Adding recidivism risk reduction therapy (3RT) to target offenders' dynamic risk needs. In G. A. Marlatt & D. M. Donavan (Eds.), *Relapse prevention* (2nd ed., pp. 333–362). New York, NY: Guilford.

9

POSSESSION OF CHILD PORNOGRAPHY

A Case Study

David L. Delmonico and Elizabeth J. Griffin

Introduction

In recent years clinicians treating sexual offenders have seen an increasing number of cases involving child pornography and the Internet. Estimates of the scope of online child pornography and online sexual offense behavior vary significantly from study to study. This is often due to the difficulty in measuring the online world and specifically individuals' sexual behavior in the online world. For example, it is estimated that the number of known sex offenders connected to the Internet at any given time is 750,000 (Maalla, 2009), but it is unclear how this number is derived. An estimate from Wellard (2001) suggested there are more than 1 million pornographic images of children on the Internet and 200 new images posted daily, with little description of how the author arrived at these numbers. Regardless of these difficulties in estimating online statistics, it is clear there are a significant number of child pornography images available online with a large number of consumers of such pornography. As expected, with the increased availability of child pornography and ease of access, the number of arrests related to such images has also increased. In the federal criminal system, an estimated 1,713 offenders were arrested for crimes related to child pornography possession or distribution in 2000 (Wolak, Finkelhor, Mitchell, 2005), and by 2006 there were an estimated 3,672 arrests for similar crimes (Wolak, Finkelhor, & Mitchell, 2011). Since 2006, federal and state courts continue to see a rise in the number of cases related to online child pornography. In addition, while sex offender specific clinicians report an increase in clinical cases associated with online child pornography offenses, general practitioners are also reporting an increased number of child pornography related cases in their practices.

The authors would like to acknowledge that the term *child pornography* is slowly being replaced across the globe with the term *child sex abuse images* to more accurately describe what occurred in the images. In the United States, the term has been slow to appear in the literature. The use of the term *child pornography* in this chapter is in no way an attempt to minimize the harm being done to children, but rather a reflection of the more recognized term in the United States at this point.

Cases involving child pornography and the Internet can present a challenge for clinicians. Some of the individuals presenting with online sex-related offenses are clinically different from their offline sex offender counterparts. Unfortunately many clinicians continue to use the same assessment and treatment models that often ignore many of the unique aspects of these cases. The purpose of this chapter is to examine a single case study of an individual who was court ordered to treatment following an 8-year incarceration period for charges related to the possession of online child pornography. A special webpage has been established as a companion to this chapter in order to expand on material discussed in this chapter as well as to provide addition information helpful to clinicians evaluating and treating individuals struggling with online child pornography use. The webpage can be found at http://www.internetbehavior.com/cpcasestudy.

Brief Case Description

Charles Hartfield is a 56-year-old male recently released from federal prison. He was incarcerated after pleading guilty to two counts of Possession of Child Pornography. He was sentenced to 10 years in prison of which he served 8 years after receiving time off for "good behavior." He received no treatment in prison and has been ordered to treatment as part of his release conditions.

Clinical Assessment

There are five main aspects to the assessment of an online child pornography offender: (a) case-related document review, (b) non-Internet related assessments (including psychological testing), (c) global Internet assessment, (d) physiological testing, and (e) risk assessment. These aspects should be considered in both pre/post adjudication and postincarceration.

Document Review

Prior to the clinical interview with the client, it is helpful to review all documents related to the client's case. These documents may include all court related documents, incarceration records, prior psychological evaluations, and the computer forensic analysis. These documents can be helpful in the formulation of assessment related question as well as the formulation of the treatment plan.

The most overlooked document in online child pornography cases is the computer forensic analysis. The forensic analysis can provide objective data regarding the sexual offense behavior, including the nature of the images/videos, the frequency, intensity, duration of pornography use, level of compulsivity, and other contexts important to understanding a client's use of Internet pornography. Glasgow (2012) stated that information contained on the computer is a "remarkably detailed record of what [was] accessed, downloaded, created, modified, browsed, and deleted" (p. 180). Such material can also inform and validate other assessment procedures, including clinical interviews.

In the case of Mr. Hartfield, a review of the computer forensic analysis revealed that while he had downloaded approximately 150 images of prepubescent females, his hard drive also stored approximately 500 images of postpubescent females (under the age of 18) and nearly 3,000 images of adult females. The ratio of adult to teenager to child images is an important consideration in child pornography cases and was considered in Mr. Hartfield's case when assessing his sexual interest (R. Parsons, personal communication, November 30, 2012). Additionally, digital evidence such as chatting with underage children, or digital evidence of communicating with other adults interested in underage children should be considered. There was no evidence suggesting Mr. Hartfield was involved in any type of chatting or communicating with others regarding child pornography. Figure 9.1 provides examples of other forensic data worthy of consideration in the assessment of individuals who view child pornography (Parsons, 2012).

The above captioned individual is currently under supervision of our department. We are requesting that you complete this survey to assist us in the supervision and treatment of the offender. When completing this survey, please take into consideration all material found during the investigation. Do not restrict to what the offender final convictions. With each question, please check all that apply. Place a "1" in the item with the highest percentage.

1. **What type of device did the offender use to store, trade, or view material?**
   ☐ Computer   ☐ Cell phone   ☐ Gaming Systems   ☐ External   ☐Other

2. **What type of media were used?**
   ☐ Images   ☐ Video

3. **Where did the offender obtain the material?**
   ☐ E-mail   ☐ Chat   ☐ P2P   ☐ Self-Produced   ☐ Newsgroups   ☐ Other

4. **Estimated number of probable Child Abusive Material.**
   ☐ < 50   ☐ 51–500   ☐ 501–1000   ☐ >1000

(continued)

Figure 9.1 Child Abusive Material Questionnaire

5. **What percentage of the overall pornography was the illegal material?**
   ☐ Under 25%   ☐ 26–50%   ☐ 51–75%   ☐ 76–100%

6. **What age groups were represented in the illegal material?**
   ☐ <2 years   ☐ 2–10   ☐ 11–13   ☐ 14–18

7. **What was the gender of the child victims represented in the material?**
   ☐ All Male   ☐ Majority Male   ☐ Equal   ☐ Majority Female   ☐ All Female

8. **Type of Child Abusive Images located (COPINE Scale):**
   ☐ Indicative   ☐ Nudist   ☐ Erotica   ☐ Posing   ☐ Erotic Posing
   ☐ Explicit Erotic Posing   ☐ Explicit Sexual Activity   ☐ Assault
   ☐ Gross Assault   ☐ Sadistic/ Bestiality

9. **When was the most recent Child Abusive image viewed?**

10. **Type of adult pornographic images located:**

11. **Were the Child Abusive Material categorized into specific folders?**

    ☐ No   ☐ Yes, Please explain:

12. **Were the adult pornographic images categorized into specific folders?**

    ☐ No   ☐ Yes, Please explain:

13. **Did they alter any of the Child Abusive Material?**

    ☐ No   ☐ Yes, Please explain:

14. **Did the offender attempt to hide the images either physically (e.g. thumb drives, etc.) or electronically (e.g., encryption, etc.)?**
    ☐ No   ☐ Yes, Please explain: :

15. **What other types of paraphilias were observed (legal and illegal)?**
    ☐ Sadism   ☐ Bestiality   ☐ Voyeurism   ☐ Exhibitionism Other

16. **Did the offender communicate with minors?**
    ☐ No   ☐ Yes, Please explain:

17. **Did the offender communicate with other adults to obtain Child Abusive Material?**
    ☐ No   ☐ Yes, Please explain: :

18. **What were the offender screen names or other identifying material?**

19. **Do you have any suspicions of a hands-on victim?**

    ☐ No   ☐ Yes, Please explain:

20. **Do you have any other concerns?**

Figure 9.1 cont.

Non-Internet Related Assessment

The non-Internet related assessment is the first clinical task to perform after reviewing the case documents. During the non-Internet related assessment the first phase of the clinical interview is conducted in order to collect information regarding the client's family, social, educational, relationship, criminal, and offline sexual history. This chapter assumes most clinicians have been clinically trained on conducting a standard psychosocial interview. For that reason, this aspect of the assessment is not discussed in detail in this chapter.

The following is an abbreviated history gathered during the psychosocial clinical interview of Mr. Hartfield:

Prior to his incarceration, Mr. Hartfield resided in the Midwestern region of the United States. Mr. Hartfield and his older biological sister were raised by their biological parents. Mr. Hartfield described his parents as strict, but not abusive. He described himself as a "good son" who never got into trouble while growing up. Mr. Hartfield reported his parents and sister were emotionally supportive of him during his incarceration, and remained supportive of him following his release.

Mr. Hartfield is in his second marriage (of 20 years) and he has one biological daughter (age 19) from his current marriage and no stepchildren. He indicated his wife has been supportive throughout his incarceration and agreed to remain married to him during his incarceration.

Mr. Hartfield graduated high school with an above-average GPA (3.65) and reported no educational difficulties. He did report feeling socially awkward and struggled with social skills during his middle and high school years. He reported these issues continued into adulthood. He attended college immediately after high school, but only attended for 2 years before leaving to pursue a romantic relationship. At age 25, Mr. Hartfield returned to college and received his bachelor's degree in Music.

At the time of the assessment, Mr. Hartfield was unemployed due to his time in prison. He was seeking employment. Prior to his incarceration he had been self-employed as a webpage designer, work that he had done for 15 years. There was no history of any major occupational difficulties throughout Mr. Hartfield's employment history, and he had never been dismissed from a job.

Prior to his incarceration, Mr. Hartfield reported he and his wife had been "great companions" and were very successful at parenting together; however, he described an overall lack of intimacy, romance, and sexuality in his marriage. After the pregnancy and birth of their daughter, Mr. Hartfield reported there was a significant decline in the frequency of sexual activity. The lack of sexual activity in the marriage remained a constant over the years prior to his incarceration. Since his release from prison, he was uncertain as to the status of his relationship with his wife. He reported that after 8 years of incarceration the lack of connection and intimacy had only deepened.

Before his arrest, Mr. Hartfield had one or two male friends; however, these friendships appeared to lack any emotional depth or intimacy. He was involved in his church; however, he reported no close relationships with other church members. During his incarceration he reported significant isolation and a lack of friendships within the prison. The only contacts he maintained outside the prison were with his immediate family.

Prior to his arrest for possession of child pornography, Mr. Hartfield was diagnosed with a low-grade depression and sought pharmacological intervention for the depression. He was prescribed an antidepressant, Wellbutrin, to help alleviate his symptoms which included a lack of motivation and energy as well as general sense of hopelessness. He reported that after starting the Wellbutrin his depression improved and he experienced a decrease in what Mr. Hartfield described as his "problematic use of online pornography." He has remained on Wellbutrin ever since it was first prescribed. He continued his use of Wellbutrin during his incarceration for his ongoing depressive symptoms. Mr. Hartfield reported increased depression as well as situational anxiety related to his release back into the community. Other than these episodes, Mr. Hartfield has no notable psychiatric history. Mr. Hartfield reported no history of physical, sexual, or emotional abuse. Additionally, he reported no history of drug or alcohol abuse or dependence.

Mr. Hartfield's first exposure to adult pornography was around age 19 when he discovered pornography magazines. His use of adult pornography was episodic and did not appear to cause any marked distress or difficulties. Prior to his use of the Internet, Mr. Hartfield's sexual behavior would be considered typical for a young adult male. He reported no experimentation with homosexuality, prostitution, affairs outside of marriage, or any other type of sexual fetish behavior. Mr. Hartfield denied any problematic sexual behaviors prior to using the Internet.

There were no disciplinary actions against Mr. Hartfield during his incarceration. He also took advantage of several vocational/educational courses. Although he reported interest in receiving treatment while in prison, the facility where he was housed did not offer sex offender-specific treatment. During his incarceration he served as an assistant in the prison library, and was viewed as a model inmate in many ways. This all led to his early release in 2011, after having served 8 years of a 10-year sentence.

A comprehensive non-Internet related assessment also includes a battery of psychological testing. Typical areas considered appropriate to assess in child pornography Internet related cases include:

- Mood Disorders (e.g., Beck Depression Inventory, Beck Anxiety Inventory)

- General Mental Health (e.g., Minnesota Multiphasic Personality Inventory)
- Personality Disorders (e.g., Millon Clinical Multiaxial Inventory)
- Psychopathy (e.g., Psychopathy Check List)
- Adult Attention Deficit (e.g., Test of Variable Intelligence)
- Offline Sexual Compulsivity/Hypersexuality (e.g., Hypersexual Behavior Index)
- Offline Sexual Deviance/Aggression (e.g., Multidimensional Inventory of Development, Sex, and Aggression)
- Substance Abuse/Dependency (e.g., Substance Abuse Subtle Screening Inventory)
- Intelligence/Learning Disabilities (e.g., Wechsler Adult Intelligence Scale)

Each evaluation requires clinicians to determine which tests are appropriate for the client based on current clinical information and the history of the client. The following psychological battery was administered to Mr. Hartfield: (a) Minnesota Multiphasic Personality Inventory, (b) Millon Clinical Multiaxial Inventory, (c) Beck Depression/Beck Anxiety Inventories, and (d) Hypersexual Behavior Inventory.

Mr. Hartfield's MMPI-2 and MCMI-III results indicated no significant elevations on any subscale. Most notably, there was no elevation on the "Psychopathic Deviate" scale on the MMPI-2. Elevations on this scale could be an indicator of future risk for violence, criminal acts, or hands-on sexual offense behavior. The Millon-III ruled out the presence of any personality disorder which would have been both an indicator of future risk for criminal behavior and reduced amenability to treatment.

Although Mr. Hartfield reported symptoms of depression and anxiety, they did not rise to a level of clinical concern on either instrument. Mr. Hartfield's score on the BDI–II was a 15, falling in the moderate range of concern. Mr. Hartfield's score of 16 on the BAI indicated a moderate level of anxiety. Mr. Hartfield's levels of depression and anxiety at the time of his assessment appeared to be the result of his community re-entry.

In Mr. Hartfield's case, several tests were not administered. Based on the absence of a criminal history and the benign results on his MMPI-2 and the MCMI-III, it was determined that measures of psychopathy (specifically the Psychopathy Checklist) were unnecessary. In addition, there were no indications of learning disabilities, attention-related issues, or substance abuse; therefore, tests to assess these areas were not included as part of Mr. Hartfield's testing battery. Finally, based on Mr. Hartsfield's history provided in the clinical interview, there was no evidence of offline sexual deviance or sexual aggression, and therefore these issues were not formally assessed with testing instruments.

Global Internet Assessment

Although the non-Internet related assessment (e.g., psychosocial inter-view, psychological testing, etc.) is important, equally important is the assessment of an individual's online history and behavior, both nonsexual (e.g., online gaming, gambling, shopping, etc.) and sexual (e.g., pornog-raphy, cybersex chatting, etc.). This aspect of the assessment is commonly overlooked, since clinicians do not always feel comfortable or adequate in assessing for their client's technology use (Quayle & Taylor, 2002).

In order to assess Mr. Hartfield's nonsexual problematic online behav-ior, the Internet Addiction Scale was used (IAS; Young, 2011). The IAS was created by adapting *DSM* criteria for pathological gambling; however, it broadly assesses for general problematic online behavior. The IAS mea-sures the degree to which the Internet affects an individual's daily life. There were no indicators of nonsexual problematic online behavior; there-fore, no follow-up assessment was necessary. If Mr. Hartfield had been assessed to have nonsexual Internet related problems, further assessment would be done to determine which specific areas of his Internet use were problematic (e.g., gambling, gaming, shopping, etc.).

In order to assess for online sexual problems, a semistructured clinical interview designed for such purposes was used. This instrument is known as the Internet Assessment (IA-3; Delmonico & Griffin, 2012). The full version of this instrument provides a list of 50 common questions that should be addressed during a clinical interview for online problematic sexual behavior. There is an additional supplement to this instrument that specifically addresses the use of online child pornography. A sampling of questions from this instrument is provided in Figure 9.2.

The IA-3 assesses issues such as the client's arousal interests, techno-logical skill level, risky and illegal online behaviors, level of secrecy, and presence of online compulsive sexual behavior. The IA-3 is useful in deter-mining the breadth, depth, and progression of online pornography use as well as psychological, emotional, and social issues related to problematic online sexual behavior.

The IA-3 also includes questions related to the "Psychology of the Internet" and how the online environment may have affected a client's online sexual behavior. Wallace (1999) discussed the "Psychology of the Internet" as a way to understand why individuals do things online they would never do in real life. Kiesler, Siegel, and McGuire (1984) suggested the lack of social cues interfered with computer mediated communica-tions, including a decrease in empathy. It was hypothesized that the end result was that individuals were less inhibited when using technology. Suler (2004) coined the term "online disinhibition effect" which included a series of factors causing individuals to decrease their online inhibitions and contributing to behavior such as viewing online pornography. The

Section I: Internet Knowledge and Behavior

1. Over the past 6 months, on average how many hours per week is your computer logged on to the Internet? On average, how many of those online hours do you sit in front of your computer and use the Internet (not necessarily for sexual purposes)?
2. Over the past 6 months, on average how many hours per week have you actively engaged in Internet sex, including downloading images, sexual chats, etc.?
3. Have you ever posted/traded any sexual material on or through the Internet? This would include self-photos, photos of others, sexual stories, videos, audio clips, sexual blogs, sexual profiles, etc.
4. Have you ever viewed child pornography or images of individuals who appeared to be less than 18 years old?
5. Have you ever tried to conceal yourself or the places you have been online (e.g., clearing your history or cache, using programs to hide/clean your online tracks, deleted/renamed downloaded files, used anonymous services, stealth surfers, etc.)?

Section II: Social, Sexual, and Psychological

6. Has your offline sexuality ever been impacted by your online sexual behaviors?
7. Has there ever been a relationship between your masturbation and cybersex behaviors?
8. Have you ever noticed a progression in your sexual risk taking behavior (either on or offline) as a result of your cybersex behavior.
9. Have you ever experienced consequences, or jeopardized important life areas (e.g., work, family, friends) as a result of your online sexual behaviors?
10. Has your partner ever complained about your Internet sexual behavior?

Section III: Child Pornography Supplement

11. What is your definition of a child pornography image? (Should include all children up to age 18)
12. Describe a typical child pornography image/video/story that you would be aroused to (e.g., age, gender, image, type of activity—BDSM, penetration, oral sex, etc.).
13. Approximately how many child pornography images/videos have you seen on the Internet?
14. Approximately how many child pornography images/videos do you have stored electronically somewhere? How is this collection maintained/organized?
15. Describe the process by which you access child pornography online?

Figure 9.2 Internet Assessment Sample Questions

Internet Assessment is one tool to assist the clinician in determining the role the psychology of the Internet may play in an individual's online sexual behavior.

While there is no "score" on the Internet Assessment, the data gained from following the structured clinical interview was helpful in gathering data to complete Mr. Hartfield's history of online sexual behavior.

In 1999 Mr. Hartfield discovered pornography on the Internet. Over the next 10 years he reported a slow, but steady increase in the frequency and intensity of viewing online adult pornography that in his words became "very compulsive and addictive." It was the clinician's opinion that the psychology of the Internet contributed to Mr. Hartfield's initial use of online adult pornography as a way to escape his depressive symptoms and self-medicate his social awkwardness as well as his lack of intimacy, especially related to his relationship with his wife. He admitted his pornography use eventually developed into curiosities about fetish behavior. In the process of this progressive escalation and pursuit of adult pornography, Mr. Hartfield discovered Japanese "Chan" sites. It was in these sites that he first viewed child pornography. Following his initial discovery of child pornography, Mr. Hartfield reported his "curiosity" contributed to his continued viewing of child pornography. This curiosity, combined with the psychology of the Internet appeared to lead to an escalation in the frequency and intensity of Mr. Hartfield's pornography use, which now included both adult and child images. Mr. Hartfield admitted he masturbated to images of both adults and children, indicating a level of sexual arousal that included both types of images. Data from the forensic analysis and the IA-3 supported claims that Mr. Hartfield viewed both adult and child pornography. Data also supported that there was a progression from viewing adult pornography to viewing child pornography over a period of time.

Another instrument useful in assessing online problematic sexual behavior is the *Internet Sex Screening Test* (ISST; Delmonico & Griffin, 1999). The ISST was developed as a screening tool for helping professionals to determine if an individual may have a problem with their online sexual behavior. The instrument consists of 34 true/false questions including nine items designed to measure offline sexually compulsive behavior (See Figure 9.3). Results can be interpreted as an overall scale score to measure online sexual compulsivity, as well as the nine-item measure of offline sexual compulsivity. Initial psychometrics were established for the ISST by Delmonico and Miller (2003). After initial screening with the Offline Sexual Compulsivity subscale on the ISST, if indicated, several other *offline* sexual compulsivity scales may be used. These scales include the Sexual Addiction Screening Test (Carnes, 1989), and the Hypersexual Behavior Index (Reid, Garos, & Carpenter, 2011).

Mr. Hartfield scored zero on the nine-item offline sexual compulsivity scale, indicating no concerns or problems with compulsive offline sexual behavior. However, his score on the total score for online sexual compulsivity was 21 out of 25. Scores at 19 or above are clinically significant and are likely an indicator of online compulsive sexual behavior (Delmonico & Griffin, 1999).

Physiological Testing

Although the data from the clinical interview and the comprehensive testing data are critical components of a comprehensive evaluation, it is important to consider a client's sexual interest or sexual arousal in cases where child pornography is involved. In addition, it is important to measure

Directions: Read each statement carefully. If the statement is mostly TRUE, place a check mark on the blank next to the item number. If the statement is mostly false, skip the item and place nothing next to the item number.

____ 1. I have some sexual sites bookmarked.

____ 2. I spend more than 5 hours per week using my computer for sexual pursuits.

____ 3. I have joined sexual sites to gain access to online sexual material.

____ 4. I have purchased sexual products online.

____ 5. I have searched for sexual material through an Internet search tool.

____ 6. I have spent more money for online sexual material than I planned.

____ 7. Internet sex has sometimes interfered with my certain aspects of my life.

____ 8. I have participated in sexually related chats.

____ 9. I have a sexualized username or nickname that I use on the Internet.

____ 10. I have masturbated while on the Internet.

____ 11. I have accessed sexual sites from other computers besides my home.

____ 12. No one knows I use my computer for sexual purposes.

____ 13. I have tried to hide what is on my computer or monitor so others cannot see it.

____ 14. I have stayed up after midnight to access sexual material online.

____ 15. I use the Internet to experiment with different aspects of sexuality (e.g., bondage, homosexuality, anal sex, etc.)

____ 16. I have my own website which contains some sexual material.

____ 17. I have made promises to myself to stop using the Internet for sexual purposes.

____ 18. I sometimes use cybersex as a reward for accomplishing something. (e.g., finishing a project, stressful day, etc.)

____ 19. When I am unable to access sexual information online, I feel anxious, angry, or disappointed.

____ 20. I have increased the risks I take online (give out name and phone number, meet people offline, etc.)

____ 21. I have punished myself when I use the Internet for sexual purposes (e.g., time-out from computer, cancel Internet subscription, etc.)

____ 22. I have met face to face with someone I met online for romantic purposes.

____ 23. I use sexual humor and innuendo with others while online.

____ 24. I have run across illegal sexual material while on the Internet.

____ 25. I believe I am an Internet sex addict.

____ 26. I repeatedly attempt to stop certain sexual behaviors and fail.

____ 27. I continue my sexual behavior despite it having caused me problems.

____ 28. Before my sexual behavior, I want it, but afterwards I regret it.

____ 29. I have lied often to conceal my sexual behavior.

____ 30. I believe I am a sex addict.

____ 31. I worry about people finding out about my sexual behavior.

____ 32. I have made an effort to quit a certain type of sexual activity and have failed.

____ 33. I hide some of my sexual behavior from others.

____ 34. When I have sex, I feel depressed afterwards.

Figure 9.3 Internet Sex Screening Test

"truthfulness" as to a client's past and current sexual behaviors. To date, there are several physiological instruments that can assist in measuring sexual interest/arousal and client honesty.

In cases involving child pornography, clinicians should always screen for sexual interest or sexual arousal patterns. Common physiological measures include the Abel Assessment for Sexual Interest (Abel, Huffman, Warberg, & Holland, 1998), a viewing time procedure measuring sexual interest, and penile plethysmographic (phallometric) testing which measures sexual arousal (e.g., Marshall & Fernandez, 2003). An additional method is the Affinity Measure of Sexual Interest (Glasgow, Osborne, & Croxen, 2003). The Affinity combines reports of individuals' ranking and ratings of sexual attractiveness to prototype images with covertly measured viewing times. While there is research that supports and refutes the use of these measures of sexual interest and arousal, in cases involving child pornography it is the authors' belief that the benefits of the information gained from these instruments outweigh the weaknesses associated with them.

In recent years it cannot be assumed that simply because an individual views or collects child pornography that the individual is either interested in or aroused by such material. The relationship between pedophilia and viewing child pornography online remains an area of investigation for researchers. While some studies suggest viewing child pornography may be an indicator of pedophilia (Seto, Cantor, & Blanchard, 2006), others have observed alternative motivations for viewing child pornography unrelated to pedophilia, such as curiosity, accidental, and hypersexuality (Seto, Reeves, & Jung, 2010). The reality is that all three are likely to be true, and the assessment process in such cases must carefully separate individuals who are truly pedophilic from those who are not. Delmonico and Griffin (2008a) suggested the term *Pedophilia 1.0* could be reserved for those who have lifelong, consistent, and primary sexual interest in prepubescent children, while the term *Pedophilia 2.0* may describe the group of individuals who may meet diagnostic criteria for pedophilia for a period of time, but the pedophilia seems more related to other factors than true sexual interest in prepubescent children.

Unfortunately, many clinicians work from the assumption that all individuals who view child pornography are 1.0 pedophiles. While this may have been more likely the case 15 years ago, the widespread availability, ease of access, and anonymity afforded by the Internet has changed our thinking about the nature of pedophilia.

It is important for clinicians to keep in mind that there may be many possible functions Internet child pornography may serve, and measures such as the Abel Screen or phallometric testing will assist in identifying individuals with a true interest/arousal to such material, versus those who are motivated by other psychological reasons (Quayle & Taylor, 2004).

Another physiological measure useful in the assessment of cases involving the child pornography process is the polygraph. Hindman and Peters (2001) outline the basic historical and more recent use of polygraph in the assessment and treatment process of both adult and juvenile sex offenders. The use of polygraph is particularly important in child pornography cases since it is one way to assist in determining if the client has a hands-on offense in his history. The research on past hands-on contact offense is mixed; however, Eke and Seto (2012) conducted a meta-analysis of 21 samples of online offenders. They reported that within a subset of six studies where data was available, approximately 50% of subjects self-reported a past, hands-on contact offense with a child. Eke and Seto cautioned that there was one outlier in the study, and this study may have skewed the sample toward a higher than actual percent. Following the data analysis, Eke and Seto asserted that there is a "large proportion" of online offenders who do not have a past contact offense. The use of a polygraph can provide one piece of objective data in separating those who have a past contact offense from those who do not. Most polygraphers believe a separate polygraph should be conducted specific to online behavior and not combined with general questions regarding offline sexual behavior.

In Mr. Hartfield's case, he was administered an Abel Assessment of Sexual Interest (AASI–3) and a polygraph. Mr. Hartfield's Abel Assessment provided objective evidence clearly indicating that Mr. Hartfield's primary sexual interest was to adult females, followed by a secondary interest in adolescent females (which is considered a normal, nondeviant response). There was no indication of any sexual interest in prepubescent children. Also there was no indication of sexual interest in males, adult, adolescent, or children. Mr. Hartfield's AASI–3 results were consistent with his self-report during the clinical interview as well as the forensic analysis.

Mr. Hartfield's Abel Assessment of Sexual Interest (AASI) results also indicated a cognitive distortion score of 6%. This score is considered low and does not reflect the typical distortions and justifications used by individuals who molest children. The AASI also computes a "Probability Score" which compares an individual's AASI with other individuals who have known sexual offenses and those who deny committing a hands-on sexual offense in the past. Although this is a new measure and should be interpreted with caution, there are few other instruments that attempt to measure the probability of a past hands-on offense. Scores can range from -5.0 to +5.0. Mr. Hartfield's probability score was −0.568. This score is considered to fall in the "Lower Probability Category" (the lowest range possible) and would suggest that Mr. Hartfield is likely being honest about not having a previous hands-on offense in the past.

Since Mr. Hartfield self-reported no history of contact offenses with children, a polygraph was administered to help determine the truthfulness of this report. The results of the polygraph indicated Mr. Hartfield was being truthful in regard to the issue of past contact offenses with children.

Results from the physiological measures are useful in determining true sexual interest/arousal patters, detecting the presence of past contact offenses, and considering risk to the community.

Risk Assessment

The final issue to address in the assessment process is risk to community. The risk assessment of online child pornography offenders with no known contact offense is somewhat problematic since currently there is no standardized risk assessment protocol for such clients. As a result, one must look to the professional literature for current research regarding risk for online child pornography offenders. Eke and Seto (2012) provided an empirically derived list of factors that should be considered when assessing risk for online child pornography offenders. Many of the same factors that apply to contact sex offenders also appear to be statistically loading for online child pornography offenders as well. The list includes:

- Age at first offense (younger is more concerning)
- Any prior criminal history (sexual or nonsexual, violent or nonviolent)
- Substance abuse problems
- Self-reported (or measured) sexual interest in prepubescent children
- Child pornography content focused on male prepubescent children
- Unmarried
- Low education level

Research is being conducted on some of the existing risk assessment tools. Initial reports indicate that with some modifications, existing risk assessment tools may be useful with online child pornography offenders. The two instruments showing the most promise at this point are the Risk Matrix 2000 (modified) and the Stable-2000 (unmodified) (Webb, Craissati, & Keen, 2007). Due to the lack of validation on Internet only child pornography offenders, these instruments are best used to anchor clinical conclusions made from other case data.

Mr. Hartfield did not have any of the potential risk factors listed by Eke and Seto (2012). Mr. Hartfield was also assessed using the modified Risk Matrix 2000, received a score of zero (0), and was therefore given a risk level of "low." Data collected for the Risk Matrix 2000 was consistent with other data gathered in this case and the assessment of "low" was also consistent with other risk related information.

The comprehensive evaluation of online sex offenders can be both time consuming and expensive. Clinicians will likely need to prioritize which assessment tools and techniques are warranted and necessary on a

☐ Family/Social/Educational History/Relationship/Criminal
☐ Offline Sexual History
    ☐ Sexually Compulsive Offline?
☐ Pornography History (Adult and/or Child)
☐ Psychological Testing
☐ Psychopathy Checklist–Revised (If Indicated)
☐ Internet Assessment
☐ Nonsexual Internet History
☐ Internet Sex Screening Test
☐ Risk Concerns / Assessment
☐ Polygraph Results
☐ Penile Plethysmograph (PPG)
☐ Abel Assessment of Sexual Interest/Affinity
☐ Forensic Analysis Review (e.g., Chat Logs/Forensic Report/Image Review Report)
☐ Legal Documents (if legal case)

Figure 9.4 Comprehensive Assessment Checklist

case-by-case basis. The "Comprehensive Assessment Checklist" compiles items that could be included in the assessment and helps prioritize the assessment data gathered. The checklist appears in Figure 9.4.

Case Formulation

The case formulation for Mr. Hartfield was based on the data gathered from the five areas of assessment, which included: (a) case-related document review, (b) non-Internet related assessments (including psychological testing), (c) global Internet assessment, (d) physiological testing, and (e) risk assessment.

Mr. Hartfield is an adult male who discovered online child pornography after a long-term history of viewing online adult pornography. Mr. Hartfield appeared to have no significant psychiatric history, other than difficulties with emotional regulation. This difficulty with emotional regulation seems to have contributed to his problematic online sexual behavior. There was no evidence of an Axis II personality disorder, specifically antisocial personality disorder was ruled out.

It appeared that Mr. Hartfield had developed online sexual compulsivity which was facilitated by the psychology of the Internet. The combination of Mr. Hartfield's emotional dysregulation and the psychology of the Internet appeared to lead to the development of online sexually compulsive behaviors and eventually the discovery and use of online child pornography.

While viewing online child pornography, Mr. Hartfield would likely have met the criteria for pedophilia; however, all data collected as part of the assessment indicate he does not have ongoing sexual interest in prepubescent or pubescent children. Mr. Hartfield appeared to be a Pedophile 2.0 given the Internet-facilitated nature of his viewing of child pornography and given that he did not seem to have an ongoing sexual interest in prepubescent/pubescent children. A thorough review of the forensic data from Mr. Hartfield's computer, combined with results from the Abel Assessment and polygraph provided objective data that supported the clinical assertion that Mr. Hartfield is not a pedophile in the traditional sense of the diagnosis.

Based on information from Mr. Hartfield's self-report, clinical interview, and polygraph data, there was no evidence of a past contact sexual offense. In addition, all future risk assessment data gathered supported that Mr. Hartfield was a "low risk" for both a future hands-on offense, as well as a future online offense with child pornography. The Risk Matrix 2000 was also administered to help solidify the clinical judgments made based on all the other data.

Although Mr. Hartfield required treatment, based on all data gathered, it appeared he did not need long term, extensive treatment, but rather would benefit from short term issue-focused treatment. Placing low risk individuals into long term, intensive treatment when it is not indicated has actually been shown to be countertherapeutic. This concept is referred to as the "The Risk Principle." The risk principle asserts that the most restrictive environments and intensive sentences should be directed at higher risk offenders; whereas, offenders assessed as low risk should be assigned to minimal levels of restriction and services (Andrews & Bonta, 2006).

Treatment Plan and Implementation

The field of Internet sex offenders is relatively new, and little has been done to empirically measure treatment approaches for Internet based sex offenders. Much of the focus of the field has been on understanding the unique characteristics of online sex offenders, and more recently the risk they pose to the community.

The research is beginning to identify dynamic risk factors associated with online sex offending. In the literature regarding online child pornography offenders, several dynamic risk factors have emerged. These include: (a) emotional regulation (Beech & Elliott, 2009); (b) social skills/intimacy (Beech & Elliott, 2009); (c) deviant arousal (Beech & Elliott, 2009); (d) online hypersexuality (Kaplan & First, 2009); and (e) problematic Internet use (Beech & Elliott, 2009).

Another consideration in treatment planning should always include victim empathy. Although research suggests that online sex offenders score higher than their offline counterparts on measures of victim empathy (Babchishin, Hanson, & Hermann, 2011), it is common for individuals who view online child pornography to minimize the impact their behavior has on the abuse of children. For that reason, it was determined that victim empathy would be addressed in Mr. Hartfield's treatment.

In addition, the treatment plan used a number of concepts from the Good Lives Model (Laws & Ward, 2011), which asserts that it is "capable of handling the issue of reintegration, because of its stress on building better lives for offenders, which acknowledges their interdependency with others, and the value of being socially embedded within intimate relationships and communities" (p. 213). It was believed Mr. Hartfield would benefit from this strength based approach to treatment especially given that he was just released from an extended period of incarceration and needed to master many of the components of the Good Lives Model.

The following sections include the main areas of treatment addressed with Mr. Hartfield and are applicable to most child pornography cases.

Emotional Regulation

In order to address issues related to emotional regulation Mr. Hartfield was referred to a psychiatrist for a medication evaluation. An evaluation by a psychiatrist is often helpful to determine if medication/dosage changes are necessary. This is especially true following an extended incarceration period.

Treatment also explored the use of progressive relaxation techniques, visualization exercises, and mindfulness to assist Mr. Hartfield in developing skills to effectively manage his anxiety and depression. Workbooks are often helpful in structuring specific exercises in stress reduction and relaxation. The workbook used with Mr. Hartfield was *The Relaxation and Stress Reduction Workbook* (Davis, Eshelman, & McKay, 2008). Exercises from two other workbooks were also used to help Mr. Hartfield manage his stress and anxiety: *The Cognitive Behavioral Workbook for Depression: A Step by Step Program* (Knaus & Ellis, 2006) and *The Cognitive Behavioral Workbook for Anxiety: A Step by Step Program* (Knaus & Carlson, 2008).

Social Skills/Intimacy

Social skills and intimacy are often therapeutic issues for individuals with problematic online sexual behavior (Beech & Elliott, 2009). Mr. Hartfield was placed in a group exclusive to other child pornography offenders. Separating child pornography offenders from contact offenders is preferred since child pornography offenders often use contact offenders to minimize their own offense behaviors.

One primary focus of Mr. Hartfield's group was to encourage interactions among members in order to build social skills and intimacy. Role play and drama exercises were often used in group to simulate situations in which these skills were important. One source used for role play and drama scenarios was the *Geese Theatre Handbook* (Baim & Brookes, 2002). As group cohesion developed the group members took the initiative to develop a "group contact list." The group members were encouraged to reach out to one another through phone calls, text messaging, e-mail, and Facebook posts. This group contact list helped achieve several treatment goals. It allowed group members to practice their developing social skills, it encouraged seeking and giving support to one another, and helped to establish healthy technology skills (discussed below).

Mr. Hartfield's attendance in group therapy was critical to the development of his social/intimacy skills. The group was process focused that used the "here-and-now" to highlight the relational aspects of the group. For example, on one occasion Mr. Hartfield was sharing a story with the group, but another group member kept interrupting Mr. Hartfield. As a result, Mr. Hartfield simply "shut down" and stopped telling the story. The group leader stopped the group and began to process the relationship aspect of the interaction—the interrupting client learned how his behavior was impacting Mr. Hartfield and the group, while Mr. Hartfield was encouraged to assert himself and voice his emotions/needs. Several weeks later, the two men reported their relationship was stronger because of the confrontation and honesty. This was used to highlight how intimacy develops and that even difficult interactions can lead to positive results.

In order to address intimacy issues within their marriage, Mr. and Mrs. Hartfield entered into couples counseling with a different therapist. As they continued in therapy, it was clear Mr. Hartfield was gaining important intimacy skills that were applicable not only to his marriage, but were being used as a foundation for all relationships. This generalization of skills was discussed in group and individual therapy.

Deviant Arousal

Based on Mr. Hartfield's clinical interview, data from his Abel Assessment of Sexual Interest and his polygraph results, it was determined that deviant arousal was not an issue that needed to be addressed in treatment. However, deviant arousal may be an issue in many child pornography cases. When deviant arousal patterns are present, it is important to consider the behavioral techniques for modifying sexual arousal that are well documented in the literature (Marshall, O'Brien, & Marshall, 2008).

Online Sexual Compulsivity

Based on Mr. Hartfield's history, clinical interview, and psychological testing results, it was determined that treatment should address issues related to online sexual compulsivity. The term *online sexual compulsivity* (OSC) is used to describe individuals whose online behavior led to significant interference with their social, occupational, educational opportunities, and who continue to engage in online sexual behavior despite the risk and consequence associated with it (Cooper, Delmonico, & Burg, 2000).

The timing of addressing OSC is important to treatment. If the concept is presented too early, some clients will use it as an excuse for their behavior and minimize their decision making role in the process. The concept was first introduced to Mr. Hartfield approximately 3 months into treatment. He agreed that at some point he felt his online sexual behavior was out of control, causing significant life problems, and certainly had legal consequences he had ignored. Although there is not official diagnosis for OSC, the pattern of behavior needed to be addressed in treatment as part of a larger relapse prevention strategy.

Earlier in treatment Mr. Hartfield underwent a medication evaluation by a psychiatrist familiar with problematic sexual behavior. It was suggested Mr. Hartfield discuss the concept of online sexual compulsivity with his psychiatrist at his next visit and discuss the ways his current medications (or possibly other medications) could be helpful in preventing relapse with online sexual compulsivity. The professional literature contains information on various forms of medications that can be helpful for people managing their sexual behavior (Kafka, 2007). Examples of common medications used include Selective Serotonin Reuptake Inhibitors (SSRIs), Serotonin-Norepinephrine Reuptake Inhibitors (SNRIs), and Naltrexone (Vivitrol), among others. Some of the medications help by treating comorbid conditions that may have contributed to the problem (e.g., depression, anxiety, etc.) while others have a direct effect on sexuality or impulsive/compulsive behavior. After Mr. Hartfield met with the psychiatrist, and a short phone consultation with the treating clinician, it was determined that Mr. Hartfield would remain on his Wellbutrin and should his online behaviors begin to escalate, additional medications would be prescribed. Mr. Hartfield seemed pleased with this outcome, and also reassured to know that there were medication interventions available should he need them in the future.

Approximately 12 to 15 weeks into treatment, Mr. Hartfield was asked to select a 12-Step support group specific to compulsive sexual issues to attend. Many clinicians who treat offline/online sexual offenders are reluctant to refer clients to 12-Step groups. They often believe the addiction model minimizes or excuses the sexual offense. However, these meetings can provide a valuable practice arena for intimacy skill development, as well as assist in relapse prevention of problematic online sexual behavior. There are a number of "fellowships" across the nation. The support groups available to Mr. Hartfield included Sexaholics Anonymous (SA), Sex Addicts Anonymous (SAA), and Sex and Love Addicts Anonymous (SLAA). After researching and discussing each of these groups, Mr. Hartfield decided to visit the Sex Addicts Anonymous group. The purpose of encouraging attendance at these groups was twofold. Many of the group members also struggled with problematic online pornography use, and Mr. Hartfield felt supported as he thought about using the Internet for the first time in years. These groups also provided Mr. Hartfield another avenue for developing new relationships and practice his skills related to social interaction and intimacy. Mr. Hartfield reported he enjoyed attending weekly groups and it was helpful to his treatment.

Finally, around the same time Mr. Hartfield began attending 12-Step groups, he also was provided a workbook specifically designed to address online problematic sexual behavior. The workbook used was *Cybersex Unhooked: A Workbook for Breaking Free of Compulsive Online Sexual Behavior* (Delmonico, Griffin, & Moriarty, 2001). This workbook takes clients through a series of exercises design to help them examine, reflect on, and change their problematic online sexual behavior. Mr. Hartfield was asked to choose an exercise each week to complete and discuss the exercise either in individual or group therapy. The workbook assisted Mr. Hartfield in assessing what may have contributed to his online use of pornography/child pornography, as well as develop relapse prevention strategies that could be used if he identified the problem recurring. Overall, Mr. Hartfield reported the exercises were helpful, especially at looking at the compulsivity aspect of his problematic online sexual behavior.

Problematic Internet Use

It is a common mistake for clinicians to employ many of the traditional aspects of sex offender treatment in cases of child pornography offense, but never really address the one issue likely contributed to the use of child pornography in the first place—the Internet. Since the Internet played an integral role in Mr. Hartfield's sexual acting out behavior, it is important that treatment also address healthy use of the Internet/technology in the future.

While refraining from Internet/technology use was an option in years past, today it is unreasonable to expect that such a requirement can or will be honored. Therefore, one of the main aspects of healthy technology use is to encourage clients to think about their use of technology prior to accessing the Internet. The authors also believe that having technology/Internet access while on probation or parole is important since the client can begin experimenting with reintegrating technology back into their lives under close supervision. Otherwise, when community supervision ends, the client will have no one to assist in determining healthy use of technology.

During treatment, Mr. Hartfield engaged in two exercises that helped him focus on healthy use of technology. The first exercise used was the "Technology/Internet Health Plan." This exercise was found in the work-book *Cybersex Unplugged: Finding Sexual Health in an Electronic World* (Edwards, Delmonico, & Griffin, 2011). In this exercise the client takes a large piece of paper or poster board and draws three concentric circles similar to dartboard rings. In the innermost circle (also referred to as the "red zone"), Mr. Hartfield listed his technology related behaviors that are never healthy and create significant problems. For example, Mr. Hartfield listed viewing child pornography in this circle. It may also be less direct behaviors, such as Mr. Hartfield's item that he could not access the Inter-net after 11:00 p.m. since he realized all of his sexual offense behavior took place after that time when he felt tired and isolated. Therefore, this became one of his red-zone, forbidden behaviors. The next ring represents the "yellow zone." In the yellow zone clients list behaviors they are uncer-tain about, or behaviors that are sometimes healthy and sometimes are unhealthy. For example, Mr. Hartfield listed "keeping his cell phone in his bedroom at night" since on occasion he had used his cell phone to view pornography; however, he also needed to be able to hear the phone ring during the night for emergency purposes. His solution was to keep the phone on his wife's nightstand to keep from accessing it. Finally, the out-ermost circle is the "green zone." In this circle the client lists technology behaviors that are permissible and healthy. For example, Mr. Hartfield listed texting group members for encouragement, and reading encourag-ing books on his Kindle as "green zone" behaviors. The technology/Inter-net health plan was one way to encourage Mr. Hartfield to be thoughtful about his technology related behaviors, and to plan his behaviors as a pre-ventive step, rather than reactive one.

The second exercise was the development of an Acceptable Use Policy (AUP). The AUP is essentially a list of rules and boundaries that helps to guide and govern a client's technology/Internet use. Hodges and Worona (1996) proposed the AUP should have six basic components: (a) a state-ment to explain the reason for the policy, (b) a statement about what the policy covers, (c) a list of the family members covered by the policy, (d) specific examples of inappropriate behavior, (e) instructions on how to report a violation, and (f) information regarding potential consequences for violations. Delmonico and Griffin (2008) and Delmonico, Griffin, and Edger (2008) created some additional dimensions for the AUP and discussed how marriage and family therapists can help guide families through the formation of the AUP. The AUP can be adapted for clients with problematic sexual behavior and allows them to set clear boundaries for their technology/online behaviors. For example, in one component of the AUP clients consider the total amount of time spent online. Mr. Hartfield determined that if he was spending more than 2 hours per day using technology, it was taking him out of relationships with others and increased the likelihood that he would engage in "yellow" or "red" zone behaviors. Therefore, he set his daily maximum use of technology to no more than 2 hours per day. Other examples of components include meeting others online (through social media or chat rooms), appropriate usernames, and appropriate places to access the Internet. Prior to being arrested, Mr. Hartfield would often go to a local coffee shop and isolate in the corner so no one could see his monitor. He would use the coffee shop network to download child pornography which he would view later when he arrived at home. Therefore, Mr. Hartfield set the coffee shop as off-limits because it was a trigger for his Internet pornography use. These are just a few of the examples of having clients think preventatively about the ways technology/Internet could lead to a relapse.

As a requirement of his release, Mr. Hartfield was given "monitored" Internet access on his home computer and his laptop computer. He was limited to these two computers, which had monitoring software installed. Although there are several monitoring products on the market, including Spector Pro and e-Blaster, Mr. Hartfield's monitoring was done through a product called Internet Probation and Parole Control (IPPC) (http://www.impulsecontrol.net). IPPC is installed by the probation officer on the client's machines and monitors all aspects of computer use. One advantage is that IPPC allows for a clinician to log in; therefore, the clinician has the ability to view reports about a client's online behavior. This can be useful to monitor time of day online, amount of time spent online, as well as websites visited. In addition, IPPC can also serve as the blocking software to block certain websites, or even certain areas of the Internet from being accessed. Should the probation officer or clinician have concerns, the Internet (on that computer) can be limited or shut down completely from a remote location. Mr. Hartfield's monitoring was helpful and certain aspects of his Internet use will be discussed later in this chapter. Perhaps the biggest disadvantage to such software is the false sense of security the software provides to the probation officer, clinician, and client. There are many ways to avoid the system—using an alternate computer, using a mobile device, or accessing computers through cybercafés or public libraries. It should be noted that while blocking and monitoring software can be useful, it should not be viewed as failsafe protection for client relapse.

Although Mr. Hartfield's computer used IPPC for blocking websites and areas of the Internet, there are also a wide variety of commercial products that can be used for blocking purposes. These are often used on a computer to protect a child from pornography, violence, and other inappropriate material, but they may also be used on a client's computer to help him be responsible and accountable for his Internet use. The same caution mentioned above, should be applied here; software is not a failsafe relapse prevention product. Behun, Sweeney, Delmonico, and Griffin (2012) published an article on various forms of blocking and filtering software available to clients. The article addresses cell phones, gaming systems, and other devices that access the Internet in addition to personal computers.

Victim Empathy

Viewing pornography online allows for the objectification of the individuals in the photographs. This is true for adult pornography, and is one of the theories as to how individuals can internally reconcile the use of child pornography. Children are translated into sexual objects without emotion. The idea of victim empathy has been long discussed in traditional sex offender literature (Marshall, Marshall, Serran, & O'Brien, 2009); however, this is particularly difficult to address in cases of child pornography. Offenders often fail to make the connection that sexual abuse of the child occurred in order for the photographs to be created. This is why clinicians will often hear the minimization from the child pornography offender that they never actually touched a child, so there was no victim. Quayle, Erooga, Wright, Taylor, and Harbison (2006) authored a workbook titled *Only Pictures?* which was designed to help online child pornography offenders work through their cognitive distortions regarding the victimization of children in child pornography images. Several exercises from this book were used with Mr. Hartfield during treatment.

An additional exercise included assigning Mr. Hartfield to read the novel *Wicked*. This book (and musical) tells the story of the "wicked witch of the West" from the movie the *Wizard of Oz*. Mr. Hartfield was asked to read this novel and then discuss the new perspective the book offers about the wicked witch. The book shared her personal story in a way that allowed readers to develop understanding and empathy for her throughout the book. In the end, the wicked witch was a person with a story. Mr. Hartfield was then asked to think about the victims in the child pornography images and create a story of what their abuse must have been like in order for the photograph to be created. Following the exercise, Mr. Hartfield demonstrated a new level of empathy in understanding the victimization of children in child sex abuse images, and his minimization of the damage caused to such children was significantly reduced. Following this discussion, Mr. Hartfield was encouraged to think about the story of the wicked witch and apply to his current situation. This allowed Mr. Hartfield to examine his own story and develop self-empathy while recognize the negative impact of his behavior.

Good Lives Model

Throughout the treatment process with Mr. Hartfield, principles from the Good Lives Model were incorporated. The "primary human goods" considered important in Mr. Hartfield's case included vocational, relatedness, community, spirituality, happiness, and inner-peace. Given that Mr. Hartfield was incarcerated for 8 years, the principles from the Good Lives approach helped him to develop or rediscover his strengths. As part of this Good Lives approach, Mr. Hartfield was encouraged to engage in activities that brought him increased life satisfaction. Beech and Elliott (2009) wrote that child pornography offenders often have a higher capacity for accomplishing these goals as compared to many of their offline contact offender counterparts. For Mr. Hartfield these included joining an instrumental group that played at his church, trying out for a part in community theater, and attending his church and singing in the choir.

The latest research on Internet sex offenders and their treatment (Webb et al., 2007) indicates that the Internet sex offender is (a) significantly less likely to miss treatment appointments, (b) significantly less likely to drop out of treatment, and (c) significantly less likely to fail in community supervision. All of these factors were found to be true for Mr. Hartfield, as he was highly successful in addressing his treatment goals.

Complications in Treatment

Even though child pornography offenders are thought to have a positive prognosis, treatment is not without its challenges. Given the psychology of the Internet, combined with Mr. Hartfield's emotional dysregulation, social skills deficits, and intimacy issues, lapses in progress were expected and witnessed.

One such lapse occurred when a quick review of the monitoring report revealed Mr. Hartfield was spending an increasing amount of time online. Further investigation showed that in a one week period he was spending an average of 4 hours per day logged on to the Internet from his monitored computer. The monitoring data indicated most of his time was being spent playing online games. In addition, a number of websites containing images of 18- to 20-year-old females in swimsuits were discovered. When confronted, Mr. Hartfield reported he was actively seeking these sites. While neither of these behaviors resulted in a parole violation, they were clinically of concern.

One of the goals of treatment was to increase Mr. Hartfield's social and intimacy skills. The increased frequency of online use was interfering with this goal—including several occasions where he admitted he skipped his 12-Step meeting in order to stay home and play online games. Although viewing adult females in swimsuits did not qualify as a violation, the "slippery slope" for Mr. Hartfield included viewing swimsuit pictures of women ages 18 to 20. He admitted many of them appeared underage and it was a concern that this could trigger a relapse into viewing child pornography. In addition, the "slippery slope" included Mr. Hartfield's increased use of the Internet, which could be an indicator of a return to online compulsive behavior

Due to Mr. Hartfield's previous progression from one form of pornography to another, and his online hypersexuality, he agreed that viewing the images mentioned above should be placed on his Technology/Internet Health Plan in the "red zone." Mr. Hartfield also placed online gaming in his "yellow zone" in order to better monitor his time online and the dangers of becoming a compulsive online gamer. Finally, in consultation with his parole officer, the monitoring program was used to further limit the number of hours his computer could be on the Internet each day, and keywords such as "swimsuit," and "model" were added to a list of words that would be included in the weekly report from the monitoring program. Mr. Hartfield was responsive to the new restrictions and at some level appeared to appreciate the external controls placed on his technology use.

Termination and Relapse Prevention Planning

After 18 months in treatment, Mr. Hartfield was placed on a therapy maintenance plan where he scheduled individual sessions once each month. He continued to attend weekly 12-Step groups, and couples counseling as needed.

Mr. Hartfield's computer continued to be monitored by his parole officer (per the court order); however, at the time of the discharge his parole officer had given Mr. Hartfield greater access to the Internet with few restrictions. Mr. Hartfield was managing his online behavior very well without the filtering of his Internet content. He continued to utilize the Technology/Internet Health Plan established during treatment, and added a weekly online 12-Step group as part of his recovery plan. In addition, Mr. Hartfield scheduled appointments with his psychiatrist once every 6 months for medication monitoring. Mr. Hartfield's emotional regulation appeared well managed; however, it was monitored during appointments with his individual therapist.

Mr. Hartfield's social and intimacy skills remained his biggest challenge. While he enjoyed attending the 12-Step group, he remained cautious in relationships with others. For example, he was invited to have lunch with others from the group, and while he was hesitant to accept, he did join them on several occasions. Mr. Hartfield recognized the importance of the principles of the Good Lives Model and benefitted from taking risks in the development of his strengths. Mr. Hartfield found a job he enjoyed and its regularly scheduled hours help him to structure his time and engage in more self-care activities.

At the end of 24 months, Mr. Hartfield was officially discharged from treatment. Mr. Hartfield planned to see his psychiatrist for medication management, attend weekly 12-Step meetings, and attend couples counseling on an as-needed basis.

Case Conclusion

At the end of treatment, the long-term prognosis for Mr. Hartfield was excellent. Eke and Seto (2012) reported that "child pornography offenders as a group are unlikely to be reported for new sexual offenses, including both contact offense and/or child pornography. This is especially true for child pornography offenders without a prior or concurrent violent/contact sexual offense" (pp. 155–156) as was the case of Mr. Hartfield.

Mr. Hartfield's treatment goals focused on four main issues: (a) emotional regulation, (b) social skills/intimacy, (c) online hypersexuality, and (d) problematic Internet use. Mr. Hartfield addressed each of these issues during the treatment process and was given a number of resources to continue to maintain his health in these areas. At the time of discharge, it was determined that if Mr. Hartfield continued to focus on these areas, his risk of recidivism would remain low.

Nonspecifics of the Case

The therapeutic alliance is important in all clinical situations; however, clinicians are often hesitant to build strong therapeutic relationships with the sex offender. Clinicians often fear they will be vulnerable and manipulated by the sex offender client. There is no data supporting that a strong therapeutic relationship undermines therapy in any way. In fact, Marshall, Marshall, Serran, and O'Brien (2011) discussed the importance of the therapeutic relationship, and identify characteristics in the clinician necessary to promote change in sex offenders. This list includes being (a) warm, (b) empathic, (c) rewarding (in the sense of affirming), and (d) directive.

The importance of the therapeutic relationship in the change process is empirically based and well documented. In numerous studies, clients consistently report the most important and effective aspect of their treatment is not the technique or method used by the clinician, but rather the positive nature of the relationship with their therapist (Duncan, Miller, Wampold, & Hubble, 2011). Clinicians need to remember that this therapeutic alliance is equally important to the online child pornography offender.

When Therapy Is Not Working

Many clients in treatment for viewing child pornography are court ordered to treatment as a condition of their release. The mandated counseling often creates an environment of resistance from the outset of treatment. While many online child pornography offenders acknowledge their viewing of child pornography, they resist being categorized as a sex offender since many of them have had no contact with a child.

It is important for clinicians to examine their own attitudes and behaviors when resistance is encountered in treatment. It is often the most basic changes in attitude or approach that can help the client let down their defenses and engage in treatment, but this requires significant self-awareness on the part of the clinician, and the ability to build a therapeutic relationship.

Finally, it is important to recognize that compliance and success can look similar, but be very different. Online child pornography offenders are often highly likable in treatment. In fact, Bates and Metcalf (2007) reported online child pornography offenders scored higher than their contact offender counterparts on measures of "impression management." However, sometimes these attributes are more about their ability to be compliant without ever addressing significant, underlying psychotherapeutic issues. Clinicians must use their skills to determine if the client is really "doing the work" or just "putting on a show" to avoid underlying issues. This is one reason why a comprehensive evaluation is necessary in online child pornography cases. Clinicians with significant amounts of data are more likely to differentiate the client who is simply "faking good" from the one who is successful in treatment.

Ethical and Legal Considerations

In cases such as Mr. Hartfield, one of the ethical challenges is the balance in honoring the confidentiality of the client, while also providing regular reports to his parole officer on his progress. It is suggested that in order to avoid confusion on the specific conditions of the court order related to technology/Internet use, a meeting be held with the clinician, client, and parole officer. Although court orders may seem clear, there are a variety of ways for interpreting the conditions.

Although Mr. Hartfield's case was governed by the fact that he was on parole, ethical issues often arise when the client is not part of the legal system. One common issue is when a clinician discovers a client is using child pornography. At this time, mandated reporting laws are confusing with regard to this issue and clinicians will need to consult with their individual state laws to determine if they are mandated reporters regarding the possession/viewing of child pornography. Currently, most states do not mandate reporting of this behavior unless the victim is known or the client is producing child pornography.

Another important ethical consideration is whether there is increased liability by having access to the monitoring data from the computer. For example, if a client does use the monitored computer to commit a crime against a child, and such behavior was available in the monitoring data, but was "missed," would the clinician be liable for any harm caused to others. Although this did not occur in the case of Mr. Hartfield, it is a significant consideration when clinicians agree to participate in the monitoring of clients.

Common Mistakes to Avoid

There are a number of common mistakes clinicians make when working with online child pornography cases. Many of these issues have been addressed in other areas of this chapter; however, the list below compiles the most common mistakes that clinicians make. These mistakes are typically due to clinicians' inability to recognize the importance of some aspect of assessment and/or treatment. Clinicians often fail to recognize:

- the subculture of technology and its impact for online offenders
- the role of psychology in the Internet (Delmonico & Griffin, 2011)
- the need for a global Internet assessment
- online child pornography users are not all pedophiles 1.0
- the importance of sexual interest/arousal testing
- the relevance and importance of legal case data (e.g., forensic analysis)
- the need for separate polygraphs for Internet versus non-Internet issues
- the usefulness of an Technology/Internet Health Plan. (Edwards, Delmonico, & Griffin, 2011)

In addition to the above list, clinicians occasionally will "buy in" to their client's minimization of the sexual offense. Although there is no contact offense per se, it is important for clinicians to not minimize the harm/abuse done to child pornography victims. Jonsson and Svedin (2012) reported victims of child sexual abuse whose images are placed on the Internet often report trauma response symptoms when thinking of the many unknown perpetrators viewing their moments of being sexually violated and abused. In order to provide the most effective assessment and treatment of online child pornography cases, it is important to avoid these common clinical mistakes.

"Art" of the Case

Clinicians should be mindful there is no single type of online sexual offender. The professional literature contains several models for understanding these online sexual offenders. One such model was proposed by Beech and Elliot (2012). They postulated there are four broad types of individuals who use the Internet for sexually abusive behaviors against children. These categories include:

Periodically prurient offender: This individual acts impulsively or out of a general curiosity in online sexuality. They engage in online offense behavior sporadically which may be part of a broader interest in pornography and may or may not be related to a specific sexual interest in children.

Fantasy driven/online only offender: This individual accesses or trades child pornography to satisfy his sexual interest in children, but has no known contact offense history.

Direct victimization offender: This individual uses online technologies as part of a larger context of both contact and noncontact offense behavior. This includes viewing sexually explicit materials *and* gaining the trust of a child online in order to facilitate a future offline contact offense.

Commercial exploitation offender: This is the criminally minded individual who produces or trades child pornography in order to achieve financial gain.

Delmonico et al. (2001) proposed a second model for understanding cybersex users. The model is applicable to individuals who use the Internet to collect and view child pornography and cases involving Internet facilitated contact offense against children. The model includes three problematic user categories; discovery users, predisposed users, and lifelong compulsive users. These categories are defined as follows:

Discovery User: An individual with no previous problematic sexual behavior and no evidence of past or current psychological concerns, but upon discovery of online sexuality develops significant sexual problems or commits a sexual offense.

Predisposed User: An individual who has a history of psychological issues that increases vulnerability for problematic online sexual behavior. Engaging in online sexual behavior triggers these dispositions and cybersex use develops into significant sexual issues or sexual offense.

Lifelong Sexually Compulsive User: An individual who has psychological vulnerabilities that have led to a lifelong pattern of compulsive sexual behavior both offline and online.

Clinicians can use these broadly defined categories as one way to better understand the dynamics of the online sexual offense behavior. The "art of the case" is combining the data with a clinician's clinical intuition about which category best describes the client. Understanding all aspects of a client and his online sexual offense behavior can assist clinicians in the individualization of the treatment. The models presented provide one additional way to conceptualize child pornography offenders.

Cultural Considerations

One of the unique skills necessary in working with online sex offenders is the ability to bring information from across various disciplines and combine it with the "culture" of technology. This integration is necessary to assess, manage, and treat the unique issues associate with online sex offense behavior.

While it may not be necessary for clinicians to have a degree in computer science, it is important that they have a basic understanding of how various technologies work, specifically, how sex is accessed via various technologies. For example, not understanding that game systems like Xbox Live provide access to grooming young children and create new opportunities for offense among high tech sex offenders is problematic for clinicians and their clients. In Mr. Hartfield's case it was important for the clinicians to understand the environment of Chan sites and the role they played in Mr. Hartfield's discovery of child pornography. In the absence of such understanding, it would be difficult to ascertain whether Mr. Hartfield's self-report was accurate and truthful.

There are many other examples of how understanding a specific technology can be clinically useful. Clinicians need to make a commitment to learn how various technologies can be used for sexual purposes. Attending continuing education seminars, watching YouTube videos, hiring a local college student, are all ways to increase knowledge about how technologies work and their potential for sexual offense behavior. Tech users have their own subculture, and as with any multicultural counseling endeavor, clinicians must know enough about that culture to interpret behaviors and ask appropriate questions. Training programs often are effective in helping clinicians understand the relevance of culture to the therapeutic relationship. However, technology is often overlooked as a culture in and of itself. It is important to consider the subculture of technology in order to effectively assess and treat online child pornography cases.

Discussion and Implications

Staying current with the research, clinical practice, and technology in sexual offenses involving the use of technology is complicated, but necessary. Not only does technology continue to advance rapidly, but research on the assessment, management, and treatment of online child pornography offenders is also rapidly evolving.

The field of online sex offenders is challenging the long-held beliefs about sex offending behavior and the development of pedophilia. What was once believed to be a lifelong pattern of attraction and arousal to children that was relatively static, may now be viewed as more malleable especially given the role the psychology of the Internet may play in fostering sexual curiosity, interest, arousal, and behavior.

There is debate as to whether the Internet is creating "new" sex offenders or if individuals online would have engaged in sexual offense behavior regardless of the Internet. It is likely that both sides of the debate have truth. For some, like Mr. Hartfield, it is likely he would not have discovered, viewed, or possessed child pornography without the Internet. However, there are others whose primary online motivation from the outset is to view and distribute child pornography images online.

The purpose of this chapter was to examine a single case study of an individual who was court ordered to treatment following an 8-year incarceration period for charges related to the possession of online child pornography and to provide an illustration of an individual that is commonly seen in clinical settings, but does not necessarily mirror our traditional view of a contact sex offender.

This chapter outlined a comprehensive evaluation process that can be applied to most online child pornography cases, and demonstrated how the data gathered helped to create an evidenced based treatment plan and approach to addressing common client issues. The topic of risk assessment is critical in cases such as Mr. Hartfield, and this chapter provided the most current research and thinking on the risk analysis of child pornography offenders. Finally, treatment, both the art and challenges, were addressed in order to help clinicians ready themselves for the challenges, but also help clients such as Mr. Hartfield to discover and develop their strengths through approaches such as the Good Lives Model.

Finally, it is hoped that this chapter provides an evidence based model for understanding, assessing, and treating child pornography offenders. While this chapter is written primarily for the clinician, it is hoped that clients such as Mr. Hartfield will be the ultimate beneficiary of the evidence based information contained in this chapter.

References

Abel, G. G., Huffman, J., Warberg, B. W., & Holland, C. L. (1998). Visual reaction time and plethysmography as measures of sexual interest in child molesters. *Sexual Abuse,* *10*(2), 81–95.

Andrews, D. A., & Bonta, J. (2006). *The psychology of criminal conduct* (4th ed.). Cincinnati, OH: Anderson.

Babchishin, K., Hanson, R. K., & Hermann, C. (2011). The characteristics of online sex offenders: A meta-analysis. *Sexual Abuse: The Journal of Research and Treatment, 23,* 92–123.

Baim, C., & Brookes, S. (2002). *Geese theatre handbook: Drama with offenders and people at risk.* London, England: Waterside Press.

Bates, A., & Metcalf, C. (2007). A psychometric comparison of Internet and non-Internet sex offenders from a community treatment sample. *Journal of Sexual Aggression, 13,* 11–20.

Beech, A. R., & Elliot, I. A. (2009). Understanding online child pornography use: Applying sexual offense theory to Internet offenders. *Aggression and Violent Behavior, 14,* 180–193.

Beech, A. R., & Elliot, I. A. (2012). Understanding the emergence of the Internet sex offender: How useful are current theories in understanding the problem. In E. Quayle & K. Ribisi (Eds.), *Understanding and preventing online sexual exploitation of children* (pp. 44–59). London, England: Routledge.

Behun, R. J., Sweeney, V., Delmonico, D. L., & Griffin, E. J. (2012). Filtering and monitoring for Internet content: A primer for helping professions. *Sexual Addiction & Compulsivity: The Journal of Treatment and Prevention, 19,* 140–155.

Carnes, P. J. (1989). *Contrary to love.* Center City, MN: Hazelden.

Carnes, P. J., Delmonico, D. L., & Griffin, E. J. (2007). *In the shadows of the net: Breaking free of compulsive online sexual behavior* (2nd ed.). Center City, MN: Hazelden.

Cooper, A., Delmonico, D. L., & Burg, R. (2000). Cybersex users, abusers, and compulsives: New findings and implications. *Sexual Addiction & Compulsivity: The Journal of Treatment and Prevention, 7*(1–2), 5–30.

Davis, M., Eshelman, E., & McKay, M. (2008a). *The relaxation and stress reduction workbook.* Oakland, CA: New Harbinger.

Delmonico, D. L., & Griffin, E. J. (1999). *Internet sex screening test.* (Unpublished instrument). Minneapolis, MN: Internet Behavior Consulting. Retrieved from http://www.internetbehavior.com/isst

Delmonico, D. L., & Griffin, E. J. (2008a). Sex offenders online. In D. R. Laws & W. T. O'Donohue (Eds.), *Sexual deviance* (2nd ed.), New York, NY: Guilford.

Delmonico, D. L., & Griffin, E. J. (2008b). Cybersex and the e-teen: What marriage and family therapists should know. *Journal of Marital and Family Therapy, 34*(4), 431–444.

Delmonico, D. L., & Griffin, E. J. (2011). Sex offenders online: What clinicians need to know. In B. Schwartz (Ed.), *Handbook of sex offender treatment* (pp. 1–25). Kingston, NJ: Civic Research Institute.

Delmonico, D. L., & Griffin, E. J. (2012). *Internet Assessment-3: A structured interview for assessing online problematic sexual behavior.* (Unpublished instrument). Minneapolis, MN: Internet Behavior Consulting. Retrieved from http://www.internetbehavior.com/isst

Delmonico, D. L., Griffin, E. J., & Edger, K. (2008, Fall). Setting limits in the virtual world: Helping families develop acceptable use policies. *Paradigm Magazine for Addiction Professionals,12–13,* 22.

Delmonico, D. L., Griffin, E. J., & Moriarty, J. (2001). *Cybersex unhooked: A workbook for breaking free from compulsive online sexual behavior.* Wickenburg, AZ: Gentle Path

Press. Retrieved from http://www.internetbehavior.com/services/cyber_unhooked. htm

Delmonico, D. L., & Miller, J. A. (2003). The internet sex screening test: A comparison of sexual compulsives versus non-sexual compulsives. *Sexual and Relationship Therapy, 18*(3), 261–276.

Duncan, B. L., Miller, S. D., Wampold, B. E., & Hubble, M. A. (2011). *The heart and soul of change: Delivering what works in therapy* (2nd ed.). Washington, DC: American Psychological Association.

Edwards, W. M., Delmonico, D. L., & Griffin, E. J. (2011). *Cybersex unplugged: Finding sexual health in an electronic world.* North Charleston, SC: Createspace.

Eke, A. W., & Seto, M. C. (2012). Risk assessment of child pornography offenders: Applications for law enforcement. In E. Quayle & K. Ribisi (Eds.), *Understanding and preventing online sexual exploitation of children* (pp. 148–168). London, England: Routledge.

Glasgow, D. (2012). The importance of digital evidence in Internet sex offending. In E. Quayle & K. Ribisi (Eds.), *Understanding and preventing online sexual exploitation of children* (pp. 171–187). London, England: Routledge.

Glasgow, D. V., Osborne, A., & Croxen, J. (2003). An assessment tool for investigating paedophile sexual interest using viewing time: An application of single case methodology. *British Journal of Learning Disabilities, 31,* 96.

Hindman, J., & Peters, J. M. (2001). Polygraph testing leads to better understanding adult and juvenile sex offenders. *Federal Probation, 65*(3), 8–15.

Hodges, M. W., & Worona, S. L. (1996, Winter). Legal underpinnings for creating campus computer policy. *Cause/Effect.* Retrieved from http://net.educause.edu/ir/library/html/cem/cem96/cem9642.html

Jonsson, L., & Svedin, C. G. (2012). Children within the images. In E. Quayle & K. Ribisi (Eds.), *Understanding and preventing online sexual exploitation of children* (pp. 23–43). London, England: Routledge.

Kafka, M. P. (2007). Paraphilia-related disorders: The evaluation and treatment of non-paraphilic hypersexuality. In S. R. Leiblum (Ed.), *Principles and practice of sex therapy* (4th ed., pp. 442–476). New York, NY: Guilford.

Kaplan, M., & First, M. (2009). Sexual and other axis one diagnoses of sixty males arrested for crimes against children involving the Internet. *CNS Spectrum, 14*(11), 623–631.

Kiesler, S., Siegel, J., & McGuire, T. W. (1984). Social psychological aspects of computer-mediated communication. *American Psychologist, 39*(10), 1123–1134.

Knaus, W., & Carlson, J. (2008). *A cognitive behavioral workbook for anxiety: A step by step program.* Oakland, CA: New Harbinger.

Knaus, W., & Ellis, A. (2006). *A cognitive behavioral workbook for depression: A step by step program.* Oakland, CA: New Harbinger.

Laws, D. R., & Ward, T. (2011). *Desistance from sex offending: Alternatives to throwing away the keys.* New York, NY: Guilford.

Maalla, N. M. (2009). *Promotion and protection of all human rights, civil, political, economic, social, and cultural rights, including the right to development* (Report of the Special Rapporteur on the sale of children, child prostitution, and child pornography: A report from the United Nations, General Assembly, Human Rights Council). Retrieved from http://www.unhcr.org/refworld/pdfid/4ab0d35a2.pdf

Marshall, W. L., & Fernandez, Y. M. (2003). Phallometric testing with sexual offenders: Theory, research, and practice. Brandon, VT: Safer Society Press.

Marshall, W. L., Marshall, L. E., Serran, G. A., & O'Brien, M. D. (2009). Self-esteem, shame, cognitive distortions and empathy in sexual offenders: Their integration and treatment implications. *Psychology, Crime and Law, 15*(2–3), 217–234.

Marshall, W. L, Marshall, L. E., Serran, G. A., & O'Brien, M. D. (2011). *Rehabilitating sexual offenders: A strength based approach.* Washington, DC: American Psychological Association.

Marshall, W. L., O'Brien, M. D., & Marshall, L. E. (2008). Modifying sexual preferences. In A. Beech, L. Craig, & K. Brown (Eds.), *Assessment and treatment of sex offenders: A handbook* (pp. 311–327). Hoboken, NJ: Wiley.

Parsons, R. (2012). *Child abusive material questionnaire.* Unpublished instrument.

Quayle, E., Erooga, M., Wright, L., Taylor, M., & Harbinson, D. (2006). *Only pictures: Therapeutic work with internet sex offenders.* Lyme Regis, England: Russell House.

Quayle, E., & Taylor, M. (2002). Paedophiles, pornography and the Internet: Assessment issues. *British Journal of Social Work, 32,* 863–875.

Quayle, E., & Taylor, M. (2004). *Child pornography: An Internet crime.* Lyme Regis, England: Russell House.

Reid, R. C., Garos, S., & Carpenter, B. N. (2011). Reliability, validity, and psychometric development of the hypersexual behavior inventory in an outpatient sample of men. *Sexual Addiction & Compulsivity: The Journal of Treatment and Prevention, 18,* 30–51.

Seto, M. C., Cantor, J. M., & Blanchard, R. (2006). Child pornography offenses are a valid diagnostic indicator of pedophilia. *Journal of Abnormal Psychology, 115*(3), 610–615.

Seto, M. C., Reeves, L., & Jung, S. (2010). Explanations given by child pornography offenders for their crimes. *Journal of Sexual Aggression, 16*(2), 169–180.

Suler, J. (2004). The online disinhibition effect. *Cyberspsychology and Behavior, 7,* 321–326.

Wallace, P. (1999). *The psychology of the Internet.* New York, NY: Cambridge University Press.

Webb, L., Craissati, J., & Keen, S. (2007). Characteristics of internet child pornography offenders: A comparison with child molesters. *Sexual Abuse: A Journal of Research and Treatment, 19*(4), 449–465.

Wellard, S. (2001). Cause and effect. *Community Care, 1364,* 26–27. Retrieved from http://www.communitycare.co.uk/articles/15/03/2001/30218/cause-amd-effect.htm

Wolak, J., Finkelhor, D., & Mitchell, K. J. (2005). Child pornography possessors arrested in Internet related crimes. *Findings from the National Juvenile Online Victimization Study.* Retrieved from http://www.unh.edu/ccrc/pdf/jvq/CV81.pdf

Wolak, J., Finkelhor, D., & Mitchell, K. J. (2011). Child pornography possessors: Trends in offender and case characteristics. *Sexual Abuse: A Journal of Research and Treatment, 23*(1), 22–42.

Young, K. (2011). *Internet addiction: A handbook and guide to evaluation and treatment.* Hoboken, NJ: Wiley.

INDEX